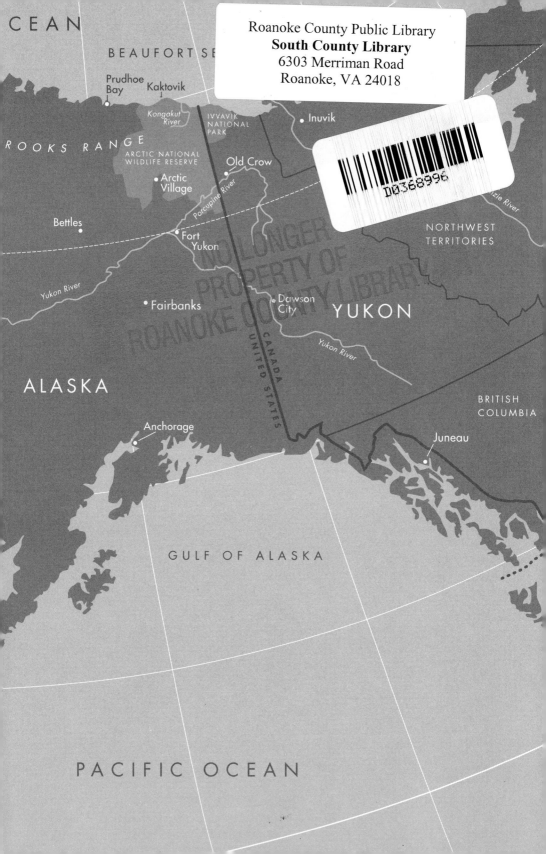

ARCTIC CIRCLE

BEAUFORT SEA

Prudhoe
Bay

Kaktovik

Deadhorse

COASTAL PLAIN

**Romanzof
Mountains**

IVVAVIK
NATIONAL
PARK

Alaska Pipeline

Hulahula River

Aichilak River

Kongakut River

Davidson Mountains

B R O O K S   R A N G E

ARCTIC NATIONAL
WILDLIFE RESERVE

VUNTUT
NATIONAL
PARK

Philip Smith Mountains

Arctic Village

Sheenjek River

Colleen River

Old
Crow

O G I L V I E   M O U N T A I N S

Porcupine River

Fort Yukon

ARCTIC CIRCLE

CANADA
UNITED STATES

Yukon River

ALASKA

Fairbanks

Alaska Pipeline

Dawson
City

ROBERT LEONARD REID

ARCTIC CIRCLE

Birth and Rebirth in the Land of the Caribou

DRG David R. Godine · Publisher · Boston

Published in 2010 by
DAVID R. GODINE · *Publisher*
Post Office Box 450
Jaffrey, New Hampshire 03452
www.godine.com

LIBRARY OF CONGRESS CATALOGING-IN-PUBLICATION DATA

Reid, Robert Leonard.
Arctic Circle: Birth and Rebirth in the Land of the Caribou /
by Robert Leonard Reid.
p.   cm.
ISBN 978-1-56792-350-6
1. Grant's caribou—Migration—Yukon. 2. Grant's caribou—Alaska—
Arctic National Wildlife Refuge. 3. Reid, Robert Leonard. I. Title.
QL737.U55R44 2010
508.798′7—dc22 2008006644

DESIGN & CARTOGRAPHY BY CARL W. SCARBROUGH

FIRST EDITION
*Printed at Maple-Vail Book Manufacturing Group
York, Pennsylvania, United States of America*

FOR JAKE

CONTENTS

The arctic circle
is a threshold
in the mind,
not its circumference.

North is
where all parallels
converge
to open out . . .
into the mystery
surrounding us
    Henry Beissel

INTRODUCTION

In the spring of 2003, I celebrated my sixtieth birthday. The occasion was a mixed blessing. On the welcome side it brought a batch of good wishes from friends and acquaintances, a cheery walk with my wife and son among radiant aspens and birches near our home in Carson City, Nevada, and several too many glasses of champagne. But it also raised some unsettling questions. Foremost among them were these: Was sixty the beginning of the end? Or was it, as I devoutly hoped, merely the end of the beginning?

Two weeks later, I found myself on a hillside in northern Alaska, two hundred miles north of the Arctic Circle. Surrounding me was an expanse of earth so redolent, so exuberant, so intoxicatingly beautiful, and yet so cold and cruel, the sight of it made me ache. If a reach of land can be personified, this one was the girl who broke your heart.

On a timetable of geological history, I was standing on the long, tapering runout from the Age of Ice. The glaciers and mastodons were gone but their scent remained vivid. Not far from where I stood was a spot the Inuvialuit people of northwest Canada call *ivvavik*, "a place for giving birth to and raising young." There, over the next ten days, thousands of pregnant females from the Porcupine caribou herd would be arriving, as they have each year since the ice withdrew, to bear their young.

The Porcupine's gallop to *ivvavik* is a marvel without parallel. Annually, herd members put nearly three thousand miles beneath their hooves, making theirs the longest migration of any land animal on earth. Most of the caribou winter in Yukon's Ogilvie Mountains. Early in April, the pregnant females catch something in the wind, and light out for *ivvavik*.

The journey is perilous, and astounding. It is an ordeal of mountains and blizzards, of ravenous wolves and scant forage and churning rivers chockablock with ice chunks as big as pickup trucks. At night, temperatures may descend to 50 degrees below zero. By a mechanism known only to caribou, the females find their way to the calving grounds on the coast of the Beaufort Sea. There, during the first week of June, they deliver their calves.

The opportunity to witness a few moments of this endlessly turning circle of birth and rebirth was reason enough for me to make the long trek to the top of the North American continent. But I had other reasons for going as well. One was to fulfill a vow I had made a quarter of a century before to an Alaskan homesteader I had known for no more than an hour, but who during that short time had transformed fundamentally the way I look at the world. Long before current proposals to develop the oil reserves in the Arctic National Wildlife Refuge, on the very site where the Porcupine herd calves, that longtime Brooks Range resident had become convinced that the caribou, the wolf – indeed, the entire arctic ecosystem – were under attack. Time is short, he had warned me. Come and see the Great Land. Then write about what you find. It had taken me twenty-five years to make good on my vow, but I was on my way at last.

I went, too, to celebrate two rebirths of a sort in my own family. After suffering from a painful and debilitating illness for more than a decade, my wife, Carol, was on the mend, entering once again into the land of the living. In ways that perhaps only the spouse of a chronically ill person can fully understand, I had suffered along with her; now, with her return to at least an approximation of good health, had come hope for my own renewal. Carol and I had weathered a very snowy winter together. Somehow we had found our way to a place very much like *ivvavik*. Amazed by the reversal of fortune, galvanized by the sudden arrival of what appeared to be a future, we looked forward now to the resumption of our own migration through the long-imagined landscape of ordinary life.

The final reason was one that no one entering his seventh decade could fail to be aware of. Tempering the renewed joy in living that I took from Carol's glad turnabout was a bleak yet curiously energizing fear of dying before I had done everything I wanted to do. For forty years I had dreamed of traveling to the Arctic. The expectations and illusions that sustained that dream, and that led at last to the journeys I shall describe in these pages, began with literature and with yet another question, one I hoped *ivvavik* would help me to answer: What is the true nature of the North? Is it generous and good, as the Inuit sing – a great day that dawns, a light that fills the world? Or is it, in the words of the Arctic explorer Elisha Kent Kane, "Horrible! *Horrible!*" – a dwelling place of darkness and death?

PROLOGUE: TO FEEL THE EARTH TURN

When you set out on your journey to Ithaca,
pray that the road is long.
    Constantine P. Cavafy

Lead me from the unreal to the real!
Lead me from darkness to light!
    Brihadaranyaka Upanishad

In the vast literature of polar exploration, certain moments blaze with almost celestial splendor. One of the brightest, arguably saintly in its proportions, is British Army Captain Lawrence Oates's transcendent sacrifice on the Antarctic plateau, a stunning, nearly inaudible whisper near the end of explorer Robert Scott's journal, when the gravely ill Oates eases himself painfully from his sleeping bag and exits Scott's tent into a blizzard, knowing that he must die if the other members of the party are to live. "I am just going outside," Oates says almost offhandedly to Scott, "and may be some time."

On an altogether different scale – big, brawling, arduous to a degree that defies comprehension – is Ernest Shackleton's miraculous eight hundred–mile journey over the tempestuous South Atlantic in his ridiculous rowboat, then foot by frostbitten foot across the brutal mountains of South Georgia; his mission, the salvation of the men of his expedition, stranded an ocean away on a flyspeck of rock called Elephant Island. Can anyone read these passages and ever again question the capacity of the human animal for greatness or the heights to which it is capable of rising?

Yet for each such moment, there are a thousand others that reveal not the nobility of our species or the triumph of the human spirit, but the rather more down-to-earth and often quite nasty details of daily life in the harshest environment on the planet. Certainly there is a kind of heroism to be found running between even the most pedestrian of lines in these riveting journals and memoirs. But let's face it: that's not why we read them. We read them for *the good parts*. We read them for the bone-snapping temperatures and the ten-day blows, the polar bear attacks, scurvy epidemics, and exploding camp stoves. Ungodly darkness, not celestial brightness, draws us to these tales, and in all the literature there is scarcely a sentence that fails to satisfy.

The shadow falls for the first time in A.D. 997. The Norseman Scargisl Orrabeinfostri wrecks his ship on the northwest coast of Baffin Bay, laying the groundwork for a two-year ordeal of starvation and madness. A millennium later the means have changed but the gloom persists. April 1998: the Russian diver Andrei Rozhkov cuts a hole in the ice precisely at the North Pole, observes a beautiful and haunting light beckoning deep in the water far below him, and dives fifty meters to investigate. His equipment fails in the demanding conditions of ninety degrees North, and he dies. (Rozhkov's demise is, *ipso facto*, the most northerly ever recorded.) Between the two events, the official record is pretty much one of hell on earth. And however sympathetic we may feel toward the condemned in their plights, something in these fiendish, callous, ambulance-chasing souls of ours makes us want to pull up a chair, pop open a beer, and watch.

"Great God! this is an awful place," Scott mourns upon his arrival at the South Pole, and we can hardly wait to find out why. Crime novels disturb us, and Stephen King scares the bejeezus out of us. But the annals of cannibalism and blackened limbs ... for sheer day-to-day horror, nothing can match 'em!

"When I awoke my long beard was a mass of ice, frozen fast to the buffalo-skin: Godfrey had to cut me out with his jack-knife." So writes the physician and polar explorer Elisha Kent Kane of his somewhat melancholy emergence from a snooze on the sea-ice west of Greenland in March 1854. The dismal scene is one of many that enliven *Arctic Explorations*, Kane's best-selling account of his attempt to become the first person to reach the North Pole. Alas, things are not going well. The doctor and fifteen of his seventeen-man crew are purple with scurvy; the expedition's precious supply of hardtack and rotten potatoes is running low; the ship in which the party has been icebound for six months has been taken over by rats.

> We have been terribly annoyed by rats. Some time ago we made a brave attempt to smoke them out with the vilest imaginable compound of vapours: brimstone, burnt leather, and arsenic, and spent a cold night in a deck-bivouac to give the experiment fair play. But they survived the fumigation. We now determined to dose them with carbonic acid gas.

Before long, half the crew will mutiny. First, however, there is the matter of the lost patrol. Five crewmen have been missing for more than a week. They are assumed to be in a desperate state. Kane and nine of his men are afoot on the ice, searching for the beleaguered five. Where are they? "Somewhere within a radius of forty miles." The temperature is minus 46 degrees Fahrenheit.

"It required brisk exercise to keep us from freezing," Kane explains helpfully. He faints twice. McGary and Bonsall are seized with trembling fits and shortness of breath. Ohlsen, who had been with the missing five and who somehow made it back to the ship to report their predicament, now returns with the rescuers, strapped to a sled. "Mr. Ohlsen, who had been without rest for fifty hours, fell asleep as soon as we began to move, and woke now with unequivocal signs of mental disturbance."

The party marches twenty-one hours without pause. Then, miraculously, they see footprints; a moment later they spot an American flag fluttering atop an ice hummock.

So: farther from help and from the good graces of God than anyone else on earth, we find fifteen cold, sick, hungry, exhausted men, plus one tent with space for eight. Lots are drawn. The eight winners pile into the shelter and fall into a sleep of desperation; the others pace outside continually to keep from freezing.

Two hours pass. The groups switch places. The thermometer reads minus 56 when the party begins the long march back to the ship. On the way Bonsall and Morton beg permission to sleep. Hans is found nearly stiff under a drift. John Blake throws himself into the snow and refuses to rise. The men camp again, without food or water. Kane's beard freezes to his sleeping bag.

> We could not abstain any longer from eating snow; our mouths swelled and some of us became speechless. Our halts multiplied and we fell half-sleeping in the snow. I could not prevent it. I ventured upon the experiment myself, making Riley wake me at the end of three minutes; and I felt so much benefited by it that I timed the men in the same way. They sat on the runners of the sledge, fell asleep instantly, and were forced to wakefulness when their three minutes were out.

Three days after leaving the ship the men are back. The missing five have been saved, if that is the word. Dr. Hayes administers morphine freely. Mr. Ohlsen suffers from snow blindness.

"The week that followed has left me nothing but anxieties and sorrow," Kane laments.

> Nearly all our party, as well the rescuers as the rescued, were tossing in their sick-bunks, some frozen, some undergoing amputations, several with dreadful premonitions of tetanus. I was myself

among the first to be about; the necessities of the others claimed it of me.

Early in the morning of the 7th I was awakened by a sound from Baker's throat, one of the most frightful and ominous that ever startled a physician's ear. The lockjaw had seized him; that dark visitant whose foreshadowings were on so many of us. His symptoms marched rapidly to their result; he died on the 8th of April.

The North! I fell in love with these amazing stories, real and true and honest as a chomp on the thigh by a rabid wolverine, when I was in my early twenties. Whatever had got into me? Was it rebellion? A cry for help? No doubt the seed was sewn early, perhaps by Jack London's *Call of the Wild*, which I read in junior high school, or Vilhjalmur Stefansson's *Unsolved Mysteries of the Arctic*, which I received as a Christmas present at around the same time. Stefansson's book fairly sang with the mystery and enchantment of the North – even more, with the peril. Those associations became my primary links with the region. A few years later I began reading the hair-raising words of the explorers themselves: Elisha Kane's *Arctic Explorations*, Isaac Hayes's *The Open Polar Sea*, Fridtjof Nansen's *Farthest North*, Frederick Cook's *My Attainment of the Pole*. Any doubts I may have had about the true nature of the North were quickly erased. The men who took on the Arctic were cool and tough as icebergs, and they had to be. They wrote about the region as though it were some distant and sinister planet to which they had been dispatched, usually by themselves, to wage war against an enemy; the more spears and cannon balls it rained down upon them, the happier they were. They seemed almost disappointed if there was enough food to eat or if the sun came out.

The idea of the North that I drew from my reading was only incidentally rooted in the physical character of the region. Partly that was because the authors rarely had much to say about geology, flora, or fauna, or even about the Inuit, who so often saved their skins. (Thoroughly at home in the North, the native people are usually consigned to a spot on the frozen edges of these high misadventures, like so many icicles; the reader can sense them shaking their heads at their strange visitors, so out of place in those harsh surroundings, and muttering, "Who are these guys?") Written as they were on the fly, with frozen fingers, in the dark, the hastily scribbled notes and diaries of the Arctic explorers are understandably deficient in scientific observation and sociological commentary.

What they brim with, however, and what formed the basis of my understanding of the place, is the notion of the Arctic as a big, empty, dangerous place where life is lived *in extremis*, and where one goes to put oneself in contact with the elements, even perhaps to risk death (or at least amputation), in order to achieve some grand reward. It was the same notion that a few years earlier had attracted me to the idea of climbing mountains. That infatuation, too, began with books. At the age of sixteen, faced with the grim task of preparing in one night a book report for a high school English class, I quite arbitrarily pulled a volume called *The Conquest of Everest* from a shelf in the public library in my hometown of Titusville, Pennsylvania. Written by Sir John Hunt, the leader of the 1953 British expedition to Mount Everest, the book told the story of the first ascent of the world's highest peak by expedition members Edmund Hillary and Tenzing Norgay.

I was a lowlander who had never before given a thought to the idea of climbing mountains. Yet something in the book's climactic chapter (the only one I read) struck a chord in me. In those sixteen spellbinding pages, the triumphant Hillary recounted in his own measured, precise, and thrilling words the story of the final assault on the summit. His tale provoked an epiphany in me. Suddenly I longed to be atop a towering peak, alone, enveloped in cold and mist and silence. I knew nothing of mountains, but I understood intuitively they were more than mere topography, that they had a spiritual side, too, and that the determined seeker could go to them, as I believed Hillary had, to find happiness and peace.

I emerged from the book on fire. I decided that I wanted to become a mountain climber. During my final year in high school, I found and devoured other mountaineering titles in the library: *Annapurna*, Maurice Hertzog's stirring account of the first ascent of an eight thousand–meter peak; *K2, The Savage Mountain*, Charles Houston's and Robert Bates's monumental, heartbreaking tale of an attempt on the world's second highest mountain by a star-crossed team of American climbers. When I went off to college I took up backpacking, then rock climbing, then the entire art of rock and snow and ice. I was never an especially skilled climber, and I set no records and gained no fame; but for a quarter century I was delirious with mountains, drunk with them. I climbed year-round throughout the Western United States and Canada: peaks, hills, boulders, crags – anything that went up. In the accepted fashion and usually with a few close friends, I put my life on the line rock after rock, mountain after mountain, and sometimes I achieved my summits. But even when I didn't, I understood myself to be a kind of pilgrim on a quest that transcended mere sport, one that inquired obsessively into eternal questions of life and death. I was not alone in this conceit: of all the reasons that motivate climbers to pursue their dangerous sport, this one is perhaps foremost.

I climbed until I was in my early forties. Then a series of lamentable events, including a divorce, the deaths of my parents, and the death of a dear friend in a rock climbing accident, caused me to rethink my commitment to mountaineering. I was growing older. I was losing the physical and mental edges I needed to climb safely. Worst of all, I was becoming afraid. When a year after my divorce I fell in love and re-married, I realized how utterly stupid it would be for me, at that joyful moment of my starting over, to perish in the mountains. Reluctantly, I hung up my rope and crampons and vowed never to use them again.

Mountaineering and Arctic exploration share much in common. Both are dangerous games conducted under difficult circumstances in extreme environments. Both beg of their players unanswerable questions about life and death, and about what in the world they are doing there, playing the game, *that* game, rather than, say, tennis. Both attract the type of person who, given the choice between flying four thousand miles in a private jet to sleep in silk pajamas at the Ritz, and hiking twenty miles in the rain to sleep in wet underwear on a pile of rocks, would choose the latter. Having fallen for Arctic literature as helplessly as I had fallen for *The Conquest of Everest* and *Annapurna*, I might have been expected at some point in my young life to make a decision to go north, just as I had made a decision to go climbing.

But I did not. I made several feints in that direction, each time slinking away having barely tested the wind. While teaching high school in New York City I attended evening classes in celestial navigation at the Hayden Planetarium. I was motivated by the romantic and requisitely crazy notion that I would one day command a dog team across some perilous northern landscape, finding my way by sun and stars. When I retired from teaching my students presented me with a handsome sextant to use on my journey. Sadly, I never fulfilled their dream for me. For a few years I kept up my navigational skills, occasionally shooting the sun to learn that, yes, I was in Palo Alto or Albuquerque. But never Greenland or Melville Island or Repulse Bay.

At about the same time I was attending classes at the planetarium, I concocted a halfhearted plan to attempt a peak on Baffin Island – real North! – with a fellow climber. The expedition died ostensibly for lack of funds, but more accurately, for me, for lack of will. As I pored over maps with my friend and studied the difficulties and dangers of living for even a short while in that forbidding environment, I began to grasp in a way that I never had before the true and uncompromising hostility of the North. If climbing a mountain on Baffin Island were simply a matter of technique, of putting one foot in front of the other, I might have gone ahead with the plan. But there was a psychological component to the exercise – that pervasive Arctic darkness – that rendered such an effort beyond my mental reach.

The difference between climbing mountains and exploring the Arctic;

the reason, I think, that I climbed for a quarter-century but never set foot north of the fifty-fifth parallel, was that for all the trouble mountains are capable of meting out, they have a bright, beautiful, spiritually grand side that I knew well and that I reveled in. No climbing account is complete without its long and painstakingly composed passages extolling the beauty and wonder of the mountain landscape, and of the act of climbing. For most mountaineers, those pleasures are central to their enjoyment of the sport. During my years as a climber I knew many scary ledges, dangerous slopes, and cold, wet nights; despite them, light and pleasure were the pre-eminent associations I always made with mountains.

By contrast, I continued to see the Arctic as an unrelievedly gloomy place. Most of the explorers' accounts that formed my understanding of the region fell into the "Great God! this is an awful place" category – riveting reading but poor advertisements for the territory. Rarely did the authors of those works throw their arms skyward and cry out in ecstasy at the grandeur of the North or at their joy in being there. With only the teeth-gritting explorer's model of the Arctic after which to pattern my understanding, I looked northward with ambivalence. The idea of the place I loved; the thought of going there gave me the shivers.

A chance encounter in 1977 with a man named Fred Meader turned my notion of the Arctic on its head. I was living in the San Francisco Bay Area, climbing as often as I could in California's High Sierra and on friendly neighborhood crags like Castle Rock and Pinnacles National Monument; attempting the rest of the time to make a living as a freelance magazine writer. Recently I had come across John McPhee's "Coming Into the Country," a long article excerpted from his book of the same name, in the *New Yorker*. McPhee's subject was Alaska. Naturally I devoured the article in one sitting. Much of the story was given over to a discussion of the Alaska Lands Bill, a grandiose piece of Carter Administration legislation that proposed carving up huge portions of Alaska's wildlands into national parks, monuments, and wildlife refuges, thereby providing them with permanent protection from development.

I had never heard of the bill, but it sounded like a good idea to me. At the time I didn't know much about the way Washington works and I assumed the bill would pass with ease. After doing a little investigation, I learned that although the legislation was widely supported in the lower forty-eight, it was stalled, perhaps permanently, in Congress. The reason: loud and cranky opposition by many Alaskans, including the governor, the Congressional delegation, the publisher of the state's largest newspaper, and most of the regulars at Rosie's Bar on Nugget Street in Fairbanks, none of whom wanted Washington laying its grubby paws on their scenery.

The thought that the bill might not pass threw me into a panic. My theoretical model of the North was under attack! That fearsome and inviolable landscape where 130 men of the Franklin expedition had perished from hunger, where Elisha Kent Kane had suffered a frozen beard on the sea-ice west of Greenland, was about to be overrun by hotels, gas stations, and fast-food joints! I had never written about a political issue before, but I made up my mind to write about this one. After querying a few magazines, I managed to nail down an assignment to write an article about the Alaska Lands Bill.

Fred Meader, too, had been goaded into action, though for reasons far more urgent than mine. He and his family lived in a cabin by a lake in northern Alaska's Brooks Range. There they had fashioned for themselves lives of almost unimaginable simplicity and self-sufficiency. Meader rarely left his homestead. But so distressed had he become when he learned that the parklands legislation was in trouble that he had uprooted himself to teeming, barbarian San Francisco to speak out for passage of the bill. He had a huge stake in the outcome. His cabin lay within the boundaries of the proposed Gates of the Arctic National Park. As subsistence hunters he and his family would be permitted to stay on if the bill passed; development over the huge portions of the Brooks Range that the new park would encompass, however, would be forbidden.

Development of the Brooks was no idle threat. Once the end of the earth, northern Alaska now crawled with petroleum engineers, geologists – even real estate agents. Anyone with a passable set of eyes and a vague sense of how the world works could see that civilization was coming to the Arctic wilderness.

One evening I got a call from a friend. He told me that some rough-and-tumble sourdough was in San Francisco, preaching the gospel of wilderness preservation to anyone who would listen. I was interested at once. The article I was writing was a hodgepodge of amazing facts and noble sentiments, but it hadn't an ounce of life. What it needed was a shot of Yukon Jack. I decided to track the fellow down. At the very worst, he might be able to jump-start my story with a few outrageous anecdotes about life on the Alaska frontier.

I met him a few days later at my friend's office on Bush Street. My first impression was encouraging. Fred Meader was clearly a candidate for All-Arctic – a towering figure, lean, strapping, a bit intimidating, with a raggedy black beard, a nearly bald head, and piercing, heavily lidded eyes. He walked into the room silently and sized me up slowly, as though he hadn't decided whether to talk to me or to tear my head off. He was outfitted in standard backwoods issue – work boots, dungarees, a long-sleeved green-and-black checkered shirt. He didn't have a long-handled axe in his hand, but I was happy. He looked perfect for the job I'd hired him for – slugging a grizzly bear, say, or whooping it up with a bunch of the boys in the Malamute Saloon.

Then he shook my hand and introduced himself, and as quickly as I had sized him up, my impression of him as combination bearslayer-shitkicker vanished. It wasn't simply that I saw at once he was no threat to man or beast; he was, on the contrary, one of the gentlest, most self-effacing people I had ever met – an old potbellied stove of openness and warmth. He thanked me for seeking him out, for giving him a chance to jawjack a bit about life in the Brooks, about what had gone wrong for the wolves and the caribou, and about what he thought the world was coming to. Despite his great height and his craggy presence, he had a voice that was feather soft, and a manner of speaking that was dreamy and allusive; he seemed more a poet or a monk just down from a Himalayan mountaintop than a frontier hell-raiser.

In one respect, at least, Meader reminded me of stateside portraits of tough-as-nails Arctic explorers I'd seen – men like Robert Peary and Roald Amundsen, and especially Charles Francis Hall, the Cincinnati printer who achieved "farthest north" in 1871, and who more than any other person showed how to accommodate oneself to the peculiarities of the North, rather than fight against them. Like the gaze of those men, Meader's was distant and pensive; he seemed unable to focus on objects in the room – desk, chair, photos on the wall. He looked frequently toward the window, not because he was ill at ease or bored, but because something beyond the glass tugged at him. What it was was obvious: latitude. Fred Meader was homesick.

But no rough-and-tumble sourdough. About all he had in common with North Slope hellbenders was an address; in the Malamute Saloon, he would have been holding belligerents apart with his cedar-branch arms, encouraging them to behave.

With no prompting from me, Meader launched into a monologue on life apart from civilization in a two-bit cabin in the Alaskan wilds. He went on for an hour, scarcely pausing to take a breath. The tale he spun was enthralling, astonishing. He spoke not of hardship or struggle or pain, but of enchantment, beauty, quiet marvels, sweet mysteries. He described a place that reminded me not of the terrible struggle for the Pole, but of the peaceful landscape I had imagined on first encountering Edmund Hillary's story of his climb to the top of the world. Meader's Arctic was rich and grand, and, most of all, *alive*. As I listened I was aware of being drawn into his world, mesmerized by it and by him. I began to wonder if years of living close to the earth might have rekindled in him powers that humans once possessed but had lost in their ascent, if that was the word, to civilization. Meader was an atavist, a throwback to an earlier type – maybe even a caster of spells. In words charged with passion, he told me about an Arctic I had never imagined: a beautiful, bountiful, generous place – not a dark and dreadful wasteland, but an abode of light.

*   *   *

He came of age in the fifties, as a graduate student in philosophy at Boston University. His view of the world, part Rousseauvian, part Jeffersonian, part Saint Jerome of the Desert, sprang from his experiences growing up on a dairy farm in upstate New York during the Depression. A background like that can lead a young man to decide early in life to get as far away from dirt and from hard work as possible, as quickly as his feet can carry him. For Fred Meader it had the opposite effect: he came to believe that there was dignity to be found in physical labor and fulfillment in the simple life lived close to the earth. Unusually for the time and place, he saw nature not as servant or foe, but as partner, teacher – perhaps even as divinity.

On the streets of Boston, in the classroom, in interactions with neighbors, community, and friends, what Meader observed failed entirely to square with what he believed. An intolerable disconnect grew. Facing a career as a teacher, a home in the suburbs, a life of commuting, shopping, mowing the lawn, he despaired. Today, hip social historians tell us that the famously bland fifties were not as bad as their reputation. To Fred Meader they were. Fancy new products, light entertainment, mindless conversation, upward mobility, luxury, power, security – those meant nothing to him.

In his wife Elaine he had found a woman who not only understood his despair, she shared in it. A nursing student at the college, Elaine Meader had, like her husband, acquired a worldview so distant from that of contemporary society, it might have seemed Plutonian. At its core lay her belief that the planet on which she lived and the universe through which it spun were more than physics, geology, and biology, and were anything but an accident. Rather, planet and universe constituted a single, eternal, and living organism through which life energy coursed like blood, and purpose like patterns of thought; whose tiniest parts were joined as molecule to molecule; whose nature was spiritual and whose central and defining properties were benevolence and love. The fully realized life was the life lived in awareness of, and gratitude for, one's small but essential role in this vast drama – one's vital *cellness.*

In the compulsively busy lives of the people she observed around her, in the arrogant, contentious chess game of neighbors and of nations, she saw little that resembled attention to this grand design. Modernity had brought comfort and wealth, but it drowned out the music of creation's heartbeat. Where others looked at a group portrait of America and saw a smiling, contented family, Elaine Meader saw fragmentation, alienation – desperate men and women out of touch with the cosmos. Civilization, she and her husband both believed, was a code word for life out of balance, even life without meaning; to participate was to risk losing one's soul. At a moment when the environmental movement was a mere gleam in the eyes of a few fantasists, these two defiant, prescient individuals understood the earth as a perfectly evolved organism whose integrity was threatened by progress. They craved simplicity, honesty, communion with the elements; moreover, they believed it was still possible to find those elusive qualities and to organize their lives around them.

Fred applied for a job at the Boston Museum of Science. He was perfect for the position, he was told, but he could not be hired unless he shaved off the small beard he had grown. The beard, it seemed, might prove disturbing to museum visitors. Meader kept the beard. With Elaine, he dropped out of school. For a few years the couple wandered – Europe, Colorado, Arizona, Mexico. Vaguely an idea began to grow: to escape from the world. They scoured maps in search of places where they might put their ideas to work. For a time they homesteaded in British Columbia, perfecting the survival skills they would need to live apart from civilization. Then, in the fall of 1960, they gathered up their three-year-old son, Dion, and a few belongings, and headed for Alaska. There they found the paradise they had been seeking: a lake in the heart of the Brooks Range, eighty miles north of the Arctic Circle, fifty miles from the nearest neighbor, two hundred miles from the nearest road.

Time was short. Winter lay just around the corner. The couple flew in provisions to see them through the long night to come. Then they set to work shoring up a dilapidated prospector's cabin they had found near the lake.

Each day they worked from dawn to dark, laboring in a kind of ecstasy. Both understood clearly the extraordinary opportunity they held in their hands. They were free and independent, as few have been. They even believed that they controlled their own destinies, though in that they would prove to be grievously mistaken.

When the first snow fell, they were ready. Tempering their anxieties over what lay ahead was a feeling of profound contentment. The sun slipped lower in the sky. The last geese disappeared over the southern horizon. Sometimes in the dimming light the couple stood with their son beside the lake and thought about friends in New England and California. Then they heard a chorus of wolves or felt an icy breeze skidding off the surface of the water, and they understood that there was no Boston or California on the distant planet where they had chosen to live, the planet that would be their home for the next seventeen years.

"We found what we were looking for. During those first years it was magnificent, unbelievable. Elaine and I came from a culture where people lived their lives in bits and pieces. In Alaska we found connection and continuity. We could watch the rhythms and patterns of life as they unfolded. There was an organizing principle, a structure to our existence. The sun returned, the ice broke up, the caribou came north, the wildflowers appeared. The seasons came and went, always bringing their expected treasures, but surprises, too, and those we learned to recognize and appreciate. I could close my eyes and feel the earth turn. I knew where the wild sheep were. The wolves accepted us as neighbors. Sometimes they left their pups with us while they were off hunting. Dion grew up in direct and intimate contact with nature in its purest form. He had innocence and joy. He wore an expression on his face that you don't often see on kids today."

To a degree that most people with a yearning for wild country could only dream of, Fred, Elaine, and Dion entered into the cycle of the seasons, the caribou, the willow, and the alder. Their goal, astonishing in its ambition and its symbolism, was to rid themselves of all vestiges of civilization – to leave the modern world behind and return to a pre-agricultural, hunter-gatherer way of life. For much of the year they subsisted on a wild diet of meat, fish, and berries. They rejected the use of sled dogs, which they believed would involve them in a master-slave relationship with the animals, a corruption of civilization. Fred continued to use a rifle to secure game. But he was learning to shoot a bow, which he had fashioned by hand, and he intended to begin using the weapon exclusively before long.

Before meeting Meader, I might have imagined such a life to be one of unrelenting drudgery, with few pleasures and little to look forward to. Those illusions vanished as he spoke.

"In spring when you first hear the water trickling and the birds singing ... there's power in that that's greater than anything I know. It teaches you something. You know that you're not alone, that you're a valued part of something that's bigger than anything you could ever understand."

The place and the way of life that Meader described were utterly beyond my experience. Yet somehow I recognized myself in his story. Odd as the details were, he invested them with a universality that anyone could relate to. I had gone to him wondering about 60-below-zero winters and caribou-skin clothing. I came away marveling at the beauty and mystery of the most common chunk of earth – even Arctic earth, which previously had seemed so forbidding to me, and of the connections that link each fragment of the natural world, one to the next. Meader's relationship to land was one of kinship; as one comes to know the patterns and habits of one's spouse and one's children, he knew the patterns of wind and snow, the habits of wolf and hare and Arctic moon. His conclusion was that the world is not a strange place, though it is quite enchanted. To grasp this, he seemed to be saying, it is only necessary to be still and watch.

Meader was one of the few people I have ever met who fully embodied the concept of "real assent." The term was coined by the nineteenth-century theologian John Henry Newman, who distinguished between what he called "notional" assent to a proposition such as "Humans must live in harmony with nature," and the far more difficult "real" assent. Notional assent is the classic liberal approach to thorny issues. It involves nodding one's head gravely, writing checks that don't hurt too much, signing politely worded petitions, scolding the riffraff for their foolishness and their profligate ways, and paying solemn lip service to the proposition, so long as doing so doesn't require one to change one's own ways in any significant manner.

Real assent is assent of the heart and the soul. Real assent is stringent, uncompromising, complete. Real assent to the proposition "Humans must live in harmony with nature" might compel a person to separate himself from the rest of humanity for seventeen years, to suffer hordes of mosquitoes stoically, to bear up philosophically under weeks of drizzly rain and months of darkness, to forgo television, films, telephones, indoor plumbing, and internal combustion engines, to raise one's son without formal schooling or Little League.

Meader possessed that rarest of qualities, authenticity. He struck me as not so much the vanquisher of the mighty mountain he had conjured in Boston so many years before, but more the mountain itself, an integral chunk of its geology. Like the title of the celebrated Aldo Leopold essay, Meader had become a man capable of "thinking like a mountain." This allowed him, like the subject of Leopold's piece, to listen objectively to wild country and to understand its meaning. That meaning was patent: wilderness is essential to human survival.

"Man has boxed himself in. He's like a caged animal. He's created something he calls civilization, a schizophrenic way of life whose primary features are alienation and disillusionment. In wilderness it's possible to overcome civilization and to find the answers that we've lost. Wilderness is a template that allows us to measure where we're going and where we've been."

Meader had come at last to the rationale for his trip to San Francisco and for his decision to lobby for passage of a bill written in a modern, schizophrenic city by civilized, disillusioned legislators: the gauge on the template had skyrocketed into the danger zone. He knew where we'd been: Eden. He feared where we were going. He had seen what the first blush of civilization had brought to the Brooks Range. Since the discovery of oil in Prudhoe Bay and the beginning of construction on the Alaska Pipeline, natural patterns thousands of years in the making had changed. Wolves no longer called at Meader's front door. The Arctic caribou population had fallen to less than half its pre-pipeline size. Meader needed fifteen caribou a year to feed and clothe his family. New hunting laws now restricted him to six. Finding even that many was becoming harder and harder, for the Western Arctic herd, which once had migrated practically through the Meaders' backyard, now some years failed to show up at all.

Meanwhile, lakes throughout the Brooks Range had become field-dumping stations for oil and mining exploration crews. Fred and Elaine sometimes saw helicopters passing overhead; hunting for game, Fred came across spools of cable, pasteboard boxes, discarded fifty-five-gallon oil drums.

He regarded development of the Arctic as flagrantly shortsighted. "There's probably a few months worth of oil to be found up there," he allowed. "There's probably enough minerals so that if you divide up the profits, everyone will get a few dollars. The cost, however, will be beyond measure. And there will be no way to go back."

In a final disaster, a Fairbanks realtor had purchased an old hundred-acre mining claim at the Meaders' lake. On the drawing boards were plans for a fifty-cabin development, in sight of the mountains where Fred stalked moose with homemade bow and arrow.

Like my encounter with John Hunt's *Ascent of Everest*, my hour with Meader changed the way I viewed the world. With a few deft brush-strokes, he had painted over the ferocious Arctic of Elisha Kent Kane, transforming that harsh and unforgiving land into a bright, vibrant, and – this was the hardest part to believe – fragile place. The transformation was enormous; it was as though I had walked into the room Norwegian and walked out Japanese. I wrote earlier that on first meeting Meader I had wondered if he might not be a caster of spells. Now I knew that he was. A few dashes of poetry and music, a dollop of philosophy, spritzes of truth, justice, and righteousness – *Here, take this . . . you won't know what hit you. . . .*

He wrapped up his story. In something of a daze I shook his hand and wished him well. As we were about to part he turned to me and, staring me straight in the eye, spoke two words that were to him as momentous as any he had spoken during the previous hour.

"Loon Lake," he said. He paused. "Loon Lake. That's where we live." He shook his head. "I've never told that to anyone before."

He waited for me to catch the significance of what he was saying. "I don't feel too good about it," he went on. "I thought that by keeping the name a secret we could prevent it from being discovered." Now, of course, he knew: the world is a small place. There are no more secrets.

"So write it in your article. Tell people where we are. I want them to know where this is happening, to give a human dimension to the threat that we all face."

Meader's final words were an invitation for me to visit him at his cabin. Come and see where I live, he said. Write about what you find. That's all you can do. Time is short. You must come.

Little realizing the commitment I was making, I promised him that I would.

Over the next few days I began thinking about making my way north. My old fear of the region had vanished. Meader had introduced me to a landscape I suddenly longed to see: not as adventurer or explorer; not as dog-team driver (a notion I now saw as bizarre), not even as tourist, but as a kind of citizen of the country who belonged there, whose inalienable rights included vastness, emptiness, and silence, whose birth certificate read "Born wild and free!", who knows that he's a valued part of something bigger than anything he could ever understand.

And then, as suddenly as this revolutionary view had been thrust upon me, it was violently snatched away. At the home of friends with whom he was staying in Bolinas, California, Meader grew restless. He gave a few public talks, spoke to a few reporters. But phantoms stalked him – dissatisfaction, alienation, that old familiar fear of being buried alive. Gazing north he saw freeways and shopping malls – the architecture of oppression. Beyond, the earth curved sharply away, and no matter how keenly he trained his eye, he could not see past the crowded horizon to the shining country of mountains and rivers, to the trackless wild.

He returned to Alaska. For a number of years, using borrowed equipment, he and Elaine had been making a film about their lives at Loon Lake. At the simplest level an adventure story about a remarkable family's struggle to survive in the wild, the film was, on a deeper level, a work about the integrity of the natural world, and about threats posed to that world by modernity and progress. Fred and Elaine knew that hunter-gatherers typically did not employ movie-making equipment. But they also saw in an honest, well-made film a powerful tool for telling their story and, perhaps, for pointing viewers in new and life-changing directions. Producing a film was a compromise with their primitive lifestyle that they were willing to make.

By the time I met Fred, he had found a distributor for the film. Back at Loon Lake that fall of 1977, he shot the final scenes. Then he made arrangements to fly to New York City to complete production of the movie and to arrange for its distribution. On the first leg of the journey south he took a bush plane to the village of Bettles, Alaska, landing on the Koyukuk River.

Of Meader's many such landings, most had been on lakes, where the routine was familiar: the plane lands and approaches the dock, the pilot shuts down the propeller, someone on shore wades out to grab the line, which is attached to the front of the plane. On this occasion, repeated radio calls failed to rouse anyone on land, so the pilot decided to dock himself. He instructed Meader to climb out onto the plane's float and to grab the tie-up rope. To prevent the plane from drifting away from the dock in the river current, the pilot kept the propeller turning.

Meader stepped onto the float and closed the door behind him. Elaine later theorized that her husband may not have understood that the rope now lay at his feet, having been carried there by the current. All he had to do was reach down, grab it, and jump to the dock.

Instead, recalling lake landings, Fred began inching his way forward on the float toward the spot where the rope attached to the front of the plane. There was a moderate swell on the Koyukuk that day, and the plane was rocking noticeably. Meader may have missed a step, or he may simply have misjudged the reach of the propeller blades, the tips of which are practically invisible when the apparatus is spinning. Whatever the reason, he failed to give himself sufficient clearance from the propeller. He was struck by the blades and killed instantly.

I heard about the accident two days later. I had called the phone number Fred had given me, to ask him a few questions about the Alaska Lands Bill and how it would affect his homestead. A grief-stricken voice at the other end of the line told me what had happened. I muttered a few inadequate words of condolence and hung up.

The news from Bettles had a curious effect on me. Naturally, I was distraught. But I was angered, too, not only at the terrible manner of Meader's death but at my own naiveté, in having abandoned so swiftly that long-held idea that I now knew to be true: the North was indeed a brutal place.

I knew, of course, that accidents could happen anywhere. But this one seemed pinned to geography. This one seemed pointedly Alaskan. Before long, the painful memory of what had happened to Fred joined in my mind with the invigorating spell that he had cast over me, to produce an ambivalence about the North that was to last for many years. I came to believe in two places – the benevolent Arctic of Fred's life, the fearful one of his death. Logically, this realization allowed me to see that good and bad, light and dark, cannot be attributes of place at all. Such words describe the acts and experiences of human beings at precisely defined points of land, not inherent qualities of land itself. When I dreamed of Loon Lake, as I sometimes did during the years to come, it was the boundless faith of that mad couple standing beside the lake with their three-year-old son, watching a small plane receding into a great sky, that informed my dream. Loon Lake was only a place; faith was the glow that lit it, the rapture that pervaded it, the color that imbued it with a sense that anything is possible.

Whenever I felt my compass needle tugging northward, I quickly brushed aside any thoughts of the promise I had made to Fred. In their place I substituted the illusion that, thanks to him, I had experienced the Arctic with an intensity that the real place could never match. Before meeting Meader, I boasted that I had visited forty-eight of the fifty states, with only South Carolina and Alaska yet to be checked off my list. Afterward, I sometimes told people that only South Carolina remained. If they asked me about Alaska, I said, Yes, I was there once, for about an hour.

In the fall of 2002 I began making plans to celebrate an upcoming milestone birthday, my sixtieth. Thirty, forty, and fifty I had released to the wind without a blink, but sixty seemed worth blinking over. Recently a small, rather high-toned voice had begun to pester me. Not often; maybe once a week, at the oddest of times. (Now that I've passed the milestone without serious incident, I hear the voice practically every day. I think that at about my age, the onboard solid-waste detector finally gets fed up with all the crap, and begins to demand of its host a measure of seriousness and honesty about things like goals, purposes, the meaning of one's life – little things! – that in earlier years it was willing to overlook.)

What the voice said went something like this: Good morning! I've been thinking about something and I believe I should mention it. Remember how you've always said that one day you were going to make up with your cousin Phil? So here's my question: *When exactly are you going to do that?* Oh, and another thing: Remember how you've always said that one day you were going to dump all that baggage about the math professor who humiliated you in front of the entire calculus class? Here's my question: *When exactly are you going to do that?*

Most of the prompts I managed to fend off. One, however, cropped up so persistently that I began to pay attention to it. It went something like this: Remember the last words that Fred Meader spoke to you twenty-five years ago? *Come and see where I live. Write about what you find. That's all you can do. Time is short. You must come.* And remember the promise you made to him that you would go? So here's my question: *When exactly are you going to do that?*

Of all the vows I had made over the years, this was the most confounding. During the short time I had spent with Meader, he had transformed my long-held fantasies about a brutal and unforgiving North into belief in a place that was bright and beautiful and benevolent, and so fragile it was in danger of being destroyed. His death a few weeks later left me unsure of what to believe. Now, at last, my uncertainty had vanished. I knew with complete confidence that the time had come for me to make good on my vow.

I had no conceits about what I might accomplish on the long-imagined journey. Balls-out, death-defying, *Outside* magazine-approved Arctic adventure, which in my younger, more foolhardy mountaineering days had figured prominently in my plans, no longer interested me. If I had once imagined that I might be willing to sacrifice a few toes to the achievement of a worthy goal on an Arctic mountain or on the polar ice, I was now firmly committed to preserving every cell I had left in my body. My greatest desire now was simply to taste, if only for a short while, the vastness and the wildness of the North.

By doing so, I believed, I might find a serenity I had not known for a very long time. For nearly fifteen years my wife, Carol, had suffered from the flagrantly misnamed disease: chronic fatigue syndrome. (Calling the illness "chronic fatigue syndrome," one wag has observed, is like calling diabetes "excessive peeing disorder." It's true that on the Center for Disease Control's list of primary indicators for the disease, one is "incapacitating" fatigue. There are fourteen others.) Years of searching for the cause of Carol's condition and procuring effective treatment for it, at stupefying prices, had drained our financial resources nearly to zero. Triple-duty as breadwinner, house husband, and soccer dad for our son, Jake, had further worn me down. We three had been adrift in windswept boreal seas, through a polar night that seemed endless.

Now, suddenly and miraculously, the end of that long night seemed to be at hand. With the help of a brilliant and caring physician, Dr. Daniel Peterson, and an experimental drug called Ampligen, Carol had turned a corner on her illness. Her symptoms had begun to recede. A significant portion of her old energy had returned. Wrenching pain, a constant companion from the first day of her illness, no longer hounded her. She still had her bad days, but no more bad weeks or months. For the first time in years she was leading something like a normal life – even contemplating a return to her career as a counselor.

At such a time I ought to have been a supremely happy man. But years of emotional ups and downs associated with Carol's illness, of alternating joy and grief, hope and despair had taken their toll. Deprived of an object for my dread, I now lay awake at 3 A.M. dreading unnamed future woes. Anticipating a phone call from a creditor, I literally shook from fear. One winter morning my car stopped dead on the highway. As I watched that faithless piece of junk being towed away, I guessed correctly that it was going to need a new engine. That afternoon I sat dazedly by the phone waiting for the mechanic to call. My entire body began to quake. I was unaware of what was happening until suddenly I was awakened from my stupor by a rapid clattering sound – the sound of my chair jackhammering against the edge of the desk.

In his poem "The Peace of Wild Things," Wendell Berry offers as an antidote to the dissonance of daily life the "still water" of the natural world:

When despair for the world grows in me
and I wake in the night at the least sound
in fear of what my life and my children's lives may be,
I go and lie down where the wood drake

rests in his beauty on the water, and the great heron feeds.
I come into the peace of wild things. . . .

Nature has the capacity to heal the frazzled soul, Berry reminds us, bringing with it freedom and "the grace of the world."

I had known that poem for years. Decades of climbing mountains and wandering the wilderness of the American West had led me to much the same conclusion that Berry had reached. But during the years of my wife's illness, I came down from the mountains of rock and snow to take on mountains that were psychological and emotional in character; I retreated from the physical wilderness into the realm of the beleaguered spirit. For reasons not hard to understand, I lost touch with the world's grace. Now, as I prepared to enter my seventh decade, I wanted to find that grace again. Something told me I could do so in the vastness and wildness of the North.

I had no idea where I would go on my journey. One evening I paid a visit to the public library. Finding my way to the section on Arctic travel, I pulled a book from a shelf and opened it at random. My eyes fell on a photograph of a knot of caribou swimming across a river. The caption said that the animals belonged to the Porcupine caribou herd, and that once a year they undertook a long and hazardous migration from their winter quarters in the mountains of northern Yukon to their calving grounds on Alaska's north coast, a section of the Arctic National Wildlife Refuge that the Inuit call *ivvavik* – "a place for giving birth to and raising young."

In that moment I knew that I had found my destination. My excitement mounted as I read on about the amazing journey of the caribou. In a vague but unmistakable way their story reminded me of my own. The animals faced enormous obstacles, met them with alternating courage and faintheartedness, bumbled toward their goal with a hit-or-miss pace that I knew well. Yet they pushed on, with something that seemed a little bit like faith, toward a place that seemed very much like still water. I wanted to do that. Ten thousand times the herd had returned to the calving grounds, to be born and reborn and reborn. In that unbreakable cycle of renewal, I found hope for Carol's rebirth, and for my own.

Six months later, seven days after my sixtieth birthday, I kissed my wife and son good-bye, boarded an Alaskan Airlines jet at Reno–Tahoe International Airport, and headed north. Caribou were descending on *ivvavik*, and I wanted to be there to see them.

PART ONE: ALASKA

What lies beyond the margin of the world often sings to us with the voice of a siren, as if calling us into its embrace. We listen, we are lured, and finally we are seduced.
James Cowan

A SURE WIND
IN SPRING

For more than sixty miles following its rise in the
Romanzof Mountains, the Kongakut River steers a steady northeasterly
course across Arctic Alaska. In winter the river is bound in ice, but in
spring, descending the steep slope of the Romanzofs, it swells in volume
mile upon mile as one nameless tributary and then the next pours from
a side canyon and joins the flood. Thirty miles from the Arctic Ocean, in
a rarely visited valley in the Arctic National Wildlife Refuge, a thousand-
foot mountain wall rises up in the river's path. Unable to bypass the
obstruction, the Kongakut is propelled in a distance of just a few hundred
yards through a wrenching ninety-degree turn to the left. As it does so
it undergoes forces of staggering proportions. The waters power through
the curve, threatening at every moment to burst from their channel.
Emerging from the turn the river straightens and widens, for several
miles running parallel to the wall. At last, hydraulic pyrotechnics concluded, the Kongakut spills off a low-angle tableland and begins its final
run to the sea.

For all the river's fury, the valley through which it flows as it executes its formidable change of direction is a place of uncommon tranquility and beauty. The river is a storm; the valley is the calm beside the storm. At river's edge the roar is deafening; a short distance away the racket gives way to a beguiling undersong – more like Gregorian chant than raging waters. Cradled in the great curve of the Kongakut is an intervale, a level spot of land perhaps a square mile in extent. It betrays no signs of previous human visitation, no boot prints or campfire scars. It is planted thickly in wildflowers and low grasses, and willows no taller than a string bass. Peaceable streams wander among the willows. Gulls circle overhead. Behind them, a newly awakened sun tumbles horizontally through an azure sky. The light at three in the morning is no different than the light at three in the afternoon. At seventy degrees north, two weeks before the solstice, time seems to have stopped in its tracks. It is always dawn in the willows by the river, always a time beyond time.

Beneath its serene exterior the valley teems with energy. Half a mile north of its mighty left the Kongakut is still shingled in ice. Every few minutes an acre of roofing collapses with a groan that rocks the entire valley. Beneath the water, Arctic char the size of third-graders circle feverishly. When an angler's lure flashes, the fish do not rise to it and take the bait: they vault, they hurtle, they *besiege* the poor hook. Every square foot of terrain is a headline: Loon quandary! Wolfprint! Grizzly kill! Ptarmigan woe! Anemone flowers concoct rapid and exotic lives in scribbles of sand scarcely fit for a weed; in a matter of hours the plants erupt, zoom upwards, come into dazzling, heartbreaking bloom. Willow buds burst from their casings like giggling nuns tossing off their frocks for a skinny-dip. Beside the river atop a rusty clutch of sticks recently converted to a nest, a male Arctic tern mounts and flutters his mate long after the eggs have been laid, then mounts and flutters again. Only humans and a few other dissolute species are known to flutter for fun. Yet what other explanation can there be for the excellent calisthenics that shake this tumbledown bungalow hour after hour. Expectations are high at the great bend in the Kongakut. Here, there is nothing one cannot reasonably expect. Things happen. It's best to be ready for them. Convention is upended, and the vigilant observer will observe a steady stream of goofy reversals – the daying of night, the screw of the tern.

The primary force animating the valley is a kind of wind. It rises first during the waning days of May and continues through the middle of June; after a break of a month or so it resumes, briefly, in a sort of reprise of the initial blow but in reverse. The wind on the Kongakut has the rhythm of the unbridled and the scent of the Pleistocene. It is a wind of caribou on the move.

The Porcupine caribou herd numbers some 110,000 individuals. The herd is named for the Porcupine River, one of many obstacles the animals must negotiate as they make their way from their winter range in Yukon's Ogilvie Mountains to their calving grounds on Alaska's north coast, on the shore of the Beaufort Sea. During that long and arduous journey the caribou travel a complex network of routes, one of which traverses the fervent valley of the Kongakut.

North American caribou, *Rangifer tarandus*, are generally referred to as either woodland or barren-ground caribou. The woodland sub-species dwells south of the tree line, in the great spruce and pine forests of Canada and Alaska. They are generally larger and more solitary than barren-ground caribou. Most woodland caribou migrate between winter and summer ranges, but the distances they cover are far shorter than those traversed by their barren-ground relatives; indeed, for many woodland caribou, the winter and summer ranges overlap, indicating less a true migration than a movement from one part of the animals' permanent range to another.

By contrast, barren-ground caribou, of which the Porcupine herd is one example, spend the greater portion of their lives north of the Arctic Circle, the region wildlife biologist George Calef, in his essential volume on the species, *Caribou and the Barren-Lands*, calls "the country of winter." Barren-ground caribou inhabit distinct winter and summer ranges. They migrate long distances between the two. Unlike woodland females, which are likely to go off by themselves to have their young, barren-ground females gather by the thousands on traditional calving grounds, to which the herd returns year after year.

The animals resemble whitetail deer; even more, reindeer, to which the species is closely related. A typical male of the species may weigh in at three hundred pounds, a female two-thirds of that. Caribou coats vary in color through the year, from snow-shadow gray in winter to tawny in spring to russet brown in fall; the necks are white. Unlike other members of the deer family, both male and female caribou bear antlers, which they shed and regrow annually. Bulls put up magnificent five- or six-foot racks that curve outward and upward like the arms of Atlas holding up the world. Each branch flattens at its end into a kind of skeletal hand with several long bony fingers. Between the two main branches, jutting forward ten or twelve inches at the animal's brow line, is a strange and slightly unsettling relic, a leathery shovel that brings to mind a back plate of a stegosaurus. Males start to develop antlers in the late winter and shed them after the fall rut. In midsummer the appendages may grow as much as an inch a day.

Females drop their antlers soon after giving birth in the spring. The animals that become pregnant in the fall grow new sets, using them through the winter to defend their calves and their feeding areas from the antler-less bulls, who remain separate from the females and in generally less desirable locations.

Calling the Porcupine a herd is a bit misleading. The term suggests a close-knit group that lives and travels together. Like the dozen or so other barren-ground caribou herds that populate Arctic Alaska and Canada, the Porcupine more closely resembles a far-flung clan of aunts, uncles, and cousins that hang in families of ten or twenty throughout much of the year, then gather at a spirited family reunion in June and July – Summerfest on the Beaufort Sea!

At other times of the year, hundreds of miles may separate the most distantly spaced members of the herd. Individuals may wander seemingly aimlessly much of the time; a few may not make the journey to the calving grounds at all.

Nonetheless, there is a pattern and a logic to the herd's movements. Both serve the demands of calving, the rules of which are as strictly ordained as those governing the production of a fine cabernet. The Porcupine winters over an area the size of Maryland. Through months of cold and darkness, the animals spend much of their time hunkered down in the snow, singly or, in the most desperate conditions, huddled with their fellows. The rest of the time they are feeding, on lichens, sedges, horsetails, cranberry. The animals can sense forage through a foot of snow. To reach the plants, they chop and shovel through the crust with their sharply rimmed hooves, forming a crater with a few inches of exposed vegetation at the bottom. (The name caribou seems to derive from a Mi'kmaq Indian word *xaibu*, meaning "pawer" or "shoveler.")

In March, the sun returns. Temperatures, which may have hit 70 degrees below zero at midwinter, begin to climb. Early in April the pregnant females read the soulful signs of spring and grow restless.

At first their activity is undirected – more a welcome stretching of the legs after the long confinement of winter than the start of a journey. Soon, however, the proceedings gather momentum and purpose. In great numbers of small, determined groups, the heavily burdened females set out north and west along a myriad of routes. Yearlings may travel with their mothers, though before the calving grounds are reached most will be driven off by the females, who must focus their attention and their swiftly dwindling stores of energy on the generation about to be born. Older juveniles, bulls, and barren females remain behind for days or weeks. Then they, too, begin the long walk.

Soon one group joins the next; the tiny tributaries lengthen and gain strength, forming streams, then rivers of animals. Now instead of tens and twenties, hundreds may move together; then, at the last, thousands. Their destination is a spot on Alaska's north coast that the Inuvialuit call *ivvavik*, "a place for giving birth to and raising young." Farther south, the Athabaskan Gwich'in call it *Izhik Gwats'an Gwandaii Goodlit*, "the sacred place where life begins." On this narrow, windswept plain, in all but the snowiest years, the females deliver their calves. The schedule is quite rigid. Seventy-five percent of the cows deliver within a span of five days; virtually all have their calves within a two-week period – some thirty thousand births during the 2003 calving.

Here, then, the wind – the longest migration of any land animal on earth. Longer than the long run of the wildebeests of the Serengeti, longer than the biannual parades of the zebra and the springbok on the South African veldt. By the time a year has passed and the caribou have returned once more to their wintering grounds, they will have traveled a round-trip of some 2,700 miles – Boston to Boise, say, without a road map.

It is a journey of the direst sort. The Porcupine plow across snow-choked mountain passes, tramp through quagmires of mud and muck, swim mad rivers in flood, march single-file in lines of a hundred across frozen lakes, ripraps of ice heaving and cracking beneath them. Many die each year when they fall through the ice or are swept away in the freezing waters. The animals are on the move twenty hours a day. Often the weather conditions are appalling. Of all the deer species, only the caribou has evolved to meet such challenges. At the height of the migration the animals may advance thirty miles a day. At such times they sleep little, lose weight rapidly, sustain themselves on snatches of reindeer moss grabbed on the fly.

The Porcupine has been making this trek for at least ten thousand years, since the end of the last Ice Age. Before the wheel, before agricultural tinkerers in the Tigris and Euphrates valley domesticated wheat and rye, caribou were setting out for the Arctic coast each spring soon after the first glad rays of sunlight touched down on their stamping grounds in the Yukon mountains. Before Hammurabi and hieroglyphics, caribou were streaming through the valley of the Kongakut as spring's first crocuses tunneled upward through the snow. Archeological evidence suggests that the earliest ancestors of the caribou may have been visiting the Alaskan coast for as many as two million years – since *Homo erectus* stepped onto the African savanna.

The forward motion of this mass of animals constitutes an immense force, one that surpasses even the force of the herd's will to procreate, the engine of evolution. Consider this: in years of heavy snow the road to *ivvavik* may be too long, and some of the females may be compelled to give birth before they reach their destination. Conflicted by competing instincts – to tend their newborns or to migrate – they choose the latter. Hours or even minutes after delivering, the new mothers crawl to their feet and resume their journeys. Caribou calves can stand at thirty minutes, run short distances at ninety, and keep up with the herd after only twenty-four hours. If their mothers are back on the trail within an hour or two, however, their fates are sealed. They quickly fall behind. Some are swept away during river crossings. Others become bogged down in deep snow, or simply drop from exhaustion. Starvation or the jaws of a wolf or a grizzly await them.

If the drive to reproduce is not behind the extraordinary journey, what is? How does one explain ten thousand visits to *ivvavik* by a hundred thousand caribou? Only one answer makes sense to me, and that is the power of *ivvavik* itself. When the Gwich'in call this spot "the sacred place where life begins," they mean sacred to the caribou as well as to themselves. When the Inuvialuit call it "a place for giving birth to," they mean a place where life begins; or, if such is desired, where it may begin again. *Ivvavik* is a kind of paradise, and the Porcupine will do anything to reach it. What the females of the herd respond to early in April, what drives them (and soon after, the others of the herd) north and west over mountain and river, is bedazzlement with a spot on the globe, a ten-thousand-year-old promise that on the cool shores of the Beaufort Sea they will find peace. It is a yearning like the yearning in the human heart for a stream or a garden or an apple orchard that one has not seen in fifty years; it is the ache that Herman Melville was thinking of when he declared that "almost all men in their degree, some time or other, cherish very nearly the same feelings towards the ocean with me." None of us is free. We move irresistibly toward destinations of the soul, seeking heaven or earth, little realizing that they may be one and the same.

Pregnant females arrive first on the calving grounds. Over the next few weeks the others trickle in – juveniles, barren females, and, lastly, the mature males. The herd remains on the calving grounds through the short summer. There they are protected from wolves and grizzlies, which den farther south, and fattened on a banquet of plants rich in protein, carbo-hydrates, and vitamins – cotton grass, willow leaves, lousewort. Cool breezes drifting off the Arctic Ocean provide relief from the torments of mosquitoes and warble flies that arrive with the first warm weather. By August the great gathering has begun to break up. Small groups meander south and east, the first step in the closing of the annual circle. Some pass through the valley of the Kongakut, recrossing the river where it makes its mighty swing to the left. The air grows cool; bearberry, willow, and birch take on fall colors that are wistful and intense. Fat, thickly furred bulls shed their velvet. For a week or two the adult males spar good-naturedly. Then the contests turn violent; occasionally one ends with the death of a combatant. In the third week of October, 228 days before their new calves must be ready for delivery, the females come into heat. For the bulls that have triumphed in the rut, a few days of recklessness follow. Then the fever ends and the animals, one and all, move quickly to their wintering grounds. One day the clouds thicken and the wind freshens, and the season's first curtain of snow unfurls across the sky.

The mechanism by which the Porcupine finds its way to *ivvavik* is cloaked in mystery. Here and there on the tundra one finds paths that have been worn in by decades or even centuries of use by the herd. These surely are useful in guiding the caribou to their destination. Addition-ally, the Porcupine, like other migrating creatures, may use the sun, the moon, or the earth's magnetic field as beacons; or, the salmon's trick, an incredibly accomplished sense of smell. The few studies that have been done to investigate these possibilities have been inconclusive.

Perhaps the most common navigational device employed by migrators, that of watching for visual clues recalled from earlier trips, would seem to be of minor use to the Porcupine. Individuals travel different routes from one year to the next. Juveniles that might be expected to take the same path that their mothers led them on the previous year set out instead on entirely different paths the first time they are on their own. We know this because several dozen of the Porcupine have been captured and fitted with satellite collars, allowing their movements to be mapped with great precision. Some caribou, it turns out, walk alone. Some travel in circles or wander off in completely wrong directions before they straighten out and fly right. Some take a year off and don't migrate at all. During their sabbaticals these stay-at-homes remain active but never stray far from their home bases. Scientists observing the animals' wanderings estimate that they put in about seven miles of walking per day. At the end of a year, amazingly, they've clocked around 2,700 miles total, the same as their more widely traveled cousins.

Beyond the standard, and unproven, explanations for the sure course of the caribou and other migrating species, there is compelling evidence that the primary mechanism of migration resides in a realm that is, for now at least, beyond the reach of science. The Manx shearwater, *Puffinus puffinus*, is a pigeon-size bird with dark plumage and white wings bordered in black. The bird spends most of its life at sea, off the coast of South Wales and Pembrokeshire, Scotland. It comes ashore only to nest and to lay eggs in rude burrows that it excavates in the ground.

Soon after the eggs hatch, the parents pack their bags, say good-bye to the chicks, and in what appears to be one of the most flagrant examples of irresponsible parental behavior in bird-dom, fly off to sunny Brazil. *Whew! Glad that's done! We need a break!* The young shearwaters, no doubt thoroughly undone by the abandonment, remain in their burrows. There they become easy targets for predators.

It doesn't take long for the chicks to realize the peril they are in. Imagine now: a shearwater chick is a pathetic little thing, a cold, hungry, mangy scruff of feathers with a brain no bigger than a pencil eraser. Yet somewhere inside that wisp of a brain there is space for two things that the bird suddenly needs very much: a friendly voice to explain that there is nothing to be gained waiting around for a fox or a rat to show up, and an escape plan.

The chicks get the message. One day soon, in a series of maneuvers that must be as thrilling to behold as the departure of the parents must be bewildering, the young shearwaters rise into the air, swoop low over the coast, circle once or twice to get their tiny bird bearings, come around – *and then make a beeline for Brazil!* One week out, they're over Madeira. Two weeks out, they tip their wings to Cape Verde. Three weeks out, they reunite with the entire shearwater family (possibly even including mom and dad) in the azure waters off Rio and Buenos Aires. Total distance flown: more than six thousand miles.

The conventional explanation for this and for other seemingly miraculous bird migratory journeys is that the chicks are born with genetically imprinted star maps. These they follow to wherever it is they wish to go. There is experimental evidence to support this theory. German scientists have demonstrated that blackcaps and garden warblers released inside a planetarium orient themselves for fall migration through reference not to true north and south, but to star patterns projected onto the planetarium ceiling.

Maps may play a role, but probably only a small one, as an astonishing episode involving a Manx shearwater reveals. In June 1952, a biologist studying bird migration took a page from Charles Darwin, who urged every proper scientist to occasionally conduct a damn fool experiment, just to see what happens. The biologist scooped up a Manx from its burrow on Skokholm Island, Pembrokeshire, plopped it into a cage, and flew it by commercial airliner to Boston. There he tagged the bird and released it.

The shearwater had never been to Boston; nor, as far as anyone knows, had any of its ancestors; nor, it must be assumed, was the bird equipped with an inborn star map outlining suggested transatlantic routes between Boston and Skokholm Island. Yet the bird was sweetly back in its nest in twelve-and-a-half days. Distance flown: 3050 miles, as the crow flies. Average distance flown per day: 240 miles.

One pauses in wonder and disbelief at such a tale. Scientific accounts of this astounding journey – or of the newborn shearwater's ability to locate ancestral waters more than a quarter of the way around the globe, or of the long, exacting runs of the salmon and the loggerhead turtle, or of the four-week cross-continental flight of the Monarch butterfly, or of the clockwork arrival of the California grunion on the moonlit beaches of the Pacific coast, or of any of the countless such sublime journeys that are routinely accomplished in nature – invariably conclude with an admission that reads something this: "How the animal accomplishes this feat is not fully understood." Despite years of study by wildlife biologists, migration remains an enigma. It is not as though investigators are slowly creeping toward a complete explication of the phenomenon, as biologists mapping the architecture of the human genome are doing. The involvement of the earth's magnetic field, star patterns, sun movements, and so on in the business of migration have been known for decades. Yet something central, a hole in the fabric, remains utterly hidden from the rational brain.

Here, then, a damn fool experiment to try at home that may provide you with a glimpse of the unglimpseable: Go outside on a moonless spring evening. Find a place that is warm and peaceful and dark. Make yourself comfortable. Open your mind suitably. Then ponder this: In the fathomless ether somewhere far above you, butterflies are winging their way north to the strains of an unheard symphony. Larks, robins, thrushes, swallows ride the breakers of night, bound for Alberta, British Columbia, and Saskatchewan. In the dark waters off North Carolina and Virginia, blue whales fresh from winter sojourns in the Caribbean plow steadily northward toward a familiar address in the Barents Sea. Three thousand miles to the west, humpbacks and fur seals traverse the outlet of the Columbia, then jog left, bewitched by the never-failing beacon of the Aleutians. Somewhere not far from where you sit, deer press forward silently in the night. Garter snakes, painted turtles, and toads make their small ways toward genial fields and ponds they remember from last year, and the year before. Far to the north, caribou as staunch as redwoods pause, lower their shoulders, launch into the silvery froth of the Kongakut.

The creatures of the earth are on the move!

"Pattern of life indelible, the fade-proof lake, the woods unshatterable, the pasture with the sweetfern and the juniper forever and ever, summer without end." That is E. B. White, rhapsodizing on the Maine lake to which, throughout his childhood, he and his family returned, with the clockwork precision of swallows swooping down on Capistrano, on the first day of August every year.

> I have since become a salt-water man, but sometimes in summer there are days when the restlessness of the tides and the fearful cold of the sea water and the incessant wind which blows across the afternoon and into the evening make me wish for the placidity of a lake in the woods.

Let us go to see the old place again. Let us find the cloud-capped hill and the path through the pine needles, and the knoll where Brownie is buried. Let us begin again.

KAKTOVIK

Emerging from heavy cloud cover, the turboprop traced
a barely discernable shadow across the narrow coastal plain of northern
Alaska, then began its descent toward Kaktovik, a hardscrabble settle-
ment clinging heroically to a clump of sod in the Arctic Ocean called
Barter Island. I was seated by the rear window of the cramped aircraft,
beneath a ceiling so low that my neck had begun to ache. On board with
me were ten or twelve others: a half-dozen passengers bound for Kaktovik; some oil roustabouts continuing on to the next stop, Prudhoe Bay;
and, across the aisle, my friend Shaun Griffin. Grizzled veteran of a hundred capricious enterprises, Shaun had signed on to this one on a cold
winter evening a few months earlier, as he and I conspired beside a potbellied stove in the bar at the Gold Hill Hotel, in the mountains near
Virginia City, Nevada. Given the location, altitude may have been a fac-
tor in his decision to join me. Also brandy. Nevertheless, I was confident
that he was sincere. Shaun belongs to the race of men and women who will
say yes if you ask them to change a tire or to sail an ocean, and who mean
it and will sweat the consequences later. Like me, he was seeing the

Arctic for the first time; unlike me, he would probably have arrived here sooner or later even without developing a sudden zest for caribou. By nature a poet, by design a tumbleweed, he travels widely and incessantly, composing quatrains and villanelles as he goes. During the previous twelve months he had circled the globe, dropping anchor in a bulging gazetteer of foreign ports: Tokyo, Bangkok, Athens, Belfast, Cape Town, Buenos Aires. Six months before Kaktovik he called at Patagonia, the antipode. He is tall and narrow and well-made, and like a good Nevada bristlecone will not topple in a stiff breeze. This and the fact that he is endlessly good-natured made him, I thought, a good bet for the North. He had recently published his fifth book, a widely praised collection of poetry; with his wife Deborah he was the subject of a new documentary in the PBS "Visionaries" series, a film that profiled the inspired community and youth development agency the two run in Virginia City. Clearly he was on a roll, and I was not surprised now to glance over and see a man who appeared to be quite at ease with the uncertain prospects before us and the treacherous landscape below.

Minutes after our departure from Fairbanks the aircraft had burrowed into yeasty clouds. There it remained for the next hour and a half. Of the Brooks Range, of the great forests, of the storied tundra, the nameless valleys, the rivers without end: of the vast, bleak, unfolding North I had seen nothing. My transition to an Arctic disposition, then, was abrupt. I saw Fairbanks, which is a green friendly place, and then I saw the coastal plain, which is not. My body ached, and not because of the low ceiling.

I gazed down on the misty world below. Surely this was the most hopeless, miserable-looking spot of planet I had ever laid eyes on. I knew that thousands of caribou females were somewhere beneath me, giving birth to a new generation, and I was very happy for them. Not even my most fervent effort, however, allowed me to imagine being down there with them.

Kaktovik is the logical jumping-off point for a journey to *ivvavik*. It is a community of some three hundred people, most of them Inupiat. As the plane began its descent to the gravel airstrip at one end of the island, I knew with utter certainty that I did not want to come down. I thought of Ralph Waldo Emerson, old and grumpy. "Travelling is a fool's paradise," he grouses. He awakens in Naples. He turns over in his bed. There beside him, to his horror, is Ralph Waldo Emerson – "the stern fact, the sad self, unrelenting, identical, that I fled from."

My stern fact shuddered. The plane circled and I caught my first glimpse of the town, a morose scatter of buildings frozen to the earth like volcanic rubble to the plains of Mars. Stretching north as far as I could see, the choking pack ice of the Arctic Ocean. In the old days, in the days of Elisha Kent Kane and Fridtjof Nansen and the other neck-or-nothing polar explorers whose exploits had done so much to bring me here, attaining the pack ice from England or Boston and then getting stuck in it, as those men inevitably did, took months. Here I was, in nearly the same pickle, and only two days from Reno. The sudden clamor of ice rattled in my ears, drowning out the drone of the engines, and my resolve.

The plane hit the airstrip hard. Moments later the door swung open and I stepped out, catching my first breath of Arctic air.

I recognized the scent at once. I knew it from high mountains and long Sierra nights, and from the Lake Erie winters of my childhood – cold, piercing, silent, alarming, liberating. The scent goes in and it goes down, and it lights up everything that it passes along the way, from the little hairs in your nose to that flappy thing at the back of your throat to your windpipe, all the way down to your lungs. Things you'd forgotten you had. Your skin jingles and your ears bristle and your lungs pump, and you notice something for the first time in a long while, your *self*, your cold glad breathing shivering self.

Gobs of wet snow pelted down. A nasty wind jabbed across the airstrip. Through a veil of pearl-gray mist I could see Kaktovik a mile away, a dim light at the end of the earth.

I looked at my friend and shook my head. Without a word we hoisted our backpacks and prepared to walk to town. Somewhere, we knew, there was a place where we could escape from the weather. Somewhere, too, there was a bush pilot named Walt Audi, who had told me by phone a month earlier that he would help us find caribou. At the time I had been impressed, and relieved, to learn how very simple the task would be. We would step out of one plane and into another, into Audi's Cessna. A short time later we would be frolicking in a lovely meadow with noted members of the Porcupine herd, who would be delighted to see us. Now I realized how badly I had underestimated the North. Not only would we not be stepping at once into Audi's plane, we might be stuck in Kaktovik for a week, or a month, or forever. As for caribou, who could say that I would ever track them down – or even that I wanted to?

I was badly in need of a lift. Miraculously, one materialized. Out of the mist came a battered brown pickup, headlights searching. The truck scooted up beside us and a heavyset gentleman in a thick jacket and a jaunty black beret hopped out. He was immediately hammered by a volley of precipitation.

However unsuited I may have been to that dismal spot of earth, the newcomer looked staunch, steady, and possibly even waterproof, as though he may have been conceived there. His skin was pale and weathered, like birch bark; his hair and mustache were the color of fine Sierra granite. On his face he wore the abstracted expression of an aging sea captain who can't decide whether to steer clear of an iceberg or to take another pull on his pipe.

The stranger smiled and squinted into the wind. I noticed a spritz of ponytail poking out from beneath his beret.

"You Bob?" He pulled off a glove and stuck out his hand. "Throw your gear in the back and get in."

"Walt?"

I never got an answer. A moment later my partner and I were sprawled in the open bed of a Chevy pickup, bouncing toward Kaktovik on a very bad road. We passed monstrous heaps of grungy snow stuffed with half-buried Arctic Cats and Datsuns, banks of utility poles jammed into the earth at crazy angles, and pools of black water whose surfaces glimmered in shimmering rainbows of gasoline; and just over there, nodding like a proper welcoming committee, the ice-clogged sea. A few days before leaving home, at a send-off dinner in a Chinese restaurant with my wife and son, I had pulled this forecast from a fortune cookie: "Soon you will be sitting on top of the world." Suddenly I recalled the thrill that that prescient dispatch had unleashed in me. I thought of Carol and Jake, and I remembered my dream of the North; and all at once I recognized the world around me – not alien, not threatening, not sopping and miserable, but comfortable and familiar as Christmas. Snow and cold I knew well. Uncertainty – that was my flesh and blood! At my side was my friend, cocked against the cab of the truck was my backpack with its bombproof tent, its dependable stove, and its fine stash of M&Ms and peanuts – and *Holy Christ!* we were bounding toward Kaktovik! The veil lifted. I felt like a million bucks. I was sailing at last – as James Cowan puts it in his wonderful *A Mapmaker's Dream*, "as if absorbed into the margins of my map, a ship embarking upon its maiden voyage."

The Waldo Arms, Walt Audi's hostelry in Kaktovik, retails for $150 per night per person. The grandeur of the fee conjures images of an elegant, refined establishment – one boasting a sauna, perhaps, or a valet laundry, or a landscaped jogging trail winding pleasantly down to the Beaufort Sea.

The images are erroneous. The Waldo Arms is not elegant and it is not refined. The fee is misleading. In a town where everything from dog kibble to steeple bells must be flown or rafted in, or carted in on the winter tractor road, $150 per night is a bargain. Everything costs in Kaktovik. For a sauna, try San Francisco.

From the outside of the lodging, which I first observed from the back of a pickup truck with snow in my eyes and possible early signs of frostbite on my cheeks, I saw what I might have mistaken for a trailer park, or a construction site, except that the name WALDO ARMS was hand-painted on its side in bold carmine letters. The building was a one-story structure composed of a shedlike entrance-way connected to a prefab mobile home, which appeared to connect at a weird angle to another prefab mobile home, which appeared somewhere in the foggy distance to have been thrust violently through the side of another prefab mobile home, perhaps during a traffic accident. The Waldo was weather-beaten and forlorn and ever-so-slightly peculiar; it was also the warmest, most welcoming sight I had ever laid eyes on. Was there a cozier-looking place on the planet? If so, I could not have imagined it.

A small lamp burned brightly in the window beside the front door. I dragged my pack from the back of the truck. The path was pitted with sinkholes of mud and puddles of oily water; piles of debris lay on all sides – engine parts, chunks of decomposing lumber, rusty fuel containers, sheets of warped plywood. Nearby stood a truck with no front end and half an engine. At a different latitude the scene might have looked squalid; here it appeared as though some very hard work was being done, when possible, under very difficult circumstances.

It was easy to see that we weren't flying anywhere soon. Audi attempted to paint a hopeful picture.

"I'll try to get you out of here this afternoon," he said. He threw open the front door, releasing to the world outside a blast of warm air and the promise of a hearty meal. "Right now the signs don't look good."

Inside, the theme of sublime disorder was taken up and raised to symphonic level. There were several large rooms, all tilting with contents. *Dances with Wolves* flickered on a television screen. Scattered about were sundry sofas and chairs of remote vintage. I saw card tables to eat on, a dart board to throw at, an exercycle, a pool table, a wok, dried flowers, another television, several power tools plugged in and ready to go, numerous cacti in various states of health. One wall held a floor-to-ceiling bookshelf of abandoned paperbacks, including what appeared to be the complete works of Danielle Steel. The walls were as busy as the rest of the place – Inupiat masks, calendars from bygone years, maps, magazine covers, a framed thousand-piece jigsaw puzzle depicting a sunny cathedral, possibly in Spain, several six-foot-long baleen feathers taken from the mouth of a locally harvested whale. Where there wasn't something else there was usually a box, often containing items of great interest.

Audi's companion, a charming and gregarious woman named Merylin Traynor, was in the kitchen frying hamburgers. Walt asked her to fix some lunch for Shaun and me. Then he was gone.

It didn't take me long to discover that to classify the Waldo Arms as a hotel is to demean it, is to fail to convey its true nature. The Waldo is not a hotel. It is a grand duchy, and Walt Audi is its duke. He authored its constitution; presides over its dramas, all of which involve weather; gives aid and comfort to its citizens, all of whom want to get out of Kaktovik as soon as possible; and orchestrates the delicious resolutions of the dramas, often while clad in a T-shirt and slippers. One tiny window of the Waldo Arms faces the town's airstrip. A pair of field glasses rests on the windowsill. On a typical day in June the patrons of the hotel – wildlife biologists, geologists, stranded bush pilots and backpackers, assorted misfits and miscreants – spend their waking hours wandering to and from the window, announcing to whomever may be listening the results of their desperate observations.

"I can see the hangar! Where's Walt?"

"Walt!"

"Damn. Pea soup."

"It's lifting. Half an hour I'd say."

"Hey, Walt. Check it out."

"Where's Walt?"

Audi will disappear for hours at a time. At odd moments he'll materialize in half-frame glasses and bemused expression to phone the weather service or to discuss flight options at a huge map of northern Alaska or to take his own long, slow gander out the oracular window. Nearly inaudibly he'll say a few words, usually in a sing-songy voice and often punctuated by a laugh. Everyone in the room listens acutely to these pronouncements, as though what he says has life-or-death importance, which it does.

Just about every book and magazine article about northern Alaska that I've read mentions Audi's name and refers to him as a "legendary" bush pilot. This is a serious charge. In an age when the term is applied willy-nilly to high-end wristwatches, men's cologne, rock stars, and practically any saloon that is more than ten years old, it ought not to be brandished carelessly.

With this in mind I did some research. I quickly reached the conclusion that the adjective "legendary" may in fact fairly be applied to Walt Audi. The reason is simple: there are actually legends about him. Many involve fog. Most pilots hate the stuff. Having lived with it for four decades, Audi has made his peace not only with fog but with its evil cousins: mist, drizzle, mizzle, and haze. He recognizes their inevitability and, being a practical man, accepts them as part of life, like indigestion. While other pilots are down on the ground pacing and shaking their fists, Audi is up yonder, jousting. Ergo, the legends, not all of them happy. One has him meeting a mountain wall in the foggy Brooks Range in early winter, going down, and spending five days on a ledge passing in and out of consciousness. Somehow he holds on doggedly until, at the last minute, a signal from his transponder accidentally intersects civilization, and he is saved. Another has him munching a ham sandwich and humming *The 1812 Overture* as he slices through cottage-cheese fog at two hundred feet; meanwhile, his passenger cowers beside him reciting the Twenty-Third Psalm. Yet another has him approaching a treacherous bank of fog, which suddenly parts mysteriously, precisely in the shape of his plane. Audi slips through safely and the fog closes in behind him.

Whether these stories are true or not is beside the point. They're legends. One admirer that I spoke with put it this way: "Walt plays his Cessna like a violin. You watch him fly, you hear Beethoven." Audi showed up on the north coast in 1965 to work the DEW line, the radar shield that the Pentagon erected along the Arctic front to detect incoming Soviet planes and missiles. He found himself in one of the most godforsaken spots on the planet. Yet he took to it somehow and stayed. Forty years later he's still there, ferrying passengers around northern Alaska as the sky allows. When he's not in his plane he's at the Waldo, holding court. He's happy, he enjoys his work, and he's very good at it. Sometimes, like a caribou, he migrates south. A few years ago he and Merylin hiked the Appalachian Trail. Every winter, when Kaktovik is dark and the temperature is insane, the two can be found on a beach in Costa Rica.

Heavy precipitation had battered the coastal plain for days. In the words of a tall, gaunt, wild-eyed helicopter pilot who stormed into the Waldo not long after my arrival, the plain was "a goddamned mess." Earlier in the day this beleaguered fellow had been called upon to yank a team of glaciologists off the McCall Glacier in the northern Brooks Range. In beating its hasty retreat, the team had been forced to leave behind a stock-pile of expensive technical equipment. The melancholy task of retrieving the materiel now fell to the chopper pilot, who was slated to return to the glacier as soon as he could fight his way through the weather.

Razor-thin, jittery, endlessly pacing, endlessly jabbering, the young man was temperamentally the polar opposite of the hotel's dispassionate proprietor. Helicopters are notoriously fussy machines. They're employed to take people where fixed-wing aircraft cannot go, on days when they cannot fly. After observing the skittish one for fifteen minutes, I con-cluded that work of this sort must have a tendency to induce cold sweats in the people who perform it and to lead to permanently frayed nerves. Helicopters require not violinists like Walt Audi at their controls but jazz drummers like Buddy Rich or Elvin Jones, who can keep five rhythms going at the same time they are working a crossword puzzle and making time with the cocktail waitress.

Again unlike Walt Audi, chopper pilots appear unsuited to enforced captivity in small hotels. They need the wind beneath their wings, or their rotors, in order to be truly happy. That, at least, was true of this one, who allowed that what he loved most about his job were the quiet times, the times when the sky was vivid and the sun warm, when he could loft through the air like a milkweed feather, and set down on a beautiful spot in the middle of nowhere with a fine view and a modest helping of peace and quiet, and pull out his field glasses to admire the view, or put on his snowshoes and go for a stroll.

Today was not such a day. Today was a day for pacing. And so he threw out his arms like an angry schoolteacher and ranted at the children. He castigated the weather, the American Civil Liberties Union, and his fate, and he delivered low opinions of the world's simpler people. Somewhere in his sermon he arrived at the mess that was the coastal plain. Two days earlier he had been called upon to pluck Karsten and Leanne Heuer out of the mud and bring them back to the Waldo Arms. In April this remarkable couple had embarked on a preposterous journey. Near Old Crow, Yukon, they had joined a wing of the Porcupine herd, just then beginning its trek northward to *ivvavik*. With everything they would need on their backs or stashed in previously stocked supply depots, the couple took off on foot and on skis with the caribou. Their plan was to accompany the herd through the entire length of its migration.

Nothing of this sort had ever been attempted. A few years earlier Karsten Heuer had warmed up for the journey, so to speak, by walking more than two thousand miles from Yellowstone National Park to Watson Lake, Yukon. Arduous though that trek was, its rigors paled in comparison with those he and his partner would face now. When they set out from Old Crow, the Heuers were committing themselves to seven months of the hardest travel on earth.

The couple's immediate goal was to call attention to the calamities they believed would befall the Porcupine herd if oil exploration were to begin on the coastal plain. Their rather more challenging existential goal was to so immerse themselves in the struggles and day-to-day lives of the caribou that they would come to know its *umwelt* – the self-world of the animal, the way it perceives and feels and understands the world. They called their journey "Being Caribou."

Few would believe that humans could achieve such an understanding. But few would believe either that humans could travel for seven months with a herd of migrating ungulates, so who could be certain that the couple would fail in its mission! Karsten and Leanne Heuer were, after all, young and fierce and tenacious. They possessed powerful imaginations. Perhaps most important, they saw themselves as flame bearers of a crucial truth that imperial science was powerless to study and that it therefore denied. And this truth was that the cultural, emotional, and spiritual differences between humans and animals are small. Get beyond the fur and the feathers, the couple asserted, and you find creatures that are more alike than they are not. Observe sympathetically and subjectively (that is, in ways forbidden to science) the behavior of amorous plovers, frolicking tiger cubs, angry trout, disconsolate coyote mothers mourning the losses of their pups – and you secure vitally important data about animals. Gaze long and hard into the eyes of a dog or a horse or a gorilla, and you gain more.

Perhaps, indeed, it was not possible to be a caribou. But if human empathy is a good thing, if it is a sign of mature, fully integrated humanness to choose to walk a mile in another man's shoes in an effort to see the world through his eyes: then surely some important revelation may await the creature that walks a thousand miles in the hoofprints of another.

Since leaving Old Crow the Heuers had lived the caribou life. Mountains, grizzlies, wolves, blizzards, bitter cold, avalanches, river crossings on boats of ice – they had seen and done it all. Approaching Kaktovik, they had come down with a critical need for French fries. They radioed for an aircraft to pull them out for a day of R and R. So entered into their lives one very frazzled helicopter pilot.

"Jesus, it's a mudhole out there. Biggest goddamned mess you've ever seen. Rain and snow and mud and they're all happy as clams and camping in it like it's a goddamned sunny beach in California. And they're, like, vegetarians, and they don't even have a goddamned gun. I told them that all you need for grizzlies is a pistol with one bullet. That's to shoot yourself. Jesus, they're hard-core, they looked like skeletons. Hey, Walt, how much weight did they lose? Twenty pounds I think."

Audi padded by on his way to the window.

"Eighteen. They gained seven while they were here." He chuckled and raised his field glasses. The room snapped to attention.

"What?"

At the Waldo Arms the Heuers ate like horses and slept like lambs. A day later they were back on the coastal plain, living like caribou. The chopper pilot set them down in "a goddamned incredible quagmire of complete shit." Now, a day later, he fretted over his impending return to the McCall Glacier. That assignment recalled another in a long history of hairy flights.

"It's flying goddamn snow and fog and I'm squinting to see where the hell we're going, and these guys figure I know what I'm doing. And I say, 'I am really uncomfortable with this, guys' and one of them says, 'Yeah, but I can see the ground.' And I say, 'Yeah, but I can't see straight ahead. . .'"

Shaun and I escaped what suddenly felt like incarceration. We headed out the door and down a boulevard of dirt and ice, our destination a spot at the end of the island where someone had reported seeing a polar bear.

The snow and rain had stopped but a deep mist lay over the town. It was late in the day. The streets were mostly empty. At odd moments I nodded to a passerby or to a barking dog, or high-stepped to avoid squooshing a mouse that scurried across my path. The houses we passed were lean, rectangular, one-story dwellings, practical as T-squares, hoisted up on stilts to keep them off the cold boggy earth. Each was fortified against the North by a yard full of paraphernalia – snowmobiles, four-wheelers, hauling sledges, engine parts. Each, too, evinced a kind of dead seriousness about existence that seemed to infuse practically everything and everyone I encountered. Who could live here without engaging unabashedly in life and its mysteries? Simply knowing that everyone else on your meridian stood south of you, was warmer than you, and was perplexed and amazed by your presence here; simply knowing that you were the civilized world's last defense, its human DEW line against lemmings and snow-borne disease, against blizzards of foolishness and ignorance, and especially against true knowledge of the dreadful emptiness that lurked to the north, just beyond your doorstep – simply knowing those things would surely alert you to the onerous weight of existence.

Strolling beside me, calling attention to each dragon and will-o'-the-wisp that rose up in our way, Shaun was upbeat. Foreign ports are good for him, and this one was about as foreign as they come. Like others of the race of poets, my friend takes sustenance from travel (Ralph Waldo Emerson is the obvious exception); somehow he is able to convert it into high-protein creative energy. He talked as he walked, but I knew that his mind was spinning. Already the mist had drifted into his subconscious, along with the sturdy houses and the mice; by morning they would be lines in his journal or images in a poem.

We rounded a corner, one of only half a dozen in the town. Our conversation turned to travel and to the awesome distance that now stood between us and our families. The next stage of our journey, the drop-off in the refuge, would multiply that distance many times over. We had purposely chosen to go without firearms, radio, satellite phone, and global positioning system. The idea was to hunt for caribou in the Arctic as we would hunt for wildflowers in Nevada, armed with only tent, sleeping bag, and freeze-dried beef stroganoff. Risks aplenty lay ahead; if one of us broke a leg or came down with appendicitis, we'd be in a jam. Yet my partner was buoyant. Would we step into a Cessna tomorrow morning and be fending off grizzlies by noon? Would we hole up at the Waldo Arms for a month or simply fold our cards and go home? Shaun was comfortable with any outcome; we would do our best and see where that led.

I was less sanguine. I was the helicopter pilot to my friend's Walt Audi – edgy, eager for resolution. The high spirits in which I had arrived at the Waldo remained. Talk of glaciers, bears, and the mess on the coastal plain, however, had given me second thoughts about the wisdom of going in without a gun and lacking the ability to summon help if we needed it. I wanted to learn grace on this journey; the knot in my stomach told me that I was still wanting.

In the tiny post office we traded stories with the postmaster, Dave Tetreau. Tetreau moved to Kaktovik to be with his son, who then up and moved to another town. That was five years before. Tetreau the elder stayed on, like Walt Audi finding here something that soothed his soul. Unlike Audi, he would not stay for forty years. He had a plan – to emigrate to exotic Michigan, where he owned eight acres and where he would sit on his porch, put his feet up on the railing, and watch the clouds go by.

Such destinations we find for ourselves! But perhaps it is the other way around; perhaps it is the destinations that find us. As we left the building, Tetreau stood at the door and aimed his finger over my shoulder at a spot near a corner of the school.

"That's where it picked me up," he said with a touch of wonder. He had been telling us about a famous blast of wind that hit Kaktovik one dark January day. He moved his finger in a wide rainbow through the air, bringing it to rest on a point fifty yards from the first one.

"That's where it put me down." A mild reverie came over the postmaster as he recalled his brief but unforgettable ascent into the jet stream. A snippet from a song by Kerry Livgren of the rock group Kansas popped into my head: "All we are is dust in the wind." Livgren probably intended the line to be understood symbolically. But in places like Kaktovik, acts of nature can make literal what songwriters intend only as metaphor. The name Kaktovik itself springs from such an incident. Once there was an Inuit named Pipsuk. One day while fishing the treacherous waters off Barter Island, Pipsuk suffered an accident and drowned. His companions retrieved his body with a type of fishing net called a seining net. In the peculiar manner of narrative, the Inuit name for the net – *qaaktugvi* – came to be associated with the site of the tragedy. Over time the name gradually transmuted to Kaktovik.

At the end of the island, on a flat, featureless expanse that is the continent's last breath of land, there is a cemetery. A score of white crosses lace the frail, snow-covered earth, as if to hold it in one piece. Land and sea are one here. Gazing toward the Beaufort Sea a short distance away you notice that sea level and ankle level are the same. And then it dawns on you that you are standing on the bottom of the ocean. Like the squall that made a rainbow of Dave Tetreau, a great wave could sweep over this desperate, defiant spot, perhaps snatching old Pipsuk's bones from the clutches of the seining net and, in a sobering example of destination finding man, returning them to the salty grave that claimed him in the first place.

Just beyond the cemetery is the town's landfill. There we had hoped (but not really!) to find the polar bear. Alas, the animal was nowhere to be seen. Looking south toward the Alaska mainland we could make out a subtle shift in the weather. The dark cloud that had hung over the coastal plain for many days appeared to have moved east, toward the Yukon border. The plain was probably still a mess, but the sky above looked one shade of gray lighter than it had since we arrived in Kaktovik.

We returned to the Waldo in a hopeful mood. During our absence, the hotel had undergone a rambunctious, end-of-the-day metamorphosis into after-hours grocery store and village social center. Each time I looked up, a new group of locals was dancing through the door. Shaun and I took the opportunity to practice our Inupiat vocabulary with four kids who showed up to purchase eggs and canned soup from Audi. As we mangled first one pronunciation and then the next, the four patiently corrected us, at once delighted and horrified at our thick-headedness.

Shaun: "*Nu-kat-pi* – Would you repeat the word?"

"Listen please! *Nu-kat-pi-a-lu-ru-aq.*"

"*Ni-pi-ak* – "

"No! *Nu-kat-pi-a-lu-ru-aq!*"

Then the slyest of the group, a fourth-grader named Yvonne, tricked my friend into saying an Inupiat word not generally spoken in polite company. At her urging he repeated the word half a dozen times, increasing the volume on each repetition, as she and her comrades dissolved into helpless laughter.

Later, two venerable village residents, Daniel and Lillian Akootchook, dropped by to chat with the hotel proprietor. Traditional Inupiats, the Akootchooks had lived off the land and the sea all their lives – Daniel fishing and trapping, hunting caribou and, with other men of the community, bowhead whales; Lillian staying home to stretch sealskins, cook, sew, make masks.

Now in their seventies, the two had moved smoothly into a world that did not exist until recently. They enjoyed their cable television, their four-wheeler, the retirement benefits from the job that Daniel held for many years with the North Slope Borough School District. With great formality, smiling broadly, they shook hands with Shaun and me and welcomed us to their town. I mentioned our unsuccessful hunt for polar bear. They laughed, and Daniel uttered the name of the great white bear: *nanuq*.

Perhaps, like most of us, the Akootchooks would describe their lives as ordinary. And yet, all I could think when Daniel, a giant of a man, folded my hand into his was, My Christ, this fellow has gone after bowhead! Twenty miles out in the misty, roiling Beaufort, he has aimed and fired harpoons into the flesh of animals the size of small office buildings! I felt a deep kinship with this gentle, self-effacing man. Adventure he had known, aplenty, as I had, too, though in ways vastly different from his; now, in his retirement, he manifested a palpable serenity and light-heartedness – qualities I was determined to acquire.

After dinner Shaun and I took a small, bare room that might have cheered a pair of Trappist monks. Late in the evening when I retired, the night beyond the window was as bright as day.

At eight the next morning, beside the school building, kids shot baskets in a dense fog. The music was atonal, the rhythm of voices hollow and haunting. At ten, Audi detected something in the air. He drove out to the landfill to take a look. Twenty minutes later he was back, with a spring in his step. He found Shaun and me reading in the library.

"Grab a bite," he said. "Then let's fly."

A LEAP OF FAITH

The Arctic National Wildlife Refuge has been much in the news in recent years, thanks to the apparently walloping reserves of oil and gas that lie beneath its surface, and the seemingly endless debate in Washington over what, if anything, to do with them. Despite its renown, the refuge remains a mystery to most people. Rarely visited, largely unexplored, utterly undeveloped, frightfully inhospitable to travelers, the huge chunk of wild country that occupies Alaska's northeast corner has become a kind of celebrity recluse that practically everyone has an opinion about, but almost no one has ever seen – the Howard Hughes of wildlife refuges.

Not surprisingly, a certain amount of myth and misconception has grown up around the place. When I told a friend that I planned to visit the refuge, she invoked both woolly mammoths and the Abominable Snowman in her flustered response. The remoteness of my destination, both physical and psychological, is at once its blessing and its curse. Inaccessible, in some ways unthinkable, the preserve likely will be saved from the convulsion of visitors, cars, and tourist amenities that have destroyed the primitive character of such lower forty-eight wonders as the Grand Canyon and Yosemite Valley; at the same time, the veil of unknowing that cloaks the region has simplified the task of explaining why its wildness may have to be sacrificed for energy production, for those who would make that exchange. In the words of Gale Norton, secretary of the interior under President George W. Bush, the refuge is the geographical equivalent of *Seinfeld* – a "flat white nothingness." Developing such an imponderable, one might conclude, would be like developing, say, Neptune. What harm could there be in that?

Some thirty thousand square miles in area – about the size of Austria, or two Switzerlands – the refuge extends from the Alaska Pipeline corridor on the west to Canada's Yukon Territory on the east. Half of the preserve lies north of the northern boundary of trees; all reposes above the Arctic Circle, the imaginary line north of which the sun remains above the horizon for twenty-four hours on June 21.

Bisecting the refuge east-to-west is the Brooks Range, one of the wildest and least known of the world's great mountain ranges. The unfriendliness of the Brooks discouraged prehistoric populations from settling the interior. North and south of the mountains, however, native peoples have flourished for thousands of years. In the birch and spruce flatlands to the south, Gwich'in Athabaskan Indians evolved a culture that centered on the caribou, and does so to this day. In the treeless north, nomadic Inupiat Eskimos learned to follow the caribou and the musk ox and to harvest the rich waters of the bordering Arctic Ocean for bowhead whales and seals. Despite the difficulties of travel, the two peoples hunted and fished the interior and came to know one another through cross-mountain trade.

The Brooks Range is the northernmost link in the thirty-two-hundred–mile Rocky Mountain chain. The tallest peaks of the range and its principal sub-ranges – the Romanzof, the Philip Smith, and the Davidson mountains – rise to a height of nine thousand feet. That's low by Sierra Nevada or Colorado Rocky standards, but woe to the mountaineer who assumes that low means easy. The Brooks are trouble. Never mind the crumbly rock, crevasse-laced glaciers, ridiculous temperatures, and atrocious weather conditions: simply reaching the peaks presents a Himalayan challenge. Because there are no roads or trails into the Brooks, access is either by bush plane, which puts them beyond the price range of many climbers, or by a long and arduous ("improbable" would be a better word for it) overland march. As a result, many of the peaks have never been visited, let alone climbed. That's good news for ambitious mountaineers. Armed with unlimited time, an audacious spirit, and a bundle of cash, the committed climber can still find remote, worthy summits on which to carve his or her name.

The northern boundary of the refuge marks the edge of the North American continent. Beyond lies the Beaufort Sea, one of the many "seas" – local arms of the Arctic Ocean (the Chukchi, the East Siberian, the Laptev, the Kara, and the Barents are others) – that circle the North Pole. From the Alaska coast northward it's all ice – or, more and more in these days of rising global temperatures, water – fourteen hundred miles to the pole. An intrepid gull heading out on that bearing and continuing beyond the pole would next make land on one of the myriad islands of northern Norway.

The Brooks and the Beaufort compose the vast proportion of the scenery in this corner of the world. Sandwiched between the two is a sliver of terrain that, despite its small size, dwarfs the others in biological and political importance. This is the so-called Arctic coastal plain. The plain forms the northern edge of the Arctic National Wildlife Refuge, but it is perhaps better understood as the ten- to thirty-mile-wide exposed portion of the continental shelf, which extends north from the foot of the Brooks Range 150 miles and more, most of it under the sea. The shelf is mightily flat. Soundings taken forty miles out in the Beaufort Sea have registered depths of just thirty-six feet; eighty miles out it's only 160 feet to the bottom. The angle of depression from shore needed to forge such a depth is about one-one hundredth of a degree. One must continue north another eighty miles before the floor suddenly drops out of the shelf at last, and it plunges more than a mile into a deep called the Mackenzie Cone.

The coastal plain is where the polar bear dens and the caribou vacations, and where millions of migratory birds nest during a blink-of-an-eye summer. It's also where the oil is. No one knows exactly how much is there, but it's a lot. Oil industry sources put the number as high as sixteen billion barrels. If they're right, refuge reserves exceed those of Prudhoe Bay, the largest-known oil field in North America. Drilling opponents have adopted a much smaller figure. By their estimate the refuge holds about an eight-month supply of oil for the United States (assuming that only refuge oil were used). An equivalent amount could be saved – and drilling foregone – by increasing the fuel efficiency of every vehicle in the United States by just two miles per gallon.

The United States Geological Survey conducted exhaustive analyses of the relevant seismic data and in 2000 published what may be the closest we'll get to an impartial estimate of the coastal plain's oil potential. The survey estimated a 95 percent chance that 1.9 billion barrels of economically recoverable oil will be found; a 50 percent chance that 5.3 billion barrels will be found; and a 5 percent chance that 9.4 billion barrels will be found. The only way to assess the accuracy of such predictions, of course, is to drill. This idea strikes some people as sensible, and others as akin to burning down a house to see if it is fireproof.

The coastal plain is commonly spoken of as land with a great deal of water upon it. It makes just as much sense to describe it as water interrupted here and there by land. Here are the final runouts of dozens of rivers that come down from the Brooks with tongue-clicking names: the Ekaluakat, the Egaksra, the Aichilak, the Kongakut, and the delightfully titled Hulahula. (For this last, legend has it, we have to thank homesick Hawaiian whalers at the turn of the twentieth century.) Following their descents, all of them rash, the rivers slow, get a grip, overrun their channels, and braid the plain in swarming silvery spiders of water. On my topo map of the region I count thirty branches of the Kongakut River fanning toward the sea. The river's westernmost fingers join the easternmost fingers of the Matsutuak, which in turn joins hands with the Egaksra, and the Egaksra with the Aichilak. Wear your hip boots if you plan to go strolling by the Beaufort.

Where rivers do not flow, there are lakes and ponds by the thousands. Most are mere puddles; a few extend a mile or more in width. Some are fed by rivers or precipitation; others are so-called thermokarst – thaw lakes – which result from the melting of the normally cement-hard permafrost that lies a foot or so beneath the surface of the ground.

Much of the remainder of the plain is goopy bog or mud flat. The great abundance of moisture on the plain is a mixed blessing for the migrating wildlife that stop over during the summer. The water sustains hundreds of square miles of nutrient-rich plants, enabling millions of creatures to bulk up before they begin their journeys south.

By mid-July, alas, it is the mosquitoes and the black flies that have bulked up. The plain becomes a buzzing, pulsating cloud of very large, very determined biting-and-sucking machines. Toward the end of its sojourn on the coastal plain, the typical caribou loses a quart of blood a week to mosquitoes. Some of the animals may be driven into the freezing waters of the ocean to seek relief; others will simply go mad from the torment. Panic spreads, and groups of caribou will stampede, sometimes trampling newborns and even adults beneath their feet.

In spring the plain is shrouded in fog much of the time. Clouds of mist ebb and flow, revealing one stretch of water and then the next. Snow may fall, or freezing rain, as the temperature edges upward above the freezing point for the first time in nine months. Bitter winds bear down from the mountains or shear off the white-capped sea. Whether the plain is land filigreed with water or the other way around, it had looked on my flyover from Fairbanks like some crackpot jigsaw puzzle of ice and mud, with interlacing ribbons of water providing the zigzag dividing lines. The puzzle pieces appeared to have tectonic significance. Gazing down, I had imagined that by giving a little shove to a tiny plate on, say, the Kongakut delta, it might be possible to induce a pleasant jiggle in a plate twenty miles away.

*   *   *

The hour following Audi's call-to-fly passed quickly. There was much to be done. I placed a call to Carol and Jake to say my melancholy good-byes. I waxed my boots, tested my stove and my water filter, loaded my camera with film and my pockets with energy – caramels, root beer barrels, lemon drops. In the tiny foyer of the hotel I unpacked and reassembled my backpack, then immediately repeated the operation to keep pace with the swiftly changing weather conditions. A few feet from me Shaun did the same, tossing T-shirts in my direction as I threw socks and mittens in his. When I was finished, the rain gear that had topped my stockpile when I began lay buried at the bottom of the pack; at the top were items that a day earlier I could not have imagined I would be needing: hiking shorts, sunscreen, a gargantuan canister of mosquito repellent.

Merylin showed up from the kitchen with BLTs on a red plastic plate. She offered a few words of encouragement, then disappeared just as Walt flew by on his way out the door: "You guys about ready?" I threw down my sandwich and checked off all but the final item from my mental to-do list; then, in soot-encrusted snow at the front of the hotel, paused to face the last – the leap of faith that would commit myself fully and irreversibly to the enterprise that had brought me to Kaktovik.

Through the furious hour just completed, I had brooded obsessively over the risks I was about to take. Chief among them were the dangers of a long flight in a small plane in a remote part of the globe in changing weather conditions; and the chance of an encounter, should I survive the flight, with a grizzly, a possibility that had haunted me since the moment I made my decision to go north. My phone call to Carol brought these risks to light with great clarity. I had her full support in what I was about to do, but at this moment of truth I could not help questioning my motives, and even my sanity. Was I mentally and physically prepared for what lay ahead? And what exactly were my responsibilities to a teenaged son and to a wife who had been ill for a decade, whose health, though growing sounder by the day, remained fragile and unpredictable?

Aggravating my ambivalence was the fact that during my short stay at Audi's hotel, I had grown immensely fond of the place. The Waldo

Arms was a warm blanket and a cup of tea. Here, a short hop from the top of the world, I could vegetate before a television set, or shoot the breeze with local dignitaries like Daniel and Lillian Akootchook, or curl up with a good Danielle Steel, or not, as I chose. Why die in a plane crash when I could be shooting pool at the Waldo?

Mine were not idle fears. Alaskan bush planes serve up scores of accidents annually. A potential passenger is foolish not to weigh the odds soberly before stepping into a four-seater for a flight into the wilds. A year earlier, three of the four members of an Albuquerque family of my acquaintance had been killed when their plane went down at the south end of the Arctic National Wildlife Refuge. And then, of course, there was the grim example of my friend Fred Meader, a quarter century in the past but never far from my mind.

As for grizzlies, though hundreds make their homes in the refuge, the chance that a visitor will suffer an unpleasant encounter with one of these occasionally violent animals is practically zero. Yet no one who has ever survived such an encounter has argued later that the Latin name for the species, *Ursus horribilis*, is meant to be taken ironically.

For this would-be Arctic adventurer suffering from suddenly cold feet, the Waldo provided an additional and quite unexpected benefit: like the Porcupine caribou herd, the hotel had become my ally in the very search that had brought me to the Arctic in the first place. I had latched onto the Porcupine because of the way their journey so strikingly reminded me of my own. Grouchy, gimpy-legged, they pressed forward obstinately in spite of avalanches, wild rivers, and wrong turns, all in the vague belief that something better lay just around the corner. Biologists attributed this behavior to instinct but I didn't believe that for a moment, any more than I believed it was instinct that led the storied swallows to Capistrano year after year. The caribou I believed in galloped halfway across hell because they had a vision of peace at the end of the road.

So did the Waldo Arms, and in a quite remarkable way. To take advantage of this unique amenity, all a hotel guest had to do was to peer through that innocuous backroom window that faced the Kaktovik airstrip. Far more than an observation post on the weather, the window was the perfect crystal ball. For no matter how wretched the elements, no matter how thick the fog, if you gazed into that dingy piece of glass long enough, *you were bound to receive good news.* At the Waldo Arms, there was always a clear sky just over the horizon, always a brighter day ahead! Could the Waldorf or the Plaza make such a claim?

With our packs ready to be strapped shut, Shaun and I turned to our host for two final pieces of equipment, both of which had been prohibited on the flight up from Fairbanks – stove fuel and bear spray. Audi topped our fuel bottles with white gas, then handed each of us a black-and-white container about the size of a large can of Raid. The label featured a drawing of an unhappy-looking bear, surrounded by mountains of instructions and disclaimers in very small print.

I had no idea how to fire the weapon I held in my hand, but I was happy to have it. It wasn't a .300-Magnum rifle but it beat the only other deterrent in my arsenal, a mishmash of highly entertaining bear-safety tips I had found on a rack of travel brochures at the Fairbanks airport. Sample, from a pamphlet called "Bear Facts," published by the Alaska Department of Fish and Game: "If a bear approaches while you are fishing, stop fishing. If you have a fish on your line, don't let it splash."

While I inspected my ammo, a young man who worked for Audi presented a crash course in bear spraying. I listened closely. The whole idea ran counter to everything I knew about establishing good relations with bears. The ones I had encountered – all of them black bears in the lower forty-eight – were grumpy and unprincipled, but never so uncharitable as to invite a stream of hot chemicals in their faces. Years before, one, a big one, had sat on me emphatically as I slept out alone in the northern reaches of Yosemite National Park. Having made her point, she proceeded to eat all my food and to destroy my pack. But as far as I could tell, it never crossed her mind to tear my arms off.

The young man borrowed my canister. A determined expression came over his face. Suddenly he dropped to a half-squatting position. He raised the can smartly, as though he were about to clean a window.

"Aim it at their eyes," he said. "You have seven seconds. After that the can goes dry."

He paused. Shaun and I looked at each other. I felt my can going dry.

"And be sure the wind is behind you. Otherwise the spray blows in your face."

"I've heard that some of them actually like the stuff," Audi interjected. "Someone told me that he saw a grizzly take a bite out of a can and then swallow the whole thing."

He must have seen the look in my eyes. Quickly he backed off. "Probably not true," he said. "Probably just a bear story."

It occurred to me that maybe everything I was afraid of was a bear story – grizzly maulings, plane crashes, bad weather, creditors, my wife's illness; and that a sensible remedy would be to arm myself with all the recommended sprays, study the labels, practice shooting the stuff, and then cheerfully go about my business. I suddenly felt an Alaska-sized lift. Maybe it was the generosity of the spraying lesson, or Audi's flimflam, or the crazy splotches of blue opening up like forget-me-nots in the mist above, or the great good will of my pal Shaun exclaiming "Saddle up!" as he heaved his pack into the back of the truck, or the echo of my son's voice on the telephone assuring me that all was well at home and reminding me of something I'd told him a thousand times, that dreams are for following. Suddenly the icy river I'd been attempting to cross for the past hour didn't look so forbidding; suddenly I was able to see beyond the river again, to the far side and to the fabulous landscape that had brought me so far – vast, empty, silent, braided in trains of caribou as long as the sky.

Audi hopped into the truck and gunned the engine. I paused for a moment to measure the gap before me. Then I offered up a brief incantation, took a deep breath, and leapt.

DRIFTING

Walt's four-seater Cessna looked sassy and dauntless in its parking spot at the edge of the airstrip. Blizzard-white on top, royal blue beneath, it brought to mind a rascally blue jay, scarcely big enough to notice, but ready to dive-bomb an eagle if the occasion demanded, or to rip off a kid's jelly sandwich, just to see him cry.

The air was cool, the wind calm. Audi went over his craft meticulously, circling, probing, passing his hand along the fuselage, fussing with gauges and with struts. When he was satisfied that all was well he yanked out the rear left seat and in its place strapped the two backpacks, one atop the other. I shoehorned in beside them; Shaun climbed into the passenger seat beside the pilot.

Audi settled in at the controls. Within seconds he was speaking laconically into his headset. In bobbed gray ponytail, Hemingway mustache, yellow work gloves, and signature black beret, he looked like an ad for really cool adventure travel. I had imagined him slipping into a new mode at this moment, an intrepid, steady-as-she-goes bush pilot mode. But that was the mode he lived in! Now, going over his instruments with

40

the scrupulousness of a surgeon preparing for a difficult operation, he was the same intrepid, steady guy I'd been observing for the past twenty-four hours as he navigated Air Waldo through the stormy skies of life.

Fifty yards away, a second plane was readying for takeoff. Traffic jam at the Kaktovik airstrip! The previous afternoon I'd spent a rewarding hour talking with Dennis Miller, the pilot of the second aircraft, about the project that had brought him to town. Once every two years Miller and a team from the Alaska Department of Fish and Game travel to the north coast to conduct an aerial photo-census of the Porcupine caribou herd. On a single day when the bulk of the herd is gathered on the coastal plain, the team crisscrosses the area taking hundreds of photographs. After allowing for overlap, team members count the dots on the photos. So complete is the family portrait obtained on these occasions that the dot total is likely to be within a very small percentage of the actual population.

Miller is not a wildlife biologist, but he knows his caribou. With his wife Debbie, a distinguished writer known for her detailed and engaging accounts of travel in the Alaska wilds, he lived for a number of years in Arctic Village, a Gwich'in Indian community at the south end of the refuge. The Gwich'in are a people whose lives have revolved around the Porcupine herd for thousands of years. In the words of the Gwich'in elder Sarah James, "The caribou is not just what we eat, it's who we are. It is our dances, stories, songs and the whole way we see the world. Caribou are our life." In Arctic Village, where Debbie Miller taught in the local school, the couple steeped themselves in the history and culture of the community. Both had ample opportunity to observe caribou and to speculate on the species' behavior. It was Dennis's story of newborns being abandoned by their mothers if they were born before the calving grounds were attained that alerted me to the idea that for the Porcupine, the migration instinct appears to be stronger than the instinct to protect their young. Miller observed this contradictory behavior during a high-snow year a few years earlier. Caught behind schedule due to the difficult travel conditions, some of the females delivered practically on the run; scarcely pausing to rest, they returned to the trail almost at once, leaving their calves behind in deep snow. There their fates were sealed.

Miller explained to me that in the wake of current proposals to open the coastal plain to oil development, the biannual photo survey, always an essential tool in gauging the herd's health, had taken on new and vital importance. Like that of other Arctic herds, the Porcupine population rises and falls from one year to the next. The precise reasons for the fluctuations are not fully understood, but predation, disease, weather, and certain natural cycles all play a part. So may environmental phenomena only now becoming known.

What was not in doubt was the fact that the herd size had crashed alarmingly in recent years. From a high of around 178,000 in 1989, the population had fallen to some 123,000 in 2001, a 31 percent decrease. (Since my journeys north, the decline has continued; in 2007, herd size was estimated at around 110,000.) Was the falloff simply part of a recurring natural pattern, one that would soon reverse itself and send the numbers climbing again? Or was the herd in trouble? No one knew. But before a sensible discussion of the potential effects of drilling could take place, accurate census figures were needed, along with a cogent explanation for the sharp fluctuations in population.

Audi completed his preflight routine. He recited a few safety instructions for his passengers: there were emergency items in the rear of the plane; there was a transponder, which might allow us to be found if we went down. I gave this well-intentioned lecture scarcely a thought. The propeller kicked and the aircraft lurched forward. All reflections on past and future coalesced into a vivid concentration on the present. The plane bumped along for a few yards, swung sharply left onto the gravel runway, paused for a fraction of a second, jumped, accelerated, skipped, wobbled, raised its nose, hopped, took a great gulp of Arctic air, lifted thrillingly, threw down the earth, went silent, went weightless in a vast envelope of sky. . .

*   *   *

The world changed in a breath. A map of the frozen sea opened up below. The ice looked lustrous and marble-smooth; in a dozen widely spaced locations, golden slants of light from the low-lying sun glanced off the surface, making it sparkle and quicken. Observing the ice from land I had concluded that it formed a more or less continuous sheet all the way to the horizon. Now I saw that the sheet was shattered into count-less narrow masses, each perhaps a few hundred yards long and generally parallel to the others; all pointed in more or less the same direction, as though a giant comb had been dragged through the water in an effort to shepherd the pieces into some kind of order. Shallow, shimmering lakes of very cold-looking blue-green water separated the masses. An Arctic tradition has it that all the lost ships – the ones that went north and never returned – somehow found their way to the same hidden cove. For a moment I thought we had found the cove. By the thousands, the frozen freighters and whalers and clipper ships rocked on their moorings, still genuflecting north, the only direction they knew, toward the great curve of the earth.

Audi banked and came around. For a short distance the plane followed the blue shadow of the coast eastward. We passed over several vintage Inu-piat hunting camps, tumbledown structures of canvas and pale driftwood. I thought of Daniel Akootchook and wondered if he and *nanuq* had tangled somewhere down there, and I wondered how *nanuq* had fared.

The two men in front conversed genially over their headsets. The talk was of frozen rivers and aircraft engines. Shaun grew up in Southern Cal-ifornia. He learned to appreciate carburetors and clutches long before he ultimately cast his lot with Wallace Stevens and William Carlos Williams. He was a good match for the pilot. With pistons thrumming beneath his heels and arresting images beckoning just beyond the window, my friend appeared to have found a congenial home in the Arctic skies.

Far away in the back seat, drifting like a contented snow goose over northern Alaska, I could think of nothing to say, nor would I have said it even if I had thought of it. The spectacle below was silencing. The crackle of voices in my headphones began to bug me, so, figuring that the plane would fly or crash regardless of whether I wore my headset, I pulled it off and dropped it at my feet.

With that subversive act I began my solo flight across *ivvavik*. My two companions jetted away like Armstrong and Aldrin in their moon ship, leaving the important matters to me. My craft rocked left and right, gently, like a hammock in a mild breeze. The pleasant bee-buzz of the engine filled my ears. A mild reverie came over me. I recognized the feeling at once – summit rapture, the euphoria that greets a climber after a long, scary journey to the top of a mountain. There are several causes for the condition, among them thin air, mental exhaustion, sublime scenery, elation at having made it to the top; and, most important, an acute understanding that there is a *really really* fast way to the bottom. Which is to say, exactly the conditions I now enjoyed in Walt's cloud hopper.

I settled back in my seat and gazed out the window. The plane dipped nicely; my stomach flupped. We settled in at an altitude of four hundred feet, between a gossamer mist below and pasty clouds above. My mind wandered. *Dust in the wind. Three men in a tub.* I thought of the French aviator and writer Antoine de Saint-Exupéry, who during the nineteen-twenties rode the night skies over Spain and North Africa in a crate about the size of the one I was in. He wrote about his lonely adventures in a great book called *Wind, Sand and Stars*. It was all very well, all very dashing, Saint-Exupéry allowed, navigating by compass in a sea of clouds: "But you want to remember that below the sea of clouds lies eternity."

Well, yes; and yet however sage this advice, I quickly let it slip as I warmed to my seat in the sky, and as the great North spread out before me and beneath me and around me, crowding out all thoughts not merely of eternity but of time itself. Whether my disengagement from my two cohorts lasted five minutes or an hour I have no idea. Beneath the sturdy wings of the plane the round Earth rotated smoothly and dependably. Behind me the ghost fleet – the whalers and clipper ships – pitched off the edge of the earth; ahead, one outlandish scene after another rolled my way. First, the coastal plain: water world, more ocean than the ocean, a train crash of twining rivers, mudflats, and black ice. The land looked so big and so forbidding I could not imagine that an animal heavy with calf could make her way across it – leaping, skidding, zigzagging among the ice sculptures, retracing her steps, swimming the freezing waters, mile after mile after mile. Whatever possessed those mad creatures!

Then, rising from the relentless flats, now a solid wall before me, now rushing closer and resolving into a thousand glittering stars: the long-imagined Brooks Range, a silent, snow-white, spine-chilling catastrophe.

The pilot set a southeasterly course toward the mountains. At my altitude, the altitude of flag poles and kites, the fact that I was a little bitty thing in a sky the size of the upper Midwest was pretty clear, and thoroughly exhilarating. Too intoxicated to make sense of any of it, I looked here and there, and then there and here, and then here and there again, without much of a plan. What's that? Rocks? Mountains? The asteroid belt? Having escaped from time, it made sense to me that the pokes of mist lingering below might be the last thin vapors of the Pleistocene. Gazing through them to the wrecked surface of the earth, I half expected to see a mastodon or a saber-toothed tiger loping by.

I was startled from my reverie by the sound of my own voice uttering a single word. Drifting pleasantly at the crossroads of fantasy and reality, I had failed to grasp the true coordinates of my position – the longitude and the latitude of it. Suddenly that crucial scrap of intelligence had been delivered at last, and I was able to give a name to the mysterious, stupefying landscape that was passing beneath my eyes.

"Alaska," I said, with immense pleasure. Hearing the word I had to say it again: "*Alaska!*"

Earlier in the day, with our destination still to be determined, Shaun and I had stood at the large map of northern Alaska that hangs on the east wall of the main room at the Waldo. Audi joined us and we discussed options. The coastal plain was out. Landing an aircraft in that quagmire would be nuts; camping there would be misery. We knew, of course, that at that very moment Karsten and Leanne Heuer were out there some-where, frolicking in the mud, being caribou. But they were the Heuers. Shaun and I were not, as we were pleased to remind each other several times during the discussion. Briefly we considered booking a room at the Waldo and waiting for the plain to dry out. But even that was risky. The rains might resume the following day; the plain might never dry out. In any case, at three hundred dollars a day for the pair of us, the hotel did us the favor of unilaterally removing itself from our list of fea-sible alternatives.

Audi had another idea. South of and above the coastal plain, in the foothills of the Brooks Range at an altitude of around one thousand feet, there was a gravel bar in the Kongakut River. He knew the area well. He had landed there plenty of times and had even gone so far as to fashion a primitive landing strip on the bar.

He touched his finger to the map. The Kongakut approached the area from the southwest, at what was probably a ferocious pace at this time of year. Abruptly, a thousand-foot wall rose up directly in the river's path, right where Audi had his finger. Unable to forge a route past the obstruction, the river took the only way out by executing a hard ninety-degree turn to the left. After that it ran parallel to the wall for several miles. Then the barrier fell away and the river slipped between a set of low mountains to begin its final descent to the sea.

The great bend in the Kongakut: it might be a grand spot. The over-all configuration was that of a wide valley. The great wall rose to the east of the river; to the west the terrain was level for a mile or so, promising easy camping and walking. Further in that direction and to the south rose the Brooks Range, culminating in one of its defining peaks, Mount Greenough.

Audi's plan carried with it two potentially serious complications. With the heavy rains of the past several days, the river might have swollen to flood stage, swamping the bar and making a landing impossible. And even if Audi could put down in the river, there was no assurance that Shaun and I would encounter caribou in the valley. We knew that one of the Porcupine's traditional migration routes traversed the valley in the vicinity of the right-angle turn. But there were many such routes, and there was no way of knowing whether members of the herd would choose that particular path this year. Certainly no pregnant females would be passing through; those would have crossed the river days or weeks before and were at that very moment ushering into the world a new generation of their kind, out on the coastal plain. But members of the second wave – bulls, juveniles of both sexes, malingerers – might pass by on their way to the calving grounds.

The decision was easily made: the Kongakut it would be. There was really no other choice. I was relieved to know that an option existed that might allow me to see caribou, however far from certain that eventuality was.

At the same time I was bitterly disappointed to know that I would not be setting foot on the calving grounds. The Kongakut valley, where Audi would attempt to drop Shaun and me, was scores of miles from the calving grounds. The question arose, then: Why travel to the great bend in the Kongakut, spectacular though it might be, when it was *ivvavik* and all that that name represented that had brought me north in the first place? And this: If *ivvavik* was the embodiment of hope, as I had so fervently come to believe, what exactly did the suburbs of *ivvavik* represent?

I had no answers to these questions. Paradoxically, I suddenly found myself in need of two of the very elixirs I had traveled to *ivvavik* to find: still waters to quiet the storm of disappointment that now swirled around me; and faith that the valley of the Kongakut, my distant second choice, possessed rewards sufficient to justify my journey north. To console myself I made up my mind that someday I would return to visit *ivvavik* in the flesh. For now, however, I would have to be content to view her from four hundred feet.

Emerging from my hazy speculations in the rear seat, I was suddenly aware that the man in the front, on the left, was gesturing toward the ground. Shaun turned and said something to me over his shoulder. He too pointed downward, with some urgency.

Engine noise prevented me from hearing what my friend was trying to tell me. Peering down toward the general area that the two men were indicating, I saw only the same perilous landscape I had been observing throughout the flight.

Quickly I slipped on my headset. I heard a sputter and then Shaun's voice.

"Did you see it?"

Audi came on: "There's another one."

Frantically I riveted my gaze on the ground. I scanned left and right, up and down, then went over the entire area again. I could see nothing out of the ordinary, or what I now took to be ordinary.

My heart sank. I knew what all the pointing was about. Four hundred feet below, caribou were moving across an island of ice. They might be the only caribou I would ever see. Desperately I tried to pick them out against the jumbled landscape rushing by beneath the plane. Despite my fiercest efforts, I was unable to do so.

We flew on. I could hardly believe what had happened. Bravely I tried to convince myself that I had in fact had a great success, for I had been within four hundred feet of a caribou, even if I had not actually seen it. Needless to say, the attempt went nowhere. Twice more Audi's eyes, trained by forty years of watching dots dancing on whole counties of mud and ice, saw caribou below. Both times I did not.

Now the complication of waters that was the coastal plain began to simplify. What had been a hundred streams became twenty slightly fatter ones, then four or five fatter still, then two, then one. Behold: the Kongakut. The relentless flats wrinkled, cranked upward into easy slopes bound in tundra tussocks and lichen-mantled rocks. Sprawling waters gave way to circling mountains as the predominant feature of the land. Muscles of snow rippled on ridge tops. Beneath the plane the wintry earth, black and white for so long, grew soft and tawny and springlike. We slipped between foothills and tracked the silvery river where it led. The sky was wide and blue. Perched on a low ridge like a nosy crow, the sun announced our arrival, a bold shadow racing beside the Kongakut. *Ivvavik* was history, the great bend in the river lay just ahead, and I felt a keen despair that my last chance to see caribou may have lain behind me.

THE ISLAND

Inflated fantasies of the North had led me to imagine that the spot where Audi would be dropping Shaun and me would be a rough-and-tumble place. Even the pilot's description of gentle flats beside a river, with long views and easy walking, failed to dent my mental image of the spot. As I saw it, almost until the moment I stepped out of the plane, the Kongakut valley would be steep-sided and narrow, with a raging river thundering through, threatening to snap up everything in its path and sweep it yelling and screaming into the Arctic Ocean. Glaciers would spill off the mountains practically to one's tent door. The rare places where the ground was level would be strewn with house-size boulders, each festooned in ice, and each with an enormous grizzly hiding behind it.

That was, of course, my original concept of the Arctic, the dark and dangerous place I had fallen in love with, from a great distance, through my armchair affairs with Elisha Kent Kane, Fridtjof Nansen, Sir John Franklin, and the rest of those red-blooded, pemmican-chomping, accident-prone polar explorers. Now, as the Cessna approached its destination, I saw that Audi had spoken the truth; equally noteworthy, Fred

Meader had spoken the truth. At least from the air, on what had turned out to be a fine day in early June, the spot we were heading for looked enchanting. The area to the west of the river was indeed level, a square-shaped tract perhaps a mile in length and width. The right-angle bend in the Kongakut formed two sides of the square; a wide creek also containing a ninety-degree crook formed the other two sides. A stretch of land surrounded by water it was: a small island, or a very large raft. The groundcover appeared to be sand or gravel, broken here and there by lazy streams. There was little vegetation. Low, mostly bare hills surrounded the area. The nearest glacier was miles away. The only snow I could see was at the north end of the square, where narrow swaths of the stuff powder-puffed along the streams. The Kongakut was still iced over in that vicinity; south, its waters ran free.

Far from the howling wilderness of my imagination, the island, as we would come to call it, looked like a great place to spend some time. Only one thing bothered me: a short distance from the river stood a yellow tent. It proclaimed itself on the dully colored earth like a splat of mustard on a beloved if slightly dilapidated cardigan.

"That's Toru," Audi said as we passed over. He pointed his chin in the direction of the tent.

Toru? Back at the Waldo Arms, Audi had mentioned dropping a Japanese in the refuge a few days earlier. But until this moment I hadn't computed that that delivery and this one were being made to the same address. I felt cheated. I wanted the island to myself. I wanted the whole refuge to myself! I knew, of course, that thanks to the chaotic topography of the region, the number of places where a fixed-wing aircraft like Audi's could put down was severely limited. Still, in a land as big as this one, it seemed unfair that I had to share a pinhead of terrain with a person I didn't even know. The vacant North suddenly was teeming with the wretched of the earth! There's an old story, set a century or so ago, about the first two automobiles in the state of Ohio. Ohio happens to be big and flat and well lit. That should have been enough to ensure that the drivers of the only two cars in the state wouldn't run into each other. But life is full of surprises. One bright summer day in 1900 or so, the two collided. That's how I felt: in a unit of the National Wildlife Refuge System twice the size of Switzerland, I was about to collide with a person named Toru.

Beneath the plane the river churned. Somewhere among its churns was the spot where we would be landing. Given the choice I might have said, Let's set 'er down on the island, Walt; at least it's dry. I radioed this idea ahead to Audi on my headset. He radioed back, in about three words explaining that the island was a rat's nest of bushes, rocks, creek beds, ruts, and ten other things that could snap a strut or puncture a tire or otherwise ruin a nice day, and was no place to attempt to land a plane.

So the river it would be. Along the water's edge there was a gravel bar where Audi could usually put down. Over the years he had done extensive gardening there, in the process fashioning a passable landing strip. He had used it many times. On this occasion, to add spice to the proceedings, a measure of uncertainty surrounded the proposed landing. The previous day Audi had scouted the area to see how high the river had risen. What he found was mildly discouraging: the Kongakut had swamped the strip, which was no longer to be seen. The question now was, would twenty-four hours of drying out be enough to expose the runway again?

From my perspective, I couldn't see anything that resembled a landing strip. Audi rolled left for a better look.

"River's down," he said. "We should be okay."

Shaun glanced over his shoulder at me and raised his eyebrows. We flew on, past the bend in the river. Then the wings dipped and the horizon went awry, and the Cessna embarked on a long, lazy, 180-degree turn. Flashing and flickering, the high peaks of the Brooks Range carouseled around the plane: this way to Audi International Airport! The wings straightened; a moment later we were dropping to the river.

As we fell beneath the line of hills on the right, the mountains in the background disappeared. Below, the river leaped up. I could see brown earth, choppy waters, and low trees, and beside the river, a bright yellow tent on rocky soil; most important, a place to land, just as the pilot had promised. Approaching the spot I guessed that Audi had maybe twenty yards to play with left and right, and a length that was going to require a good set of brakes. At the last moment, that moment just before touchdown when you *feel* that you're flying, we floated. Then we smacked the ground and I flew hard into my seat belt.

The plane zipped along nicely and surprisingly smoothly. A few seconds later it came to a halt near the end of the bar. Peering between the two heads in the front seat I had a nice view of the river, perhaps thirty yards in front of the plane.

As Audi taxied back to the landing spot, I saw that the river had not in fact returned to its normal level. The gravel bar, which normally abutted the mainland, remained separated from it by a slow-moving creek. This was a vestige of the torrent that had poured through the valley over the past few days. The creek wasn't wide – perhaps twenty feet – but it appeared that anyone attempting to cross it might find himself in deep water. In drawing up our list of equipment to bring to Alaska, Shaun and I had been thorough, we thought, and conservative. If we might need it, we brought it. We had our stove repair kit, our odor-tight, bombproof plastic storage canister for protecting valuable cheese and chocolate cookies from hungry grizzlies, our Vicodin for pain. Now it appeared that we had neglected to carry with us the very first item we were going to need: waders. Not a good sign; we dragged our packs from the plane and prepared to get wet.

Almost from the moment the plane had touched down I had noticed a man standing on the far side of the creek. The notorious Toru, obviously. Now he waved. Audi waved back. Toru the precursor, the man who had booked the Kongakut before me, the man with whom I was destined soon to collide. He was wearing a teal parka over a pink shirt and, on his legs, a pair of waders.

Raising his hands, the fellow signaled for Shaun and me to remain on the bar. He shouted something but I couldn't make it out over the clamor of the river and the general confusion of the moment. I was about to yell something back when, abruptly, he plunged into the water. A moment later he was standing beside us, smiling broadly. He and Audi exchanged jubilant greetings. Audi introduced the new arrival: Toru Sonohara, a wildlife photographer from Saitama, Japan.

If Sonohara felt any resentment over the sudden explosion in the human population of the Kongakut valley, he hid it well; he seemed genuinely pleased to see Shaun and me. That and his noticeable lack of pretension pretty much put an end to the resentment I had felt over his own presence here. He appeared to be in his midthirties, a sturdy-looking fellow – medium in height, broad shouldered, fit. He had bright eyes, a thin mustache, and thick, scruffy, jet-black hair that came down over his ears, bottoming out in sideburns. He had an air of awareness and alertness about him, like a badger calculating the odds and preparing to pounce. As we were soon to find out, Sonohara was an inveterate wilderness wanderer who logged several months a year in the Alaska backcountry. His face was a mirror of his travels: a month of sun and wind on his cheeks, a season of storms on his furrowed brow. When he smiled, which he did often and exuberantly, a fan of wrinkles appeared beside each eye, like cracks in the ice.

Sonohara spoke English haltingly and with a heavy accent, but with enormous skill. The weather had been "atrocious," he said, speaking each syllable carefully. The river "went on a rampage." He had spent much of the last few days lying in his tent "trying to be happy." He was open, self-effacing, and quite charming; he had an ease about him that, in this far corner of the world, reminded me of climbers I had known who suffered their city lives dutifully in order to earn time in the mountains, the only place where they came fully alive.

Sonohara painted a compelling picture of the island's possibilities. That very morning he had spotted a wolf near a creek not a mile from where we stood. By the ice on the north side of the island he had watched a crime taking place, when a jaeger swooped down and stole a fish from an Arctic tern. Toru went on in this way for several minutes, describing with some energy the kinds of things we might expect to see. Suddenly he reached down and picked up Shaun's pack.

"I will take it," he said amiably. "You stay here." A moment later he was in water above his knees. He crossed to the far side of the creek and dropped the pack, then returned for mine. Assuming he was helping with the packs so that Shaun and I could negotiate the creek more easily, I started to follow Sonohara into the water. He turned and repeated what he had said.

"You stay here. I will take you across."

Thinking back to that moment, it's hard for me to imagine that I agreed to this radical plan – that I readily assented to traveling the final few yards to the land of my dreams sprawled ignominiously on the shoulders of a man I didn't even know. But I did, and Shaun did as well. Moreover we did it cheerfully and without objection. Shaun went first. He's tall and gangly, and so was able to arrange a kind of death grip on his host, like a praying mantis about to devour its mate. Praying mantis but no butterfly: when the passenger crawled aboard, applying to the man below him the dead weight of a small set of office furniture, it appeared that Toru might change his mind and send us across on our own.

But no; the operation went forward. This first crossing was thrilling. Mid-stream, Toru missed a step. He and his cargo nearly went in the drink. The driver recovered nicely, planting one leg straight as a canoe paddle in the creek bottom to regain his balance. I cheered, and even the laconic bush pilot standing beside me mumbled a word of praise.

By the time Sonohara dumped his passenger on the far side of the creek, the two men were jabbering like cockatoos. Toru returned to the bar for the final act of the drama. I turned my ball cap backwards and climbed aboard. With several layers of clothing and ten pounds of camera equipment, I represented perhaps two hundred pounds of baggage. My porter was not elegant but he got the job done. After depositing me on the mainland, he fell in a heap on the ground.

Since it is not possible to cross a creek on a man's shoulders and think him a barbarian, at this point I was favorably disposed toward the Japanese photographer. It seemed possible that the human inhabitants of this desert island might become, not a single plus a late-arriving pair, but a trio – Shaun and I and the guy in the yellow tent.

On the far side of the creek, Audi policed the runway from end to end. He flicked aside a stick here, a rock there. To live to a ripe old age a bush pilot needs to be lucky, but he can improve his odds by being persnickety about sticks and rocks. If Audi had had a portable vacuum cleaner along I don't doubt he would have used it. Prior to our triumphant crossings of the dreaded creek, Shaun and I had said our goodbyes to this amiable and enormously skilled man and agreed upon a pick-up date. Half an hour after touching down, Audi's little Cessna was in the air again, a purr and a wisp of blue curling into the northern sky.

In this way my sojourn on the Kongakut began. It was a curiously timeless affair, partly because the sun circled the horizon at shoulder height, less a clock than a wheel, whose purpose seemed to be to reassure anyone who might be paying attention that the universe was rolling along in fairly good working order. The great disk trundled along the ridge tops with a noticeable crunching sound; the light it produced was consistently even and flat, black of night merging with white of day to produce a kind of cream-colored world.

Partly it was because my calendar was utterly clear and I had nothing to do: no appointments, no plans, no chores – nothing. I explored the island when I felt like exploring, slept when I felt like sleeping, ate when I was hungry. I'm pretty sure I chowed down what I thought of as breakfast late one what-I-thought-of-as evening. Even the idea that a particular meal was "breakfast" or "dinner" quickly became meaningless. It turns out that one can eat salami at any hour without suffering dire consequences, and Fig Newtons, too.

In this timeless time zone, in this spacious space, my normal behavior patterns changed. Sometimes I sat by the tent (cobalt blue, thirty yards from the mustard spot) just gazing at the scenery. Mount Greenough, a glacier-clad behemoth flanked by several slightly smaller but scarcely less imposing peaks, rose twenty miles to the south, as spectacular a panorama of unnerving mountains as I have ever seen. Normally I would have wanted to climb them. Now I was content simply to admire those pulse-quickening summits and to remember the fierce pleasure of *desiring* a mountain, without feeling the slightest urge to give in to it.

There were other telltale signs that I wasn't myself. For one thing, I could enjoy the river without heaving rocks into it. For another, I never cracked either of the two books I brought with me, John Muir's *Travels in Alaska* and Jack Kerouac's *The Dharma Bums*. I have since read and enjoyed both; at the time I couldn't be bothered.

Most amazing of all, this normally obsessive footslogger only once left the island, barely, and never wandered more than a mile or so from the blue tent, or even thought of taking a long day-hike hither or yon to investigate one of the many curious features of the landscape I could see from the campsite. The common thread running through all these departures from custom was their tendency toward simplifying my life. It happens that I enjoy reading, hiking, and heaving rocks into large bodies of water, and I had every intention of doing those things while I was on the island. But I didn't. For some reason, a little of my compulsive busyness rubbed off. What remained was a simple pleasure in sitting back and letting the world happen, without interference from me.

Once I had switched over to island time, I began to feel less and less like a visitor, and more and more like part of the landscape – like someone who belonged there. Every day I went calling on a pair of ptarmigan that lived in the neighborhood. Ptarmigan are a type of grouse; think barnyard chickens and you have the idea. The male was still clad in his winter whites; a blood-red comb blazoned above each eye, like bad eye shadow. The female was well along toward the brown and buff that characterize both sexes through the summer. I could always find the two in the same place in a clearing near the river, perhaps ten minutes from camp. We didn't say much to each other. I would greet them and they would cluck a couple of times and that was about it. They would go on with their business, and I would squat down in the sand, utterly disinterested in studying them or trying to figure out what their business was. I just liked being there.

This sense of belonging I felt most strongly when I lay down to sleep.

As I drifted off I was often aware that other creatures were nearby and that along with birds, wolves, ground squirrels, and other assorted critters they included trees, rocks, flowers, mountains, rolling waters, and various friendly spirits: all residents of the country, all purveyors of the peace I longed to know. My nerves began to calm; my spirits lifted.

Shaun and I talked for hours. He is an enormously accomplished man – poet and essayist, artist, teacher and patron of aspiring writers in the Nevada State Prison, social activist, world traveler, advocate for the homeless. Yet still he hungers for something he cannot name. His appetite is so voracious, perhaps he can never be filled. Or perhaps he requires nothing more than empty time, time such as he found on the island for reading, journaling, painting (during our sojourn he completed watercolors of the views in all four cardinal directions from our campsite); wrestling with the capricious angel of poetry. Certainly I have never seen him as joyously happy as he was during our days in the refuge. Only the absence of his family disturbed his contentment. Yet he is a resourceful man who knows how to deal with adversity. In his way, he scoured the alien language of the island for images of the familiar, and in those found his way home.

"For five days I have sat riverside with/migratory birds and the first wild crocus," he wrote in a poem to his wife Deborah:

> and the first wild crocus
> to risk its full height of one inch
> before tonight's killing freeze. In the haze
>
> of a quarter century's love for you,
> I think no woman would rise from rock
>
> to make her purple wings felt on this
> June day – but of course, you have, and
> have again, . . .

Shaun's son Nevada would soon be heading off to his freshman year at Bard College, three thousand miles from home. The pain of separation was already palpable; my friend wondered if nature prepares parents for expelling their offspring from the nest as well as it prepares them to build a nest in the first place. And younger son Cody: "I'm missing his fourteenth birthday," a rueful voice announced to me one day. Shaun dreamed of a future day when he could bring his boys here, to see the island and to fish its primordial waters. The three would cast their lines without ceasing, day after day, and time would come to a halt, and Nevada would be home, and Cody would be thirteen, and many worthy fish would meet their ends.

Toru drifted in and out of our lives like the clouds that sometimes crept down from the foothills to drape the island in mist. He seemed never to sleep. When I climbed into my sleeping bag he would be out on the island somewhere, and when I awoke he might be waiting outside my tent with a pot of coffee. "I saw a fox," he might say when I poked my head through the door.

"Oh? When was that?"

"About 2 A.M., I think. It was on the cut-bank over by the creek."

Sometimes during my own travels I would suddenly think of him and wonder where he was, then spot a tiny figure across the flats, still as a fawn in tall grass. When he wasn't taking photographs he would sit for hours before his tent with his field glasses pressed to his eyes, scouring the landscape for wildlife. The island was an Eden of birds and wildflowers. Toru knew them all, their English as well as their Japanese names. He was an encyclopedia of the Arctic. As the days grew warmer and new flowers appeared, he would tell us where to find them. "There are purple saxifrage behind those snow banks," he might say, and soon Shaun or I would be on our way to investigate. Toru was our eyes and our ears. We never really got off his shoulders. He carried us through the hours with a firm hold and a knowing step. Only once did I ever feel uncomfortable speaking with him. That was when, soon after my arrival on the island, I posed a question that had been bothering me. My discomfort had nothing to do with Toru, but with the answer I feared he would give.

"Have you seen any caribou?" I said.

"Oh, yes. Some came through last night."

A wave of relief swept over me.

"Really? How many were there?"

He thought for a moment. "Oh, eight or ten. I've seen a few."

"Do you think they pass through only at night?"

"I don't know. Maybe. They are hard to predict. I think there will be more."

I scanned the ridge to the east, above and beyond the river, wondering if perhaps that is where they would come from, when they came.

On the more than two dozen sallies he had made into the Far North, over a span of fifteen years, Toru Sonohara had spent collectively close to four years in the Alaska wilds. A disciple of the legendary Japanese solo mountain climber and adventurer Naomi Uemura, Sonohara usually travels alone and with daunting plans. His journeys are not for the faint-hearted. Six months earlier, as winter seized Denali – Mount McKinley – he had spent six weeks alone in Denali National Park. The wind howled, temperatures plunged to 50 below, the sun never rose above the horizon, and Toru's desire to exit his sleeping bag in the morning was sometimes quite small. But exit he did. He knows Alaska. When he travels he totes a suitcase brimming with camera bodies, lenses, and film, plus a backpack containing, among other things, a yellow tent, a gargantuan bottle of soy sauce, waders, and a Japanese translation of Barry Lopez's wondrous *Arctic Dreams*. Toru's photographs are records of true adventures, the adventures of a man alone in space. The name Toru means "iron will" in Japanese. (With his wife Itsuko he has two young boys, Yudai – "nomad of the great land" – and Noho – "walking in the wilderness.")

Toru knew how to get the most out of his travels. One day on Denali he came upon a grizzly den.

"I always wondered what they were like inside," he told me. "So I cleared away the snow at the door and stuck my head in."

It was dark inside, and he couldn't see anything. But his curiosity got the better of him.

"I decided to go in. But I thought I'd better say something first."

"Did you?"

"Yes."

"What did you say?"

Toru cupped his hands to his mouth. "I said, 'HELLO? ANYBODY HOME?'"

Receiving no answer, he crawled in and explored the place. As it turned out, nobody was home. Most people would have been relieved, but Toru was disappointed.

"I really hoped he would be there," he said. "I wanted to see him sleeping."

Observing my stupefied reaction to this story, Toru quickly intuited my soft spot. He began to have fun with it. One day I was seated on my favorite rock near the tent when Toru wandered into the campsite. He stood over me, and we chatted for a few minutes. Offhandedly, he announced that he had seen a bear.

I looked up at him.

"What kind of a bear?" I knew the question could not have an answer that would please me, but I asked anyway. There are some things a man must know.

Toru's cheerful expression suddenly turned grave. He stooped slightly, fixed his eyes on me, and drew a deep breath.

"A VERRRRY BIIIIG BEAR!!!" he boomed in a deep voice. He waited for my reaction, then exploded in laughter. He was not lying – he *had* seen a bear, a grizzly, a very big one, on a hillside a mile or so from camp. Whether the animal was a resident of the island or just a tourist wasn't clear. But after that, the very big bear became my constant companion on my travels. I never saw the animal but I was aware of it practically every step I took.

This widening of my appreciation for the island's dangers

represented a major revision in the way I took in my surroundings when I hiked. Over four decades of incessant backcountry rambling throughout the United States and Western Canada, I had passed many thousands of miles beneath my boots. Only a few, in Montana's Glacier National Park, had been on terrain where I had any reason to fear the wildlife. Glacier has a respectable population of grizzlies. It also hosts a large number of day hikers and backpackers. Many of them tramp along the park's trails dutifully shaking "bear bells" or tin cans full of rocks, or otherwise making an awful racket, the time-honored routine for warding off grizzlies. The idea is that by announcing your arrival, you avoid surprising the bears, the usual cause of trouble.

The system works pretty well, and there aren't many grizzly incidents in Glacier. That may be because bear bells do the job they're supposed to do; or it may be because grizzlies like their peace and quiet as much as anyone else, and beat it the hell over the next ridge at the first sign of a troop of musical Boy Scouts. Whatever the explanation, I saw no signs of grizzlies while I was in the park.

Outside of Glacier, my bootsteps had all been on danger-free terrain; or at least danger-free as far as wild animals were concerned. Lower forty-eight black bears I'd encountered aplenty, all of them nuisances but without an aggressive bone in their bodies. (A six-year-old girl was killed by a black bear in Tennessee in 2006, the first fatality involving the species in six years.) Wolves I had once or twice been within howling distance of, without the least concern for my skin. It took several millennia for the truth to sink in, but most people now realize that the villains of "The Boy Who Cried Wolf," "Little Red Riding Hood," and God knows how many poorly acted wolf-man and werewolf movies were innocent on all charges and presented precisely zero danger to humans. A hiker has more to fear from a falling trail sign.

Then there are mountain lions, so reclusive that I'd never seen one, though I'd spent plenty of time in places where they could see me. In recent years, as more and more of the species' habitat has been destroyed, a few of its members have come out of hiding. In several highly publi-

cized incidents, hikers have been attacked by mountain lions; a few
people have been killed. The frequency of incidents remains small, and
for now, at least, the animals cannot be said to represent a significant
danger to wilderness travelers.

The doleful fact is that most of America's dangerous animals were
wiped out long ago. On the vast majority of our nation's wild lands, a visitor has nothing to fear from animal attacks. (This raises the interesting
question, *Are those lands really wild?*) Because I'd done nearly all my hiking in nice, friendly places, the small but real danger I felt on the island
was new to me and mildly discomposing. (Actually, not new. The nagging
fear I felt when I pushed blindly through a tangle of scrub into a hidden
area beyond recalled similar fears from my childhood, when as a boy of
five or six I explored the neighborhood woods near my Pennsylvania
home with friends. We all understood that there were terrible beasts
lurking in the shadows.)

And yet, overall, the very big bear was a blessing. The mild sharp-
ening of my wits that the animal inspired seemed to fine-tune me to others of the island's countless pleasures. Certainly I do not recall ever
seeing colors as vivid as the orange and tangerine of an orchard of rock
lichens I found on one of my excursions; or, on another, as haunting as
the swirling violets of a patch of rosebay, which might have been clipped
from a canvas by El Greco. The buds on the willow trees that lined the
creeks near camp were just opening. They were the size of almonds and
growing larger every day. It appeared that they were about to explode.
I couldn't take my eyes off them. Each bud consisted of a fat core of silky
gray lineaments. Some of the threads were quite plain; others, which
seemed to have a special purpose I couldn't decipher, were tipped with
a beautiful orange-red dot. Each time I passed a willow I stopped to
admire its buds, and to judge how they had changed since my last visit;
and to squeeze a few of them, as though they were peaches at the super-
market. Thanks to Toru's bear, I became a big fan of willow buds.

And, unexpectedly, if not a fan, at least a tolerator of grizzlies. The
more time I spent in the bear's imagined presence, the less fearful I

became. I was vaguely aware that my efforts to make peace with the bear represented a small step on my long journey to find peace in the world beyond the refuge. It's true that I remained alert to the ever-present threat of grizzly mayhem, and I never traveled without my bear spray. But with Toru's example before me, I began to see that, with bears and perhaps with shadows of other kinds, coexistence may be possible.

Above the Kongakut, gulls endlessly patrolled the air space, cool and cocky as top guns. Never were more than two or three of the birds to be seen, but rarely was there a time when, glancing toward the bare hillside of the far side of the river, I didn't have my view temporarily tweaked by the sight of one of them slipping diagonally across my field of vision.

Gulls I knew, but most of the birds that inhabited the island were new to me. Northern Alaska is the Grand Central Station of the bird world. Millions of birds representing some seventy species visit each summer from around the globe – semipalmated sandpipers from Brazil, bluethroats from India, smews from Russia, northern wheatears from Egypt, wandering tattlers from New Zealand, loons and pipits from the American Midwest. Birds like Alaska.

Because the island is a spell north of tree line, the birds that summer there must build their nests on the ground. Tramping about, I had to watch my step for fear of accidentally crushing a clutch of eggs beneath my boots. Several times I unintentionally walked too close to a nest. Suddenly I was aware of a screeching sound, then a pesky dive-bomber-of-a-thing strafing my head and making repeated runs at my nose and ears. Not ten yards from the campsite, a semipalmated plover contrived for herself a nest of pebbles and dead grasses. In it she deposited four lovely brown-speckled eggs. So successfully were she and her digs camouflaged that several days passed before one of us – Toru, as it happened – stumbled onto the thing.

It was a valiant life she led. Rain, snow, foxes, photographers: they meant nothing to her. Because her headquarters were so close to our camp, it was inevitable that several times a day one of us would pass nearby. Each time, she put up a terrible fuss and rose fiercely to defend her nest. Pulling herself up as tall as she could (not very tall, as it happened; maybe six inches), rocking back and forth from one foot to the other, she dared the intruder to take another step. Such courage! A human being must look like a battleship to a plover. She held her ground successfully, and the last time I saw her she was still at her post, her eggs and her resolve unbroken.

Except for a few year-round residents – ptarmigan, ravens, snowy owls – the birds on the island had traveled great distances to get there, none more so than the Arctic terns. Shaun and I found a pair of them nesting not five minutes from our campsite. The two had appropriated a snarl of sticks and twigs that looked as though it had probably begun life as part of a very disorderly shrub upriver, then got swept away, finally running aground on a spit of sand and gravel at the island's edge. The nest reminded me of Le Corbusier's famous church of Notre-Dame-du-Haut in France; it had the same curvy boat shape sweeping up to a peak at one end, the same sense of the calm and the primitive teetering on the edge of chaos.

In such a place the terns settled down to a short but event-filled residency. She was a beautiful thing, and both of them knew it. The male worked his tail feathers off for her. Not yet having laid her eggs, she spent most of her time perched very still and regally on the steeple of the church, pretending not to know her mate. Terns are of the same lineage as gulls but generally smaller – perhaps a foot in length. The Arctic model wears a trendy black beret down to its eyes; below, the head is white. The bill is a nasty-looking red dagger as long as the bird's head. The breast, back, and wings are mostly gray. The tail is long and narrow; in flight it opens into a two-pronged fork.

What a fuss the female's partner made, and what he wouldn't do for her! Hour after hour he took to the air in search of insects, small fish, snacks and desserts of every description. North and south he prowled, east and west, long angel wings carving marvelous love letters in the sky.

Spotting a delicious minnow below he would hover for a few seconds, reading his instruments, furiously beating off gravity with his wings. Then he would fold them and drop like a flaming arrow to the water.

He rarely came up empty. Obviously pleased with himself, trophy dangling from his bill like a hipster's cigarette, he rose into the air. He always took the long way home – three or four extended swings across the river, swooping down at the right moment on each pass so that his mate would see him cutting his fancy route. She, of course, feigned indifference – but was anyone fooled? Hardly! On his arrival home she shivered like a bumblebee. But the drama was not yet over: now he would hover above his darling, his back arched, his wings pumping, and she would look straight up and crank open her bill, and he would look straight down and take aim, and then – *bingo!* – he would poke his catch into her mouth as though it were his tongue and they had just discovered French kissing.

Sometimes the lady's beauty and the male's excitement and their pleasure in each other overcame them, and he would mount her and flutter above her, and she would flutter below, both of them quite flushed with passion. As far as I could tell, this orgy of spooning and feeding and fluttering and carrying on continued twenty-four hours a day. They were quite a pair; they knew how to enjoy life.

What they had done to reach their cozy love nest by the river defies reason, common sense, and quite possibly the Second Law of Thermodynamics. The annual migration of the Arctic tern is one of nature's great stupefactions. The birds summer in the Arctic. They winter a world away, in the pack ice off Antarctica. Twice a year they fly from one end of the earth to the other, some eleven thousand miles in each direction; with added mileage for normal deviations from a straight line, each bird logs perhaps twenty-five thousand miles annually. That is a distance equal to the circumference of the earth. Arctic terns have been found wearing leg bands placed twenty-five years before. A twenty-five-year-old tern must have seen some two-thirds of a million miles pass beneath its wings – to the moon and back and then some. All this by a creature weighing no more than a bran muffin.

How to understand such a journey? It seems to me that the migration of the Arctic tern is most usefully viewed not as a record-setting flight, or an oddity of nature, or one stage in the life cycle of an interesting bird; but rather as a work of epic poetry – *The Odyssey* of migrations. Understanding the journey – no, not understanding it: *glimpsing* it, tentatively, distantly, imperfectly – requires not a map or an odometer but an imagination, the more fanciful the better. After all, beyond mileages and flight times – beyond what one might learn in the *Guinness World Records 2008* – we know nothing. We have no photographs of Arctic terns in clouds. We do not know if they sing while they fly, or if they chant tern-ish chants. We do not know if they fly in a vee or in a straight line, or in long swoops left and right, or in roller-coaster curves up and down. We do not know if they travel with other birds who happen to be going their way – sandpipers, say, or cranes – and we do not know how far they fly each day, and we do not know how they apportion their time. Do they fly for a few hours, then stop somewhere to feed for a while, like most birds. Or do they fly for days before taking a breather? We do not know.

Imagine them over the coast of British Columbia. Do they fly in tens or twenties or hundreds, or do they fly alone, each bird miles from its neighbors? How high above the ground do they fly? Small birds sometimes fly as low as two hundred feet on their migration paths; we could see them if we looked up, which we don't. Big birds fly higher, a mile or two or three.

A mountain climber in Nepal did look up and was amazed to see a goose flying over Mount Everest. That's up there. Arctic terns are medium-size birds, so you would expect them to fly one or two miles up. But they fly so much farther than other birds – maybe they fly higher too! Maybe they fly in the stratosphere, at the altitude of test pilots and ozone holes. I know, there's not enough oxygen up there to keep a bird alive! But this isn't just a bird, it's an Arctic tern! Maybe they store oxygen in the hollow quills of their tail feathers, and sip it when they get thirsty. There are big advantages to flying in the stratosphere. It's less crowded up there than it is down below with the riffraff. Plus, you can see Antarctica sooner! Imagine them over Peru. Peru! A storm front is ahead. Do they see it? Do they care? Perhaps they'll fly above it.

Perhaps they'll fly through it. What's it like in a storm cloud? Is it cold? Is it eerily silent? Is it dark and scary? Do Arctic terns worry about falling behind schedule when they're flying through storm clouds? No one knows.

Imagine them over Patagonia. What do they do to pass the hours?

The film director Stanley Kubrick once speculated that dolphins spend their free time solving complex mathematical theorems. Do Arctic terns play games or write poetry or find new solutions to the longitude problem? They would be good at that. In any case, no one knows.

Bulletin! We know this: Arctic terns love the sun. Arctic terns know the sun better than any creature on earth. The birds summer in the Arctic, where the sun is above the horizon twenty-four hours a day. They winter in the Antarctic, where the sun is above the horizon twenty-four hours a day. Late in the summer, as the long days begin to move south from the Arctic, Arctic terns move with them, following the light. Late in the winter, as the long days begin to move north from the Antarctic, Arctic terns move with them, following the light. As bats and worms spend their lives in darkness, Arctic terns spend their lives in light. They go where the light goes. Does this explain their inexplicable journey – that they love the light? No one knows.

Years ago, when I first imagined that I might someday like to write a book, I came up with a vegetable-stew-of-an-idea for a novel that involved Arctic terns, the legendary blues guitarist Robert Johnson, and the notion that the earth is a spaceship forever crisscrossing the cosmos, calling at various interesting destinations as it goes. As I saw it, Arctic terns would symbolize the indomitable spirit, Robert Johnson would symbolize art, and Starship Earth would symbolize the hope for eternal life. It all made sense until you tried to write a novel about it. Mine, if I had ever written it, which I didn't, would have been all symbols. It represented everything: struggle, hope, art, life, death (what else is there?) – and so it represented pretty much nothing.

What I had was more a novel idea than an idea for a novel. It happened that, at the time, I was interested in Arctic terns, I was interested in Robert Johnson, and I was interested in space travel; so I tossed the three willy-nilly into my stew and figured that that was how you outlined a book. But when I tried to turn my outline into pages and chapters, I had no idea what to do. I had no characters and no plot. I couldn't find a single connection among my themes. My novel collapsed under its own weightlessness.

I hadn't thought about the book for years. One day as I watched my beautiful, giddy terns whooping it up beside the Kongakut, I suddenly recalled my masterpiece in all its weirdness. It occurred to me that the reason the project had foundered wasn't the lack of a plot or of characters or of connections among its themes; it was that I had chosen the wrong form for my material. What I'd dreamed up wasn't a novel at all. It was a song. What's more, someone else had dreamed it up before me. His name was Robert Johnson, and the song was "Honeymoon Blues." It was about spirit, art, and the hope for eternal life. Johnson wrote it during the 1930s. He recorded it in 1937, six years before I was born.

Robert Johnson spent the bulk of his brief and mostly unlucky life (he died at the age of twenty-seven, probably a murder victim) in the Deep South, a long way from the island. Nevertheless, on the evidence of "Honeymoon Blues," it's clear that he would have recognized the place at once if he had suddenly been transported there. He would have seen that the Kongakut is just a big old guitar strumming a heartfelt blues down the rocks and gravel bars of the valley, and that sometimes the song is fast and wild, and sometimes it's slow and peaceful. He would have known that the island is the words of the song, and that some of them are joyful, and some of them are sad. He would have understood that the theme of the song – and the theme of the novel I never wrote – is simple human yearning, for a good and a happy and a useful life that will never end.

I could probably have figured out most of that if I had been in some other wild and musical place. But I needed to be on the island, situated among its multitudinous vagaries and curiosities, to grasp something I had never known before. And that was that no one is willing to go farther or to search harder for a good and a happy and a useful life than the little birds with the black berets and the forked tails. Robert Johnson was no ornithologist but he came to that same conclusion, and decades before I did. Even more amazing, he knew the name of one of the birds. She was the one who spent her days perched on the steeple of the cathedral at the edge of the river, pretending to be bored. Her name was Betty Mae, and he wrote his song for her.

"Honeymoon Blues" by Robert Johnson

Betty Mae, Betty Mae, you shall be my wife someday.
Betty Mae, Betty Mae, you shall be my wife someday.
I wants a little sweet girl, that will do anything, that
    I say.
Betty Mae, you is my heartstring, you is my destiny.
Betty Mae, you is my heartstring, you is my destiny.
And you rolls across my mind, baby, each and every day.
Li'l girl, li'l girl, my life seem so misery.
Hmm hmm, little girl, my life seem so misery.
Baby, I guess it must be love, now, hoo mm, Lord that's
    takin' effect on me.
Some day I will return, with the marriage license in my hand.
Some day I will return, hoohoo, with a marriage license
    in my hand.
I'm gon' take you for a honeymoon, in some long,
    long distant land.

This was the island. It was a peaceful, earnest place where life unfolded effortlessly and seamlessly, where you could drop in at an arbitrary moment and get swept up in the flow and the feel of the place, as though you were part of the plan, even if you didn't understand a word of it, even if you didn't know that there was a plan. Where you felt a kind of deliverance from everything that had come before your arrival, and where mysteriously you could find the patience to await whatever was to come next. Each moment was the same as the last; both had a familiar shape and sound and taste. But each was different, too, for it always brought something new – a breeze, a crocus wakening on a logjam, the plaintive cry of a curlew, blue clouds crowding over bare brown hills. Lichen and fox, plover and ground squirrel: each was inventing a life, each was going about a business I couldn't fathom but which I understood to be quite important. The island was a diligent, deadly serious place, but one without airs.

If there was a purpose here it was new life – new buds, new eggs, new leaves; and, to my mind at least, new beginnings. One particularly exuberant morning, watching the grand preparations for the next generation of every kind, I realized that I was witnessing nothing less than the first day of creation. The Sioux believe that all animals came from the same valley. Now I knew that they were right, and the valley was here. The world was being born before my eyes.

And such a nursery the parents had contrived! Icy mountains to grace the walls, lullabies of wings and waters, spinning mobiles of gulls and dragonflies, cuddly blankets of phlox petals and willow buds. Twenty-five years earlier Fred Meader had told me this was going to happen: "In spring, when you first hear the water trickling and the birds singing . . . there's power in that that's greater than anything I know. It teaches you something. You know that you're not alone, that you're a valued part of something that's bigger than anything you could ever understand."

And, millennia before that, that old backcountry traveler Isaiah: "Let the wilderness and the dry land be glad, let the wasteland rejoice and bloom . . . let it rejoice and sing for joy. . . . "

I am not a fisherman but Shaun is, and during our stay at the Waldo Arms he had been disheartened to learn from several leading authorities that he was not likely to have any luck with a hook and a line on the island. The season was too early, the jittery helicopter pilot told him. The fish were still comatose beneath the ice; even those that were stirring would be too stupid to recognize a decent worm if they saw one. The young man who initiated Shaun and me into the dark mysteries of bear spray explained that the issue was not stupidity, it was visibility. Because of melting snows in the Romanzofs and the furious rains of the past few days, the Kongakut would be so choked with mud and debris that even smart, happy, hungry fish would be unable to see anything my friend might dangle in front of their noses, no matter how tempting.

Discouraging words, these. And yet, such words mean nothing to members of the brotherhood of bullheaded anglers, of whom my friend is a regional vice president. During Shaun's final moments at the Waldo, after he had climbed into the back of Audi's truck for the hop to the airport, and many minutes after he and I had made our final and irrevocable decisions on what we would take to the island, a look of profound fear came over his face. It was the look of a man who has seen the future, and it is bad. He leapt from the truck and raced into the Waldo. Moments later he was back, pole and tackle box tucked safely under his arm, a sigh of relief murmuring devoutly on his lips.

Not long after we took up residence on the island, Shaun mentioned to Toru his disappointment that, because of the poor conditions, there were no fish to be angled.

Toru's forehead wrinkled.

"I saw fish," he said. He pointed at a pool of melt water that had calved off from the river. "Over there. Big ones. You can catch them."

The words were scarcely out of the man's mouth before Shaun was ransacking his backpack for tackle and pole, as though a phone were ringing in there. Minutes later the two men were poised at the edge of the pool, peering down into blue-green water for signs of life.

What followed was one of the great chapters in the annals of fishing. Shaun tied a rooster tail onto his line and aimed it at a spot by the edge of an ice shelf on the far side of the pool. The plash of feather and hook on water was enough to wake the fish, of which many were present. He tried again, this time securing their attention.

On the third cast the lure had barely touched down when it was assaulted by an Arctic char of great length and volume. Toru let out a hoot. Shaun dug in his heels. Man and fish battled briefly; fish lost. In a minute, the creature was flopping in the gravel at Shaun's feet.

He cast again. This time he reeled in a cousin of the first catch, slightly less handsome, but bigger. I was on the other side of the island during this developing story and learned the details only later.

"I was feverish," Shaun told me. "I was crazy. I was casting like a mad man. I'd reel one in, take it off the hook, cast again, reel in another one." The look in his eye as he talked was new to me – and unsettling. "I've never had so much fun in my life." At some point he passed the rod to Toru, whose results were the same.

The pair's final tally was eight Arctic char in ten casts in twenty minutes. None of the fish taped in at under twenty inches. With visions of a grand banquet in the wilderness forming in his mind, Shaun kept three of his catch and threw the rest back.

As I said, I am not a fisherman. But I know a thing of beauty when I see it, and these babies were centerfold material. Arctic char belong to the salmon family. Some exhibit red or green coloration; the three that Shaun had selected for dinner were electric silver in hue and dotted with tiny pink spots. In their essential qualities they presented reasonable facsimiles of Jennifer Lopez's legs in silk stockings: long, slender, supple, muscular, curvy, delicious looking. Toru offered to clean the three chosen specimens. Shaun gallantly accepted. On their way back to camp, the two men cut willow branches, one for each fish.

I had returned to the tent by this time and was privileged to witness the homecoming. My two friends strolled into camp like Peter returning with the wolf. For the first time I understood the expression "drunk with victory." One welcome result of our warriors' giddiness was their conviction that only they were worthy of preparing dinner. I was put in charge of snacks and drinks, but otherwise ordered not to interfere.

I found a rock and flopped down in the dirt beside it to watch. Above, long trains of ashen clouds chugged across the sky. They were harbingers; soon a light rain began to fall. I slipped on my rain parka and flipped the hood up over my head. Blue mist crept through the gate of bare hills to the north, dropped to ground level, skulked across the rocks and into the banquet hall. Rain fell intermittently but never with any conviction; before long it gave up. Left in its wake were a slow, loping wind and a deep chill.

My hosts collected driftwood and fashioned a tidy fire pit. Toru whittled points on the willow branches. Earlier, cleaning the char, he had slit each open to the neck; now he mounted a fish on each branch, poking the stick clear through from tail to mouth. When the fire was blazing, he and Shaun angled the branches over the flames, securing them with rocks. A patient grilling began. The two men planted themselves beside the fire to await the outcome.

I sprang into action. I located crackers. I located some lovely Japanese cookies in Toru's pack. I located a hefty bottle of Canadian Mist in my pack. I showed the bottle to Toru, and he expressed interest.

"Yes," he said, his eyes narrowing. "I believe I would like to try that."

I rounded up coffee cups. We made a toast, to international peace, to the gallant fish that had donated so generously to our meal, and, of course, to the very big bear.

As the fish smoked, as we delved deeper into the bottle, crystalline silence drifted into the campsite. Just beyond my extended arm, a creamy moon joined the party, hunching down musefully on a hilltop behind gusty clouds. A pair of gulls grabbed a small breeze and rode it down the valley. Moon glow, bird flight, firelight: how quiet the evening was!

Or was it morning? I had no idea.

We were very far from anywhere. Gazing into the fire I tried to process that fact, without success; it seemed so clear that we were very close to everywhere. Now the flames crackled, shattering the silence. The steel-stringed river broke into song. We spoke of the animals that had lived here. How many? A million? Ten thousand grizzlies? Imagine! All seemed to be present, all went about their business in the shadows, pausing at intervals to take in our words. With the animals were Inuit and Indians of a thousand years ago, following the river north or south to whatever it was that animated their dreams. The world seemed like firelight, something you gazed at with a faraway look in your eyes. Shaun moved one of the willow branches closer to the flames. Toru added a stick to the fire and spoke lovingly of his family in Japan. His words, all of our words, were simple and fervent and true; they seemed more important than usual; they had a sparkle and a glow, like the driftwood coals that glimmered beneath the flames.

Long after we flopped down in the dirt, the char began to droop from their supports. The flesh was deep orange by now, and flaking from the bones. The two chefs lay it on hot rocks at fireside to allow the flames to do their final subtle work. Toru collected his giant bottle of soy sauce. I ate slowly and in amazement, with my fingers, with the knowledge that like the creeks and the ptarmigan and the Indians of a thousand years ago, I was now part of the history of this place, etched onto its rocks like a petroglyph, celebrated in song like the little bird that lived by the river: an intrepid explorer in some long, long distant land.

At some point it was over. Toru had returned to his tent, or perhaps he was out searching for wolverines. Shaun and I lay in our sleeping bags, with the side flap of the tent pulled open. We chatted quietly. The north half of the earth lay before us, damp, bright, cold, misty, full of promise. The sky over the ocean was yellow and gray. I started to move away from the door when I heard my friend say something. His voice was quiet and calm.

"Caribou at twelve o'clock," he said.

It took a moment for the words to sink in. I looked north, toward the hill that fell to the river's west side. There atop the ridge, silhouetted against the sky, were seven caribou. They were perhaps a quarter mile from us, one a male with a modest set of antlers. Several were feeding; the others stood motionless but alert, as though they knew they had been spotted.

We watched, rapt, for a few seconds. Then one of the seven moved, and then they were gone, over the ridge, slipping silently toward *ivvavik*. Shaun and I said a few words, expressing a well of gratitude for what was surely one of the grandest days we had ever known. Then I scrunched down in my bag and fell into a deep and dreamless sleep.

TRAVELS WITH LUCKY

The Porcupine caribou herd is one of more than a dozen barren-ground herds that endlessly crisscross the bleak, treeless latitudes of northern Alaska and Canada. With a population estimated at around 110,000 in 2007, the Porcupine is a considerable collection of animals, but by no means the largest of the barren-ground herds. Several others, including the Bathurst (128,000 in 2006), the Western Arctic (490,000 in 2003), and the Qamanirjuaq (496,000 in 1994, the most recent year for which an estimate is available) are larger. In all, as many as two million barren-ground caribou may inhabit the North American Arctic. (Even larger aggregations of forest-dwelling woodland caribou are to be found. The Leaf River herd of northern Quebec was reckoned at some 550,000 animals in a 2003 census. A decade earlier, Labrador's George River herd was judged even bigger, around 800,000 animals. In the years immediately following, the size of the herd plunged drastically, for reasons that are not fully understood. By 2001, the George River herd had fallen to an estimated 400,000 to 500,000 caribou.)

Given the huge numbers of animals, and the fact that at certain times of the year major portions of a given herd move together toward the same destinations, it's little wonder that Arctic travelers sometimes return home with stories of throngs of caribou streaming across the tundra, grunting and bleating, hooves clicking *en masse*, like Alaska-size orchestras of castanets. (Caribou hoof clicks are produced by ligaments slipping over bones in the feet.) In *Midnight Wilderness*, an engrossing account of her travels in the Arctic National Wildlife Refuge, Debbie S. Miller recalls a warm July afternoon on the Egaksrak River when what she at first thinks is a mirage shimmering in the distance turns out to be "a living, breathing, pulsating mass of animals." Later she learns that the multitude, which eventually surrounds her, contains some ten to twenty thousand caribou. Visitors to caribou calving grounds may see practically entire herds gathered in one place. Writer and photographer Kennan Ward camped at *ivvavik* with most of the Porcupine herd, a number that, in Ward's passionate work *The Last Wilderness*, he estimated at some 100,000 caribou.

Before heading north I had read so many of these accounts that I had come to think of the sights they described as commonplace. I began to imagine that when I first saw caribou I would see a ton of them – perhaps hundreds swimming an ice-choked river, or thundering thousands such as Debbie Miller saw, a sight some writers have compared to the great herds of buffalo that once romped over the American West.

Like my fantasy of the Kongakut valley as a glacier-strewn wasteland, my idea of what I would see when I at last laid eyes on *Rangifer tarandus* turned out to be somewhat overblown. Instead of hundreds of caribou furiously dog-paddling across a river, or thousands steamrolling over the tundra, I saw, well, seven, and they weren't doing much of anything. Grazing is what they were doing, like cows, atop an unremarkable ridge beside the Kongakut River.

But such a seven! Having lowered my expectations considerably since seeing exactly nothing as Walt Audi pointed first at one spot on the ice and then another, during the flight in from Kaktovik – "There's one! There's one!" – I didn't need thousands of caribou, or even hundreds, to count my trip a success. One would do. Even a small one. Even a sick one. Even a homely one whose hooves didn't click.

But seven! Now that was something! By the time I crawled from my sleeping bag many hours after last call at the Grand Fiesta of the Humongous Char, the seven had grown in my estimation to a newly discovered herd, the noblest and bravest caribou of them all: the Canadian Mist herd! If I had observed its members for mere seconds, I nonetheless held a vivid picture of each: two handsome ones on the left, one grazing expertly, one with her head cocked in my direction, perhaps in a gesture of welcome; next, the antlered male, a bit arrogant, pushy, one of those tiresome fellows who never admits he's wrong; then two grazers; then a sentinel; then the last, somewhat apart from the rest, the rebel of the bunch, headstrong, rascally, impulsive. Certainly as fine a team as has ever been assembled on an unremarkable ridge beside the Kongakut River! I felt that I knew those stalwart beasts. I felt that we had communicated with one another, using the same trippy, mysterious, Esperanto-like dialect that my golden retriever and I employ to talk to each other, even though I wasn't sure what the message from the other side had been. I even believed that one of the seven might have been Lucky.

Lucky was one of ten female caribou that were captured in late 1997, outfitted with satellite collars, and then released. The operation was carried out near Old Crow, Yukon, by two Old Crow residents, Robert Kay and William Josie, and a team of wildlife biologists representing a consortium of Canadian and U.S. agencies. Schoolchildren in Alaska and Yukon competed in contests to christen the ten. The winning names were Dasher, Gus-Gus, Homer, Blixen, Lynetta, Cupid, Donner, Vixen, Springy, and Lucky.

With their collars sending out steady streams of data, the test subjects could be followed on their meandering journeys across the North with great precision. This was true not only for the scientists who were studying the animals, but for anyone with a connection to the Internet. Maps pinpointing the caribou's positions were posted and updated regularly on the project website, *www.taiga.net/satellite*. As a security measure, the animals' locations were kept at least two weeks behind, to prevent anyone with a hankering for a certain dim kind of notoriety from going out and plugging one of the famous caribou. When you checked a map you didn't see where the animals were at that moment, only where they had been a few weeks before.

With the aid of the maps, a visitor to the website could play a humbling and thoroughly exasperating game of Where Will the Caribou Be Next? This exercise was based on Aldo Leopold's exhortation to "think like a mountain" but with a new twist that asked players to think like a caribou. The idea was to attempt to get into the head of, say, Blixen, following her progress over several weeks, making sense of it, sort of, and then predicting where she would be when the next map came out.

Of course, Blixen was never where you thought she would be when the next map came out. To anyone with an ounce of sense, it was obvious that she should have headed straight for Timber Creek, to avoid the Terrible Mountains. Instead, she turned left and ran straight for the Terribles. Two weeks after that she had reversed course completely and was heading back in the direction from which she came. *Hey girl! Where you going?* There was surely logic behind the movements of the animals, but it was caribou logic, which marched to the beat of a different drummer. The ten collared females demonstrated that caribou navigation was one part horse sense, one part goofiness, and one part riddle wrapped in an enigma wrapped in a great big clump of pickled reindeer moss.

Back in Nevada, where betting on caribou positions had not yet been discovered by the bookmakers, I happened onto the website early in 2003. Tables of historical data brought me up to date on the adventures of the fab ten since they had gone online more than five years before. The hard life of a caribou was manifest at once. Springy, collared in October 1997, died in August 1998. Vixen, collared in October 1997, died in June 1998. Dasher, collared in November 1997, died in August 1998. By May 2000, five of the original ten were dead. By that time several new herd members had been captured and collared to augment the team. (The process of replenishing the group as old members fall by the wayside continues to this day, as does the satellite project itself. In 2007, biweekly updates of herd locations on the Internet were switched to four updates a year in the face of mounting evidence that the two-week delay did not provide sufficient protection for the herd from hunters.)

Several months before my departure for Alaska, I decided to follow one of the caribou on her passage to *ivvavik*. In homage to my home state, I chose the animal known as "Lucky." Lucky had originally been collared in October 1997, as she swam the Porcupine River some forty miles upriver from Old Crow. River captures do not allow for the collection of physical data, so at the time nothing much was learned about the animal herself; the entire process of roping a caribou, maneuvering it into position beside the capture vessel, attaching a collar, and releasing the animal takes only two or three minutes.

In March 1999, Lucky was recaptured, as each of the caribou must be, every couple of years, to replace her batteries. This time she was apprehended on land, with the aid of a gun-activated net fired over her from a helicopter hovering above. Blood samples and other measurements determined her to be a healthy animal, about five to six years of age – middle-aged in caribou years. Her weight was 200 pounds, her total body length just over 6 feet 1 inch, her height at the shoulders 3 feet 10 inches.

Thanks to the website's huge database of position coordinates, I was able to review in great detail Lucky's travels since her initial capture. Far from an immutable route followed year after year, this caribou's peregrinations more closely resembled the path of a shnockered soccer fan trying to find his Toyota in a stadium parking lot after a game. Each annual cycle took Lucky to territory different from any she had set foot on before. Except at the northern and southern termini of these circuits, where there were occasional return visits, she appears never to have set foot on the same spot of ground twice. The idea of a "migration route" followed by members of the herd was clearly erroneous.

A look at Lucky's positions at the same time each year shows how widely she wandered. In October 1998, a year after her capture, she was 160 miles south of her capture spot, in Yukon's Ogilvie Mountains.

A year after that she was 250 miles to the northwest, in the Davidson Mountains in the Arctic National Wildlife Refuge. The next year she was back very near where she had been two years earlier, in the Ogilvies. October 2001 found her 140 miles to the northwest, at a spot near the U.S.–Yukon border, southwest of Old Crow. Twelve months later she was 80 miles farther northeast, not far from her original capture spot. In October 2003 she was thirty miles east of her 2001 location. Each of those positions was a single point on an erratic, circuitous path several thousand miles in length, which changed utterly from one year to the next.

Equally characteristic of her species' fanciful nature is the fact that Lucky's October locations were often far from where her collared mates were at the same times. In October 2003, when Lucky was near Old Crow, Donner was one hundred miles south, in Yukon's Mahoni Range. Helen, meanwhile, was 150 miles northwest, in Alaska's Davidson Mountains. The entire herd was dispersed over an area in excess of 20,000 square miles.

Spring is the one time of the year when a pregnant female caribou might be expected to behave in a somewhat predictable fashion. And, indeed, in the spring of 2003, Lucky did just that. Through March, the traditional final month of an expectant female's winter gestation, she headquartered in the vicinity of the Eagle River, some forty miles north of Eagle Plains, Yukon. She hardly moved. During the week of March 22–29, she wandered south a few miles, where she remained until around April 5. Over the next seven days she moved slowly north again, about a mile a day.

Around April 12, she caught the fever. The following week she put sixty miles beneath her hooves, due north. The week after that she did sixty more, altering her course to the northwest. The migration was now in full swing. By the time I left Nevada for Kaktovik, at the end of May, it had long been clear from the website maps that Lucky had one thing in mind, and that was the calving grounds. By my reckoning, she should have dropped anchor in *ivvavik* a week or two before Shaun and I pitched our tent in the Kongakut valley. Even if she had visited the island along the way, she would likely have done so many days before we arrived.

Was Lucky one of the seven that I saw poised atop the ridge? Probably not. Still, this was one happy-go-lucky caribou. Maybe instead of heading for Timber Creek, she had turned left and steered straight for the Terribles. Maybe she decided to lay over beside the Kongakut for a few days – you know, put her hooves up and listen to the grass grow. Maybe she was the appointed emissary from the other side. If so, she would have been expected to hang around until I arrived, so that she could deliver her message. *Welcome to caribou land, my friend. Geez, I thought you would never get here! Anyway, look fast, I have to am-scray. And, oh, by the way, you owe me one.*

And if she was not one of the seven, it didn't matter. Lucky or Unlucky, seven caribou or seven thousand, I emerged from my tent that day with a sense of a job completed, a goal fulfilled. It's okay, Shaun. I'm fixed. We can go home now.

Fortunately, I did not go home. If I had, I would not have learned what I was about to learn, which was that the esteemed members of the Canadian Mist herd were not the only caribou in the valley. Not by a long shot. Sometime later that day I was shuffling about the campsite, mulling over at interminable length, and quite contentedly, what I would do next, if anything. Shaun had pulled out his portable watercolor kit and set himself the megalomaniacal task of squeezing the monstrous stack of peaks that hovered over the island's south end onto a canvas the size of a large Post-It. Suddenly I heard a shout.

"Caribou!"

I glanced left. There was Toru, posted straight as a shovel beside his tent, eyes glued to a pair of field glasses. With one hand he gripped the glasses. With the other he was jabbing a finger at a spot on the opposite side of the Kongakut.

I was beside him in a moment.

"There are I think nine," he said. He was excited. He showed me where to look, indicating a small peninsula that jutted into the water a short distance downstream. Ever attentive to my needs, he passed the field glasses to me, then hurried off to collect his camera equipment.

I raised the instrument to my eyes. My hands were shaking. I had pretended to myself that seven caribou were enough. Now I knew that they weren't: I wanted more! Yes, this was a bonus I hadn't expected, but I deserved it! In an effort to steady the view, I held my breath, braced my elbows against my sides, and began reciting a ridiculous mantra I hadn't thought of for years.

I panned left and right, locating the peninsula. I gave it a quick once-over, petrified that any creatures that might have been standing on that minuscule patch of ground a moment before might have hightailed it away, never to be seen again. If I could at least glimpse. . . .

Something was there. Yes – *Jesus!* – caribou! They were tiny. They were little statues. I began to distinguish bodies: three at first, then five, then another I hadn't noticed, half-hidden by one of the first.

Finally, perhaps, stretching it, nine caribou, now moving, pacing at river's edge. I drank them in, cool water after a long day in the sun. I counted again, watched one put its nose to the icy Kongakut, watched another walk away from its mates; attempted desperately to make sense of what I was seeing. *Caribou!* Just gazing seemed insufficient. I wanted to be closer to them. I wanted to *touch them!* I was crazy with excitement, at the same time thoroughly flummoxed by the fact that I had no idea what to do with my craziness. My rational mind pestered me: What does it mean to see something after months of *imagining* that you are seeing it? Which is better, the seeing or the imagining? At the same time some other part of me simply wailed: *How can I hold on to this moment?*

Behind the caribou and perhaps half a mile to the north, a narrow shadow cleaved the mountainside. It appeared to be the entrance to a canyon, or a notch in the mountain, though from my perspective its exact nature was impossible to tell. Shaun, standing beside me now with his own set of binoculars, speculated that the animals might have come through the notch to reach the river. It made sense. My topo map of the region showed passes both north and south. The southern one was known to be used in some years by some members of the Porcupine; that was the route Walt Audi had in mind when he put forward the Kongakut as a feasible destination for Shaun and me.

But Toru had not seen any wildlife in the vicinity of the southern pass. From the map it appeared that the northern route – the shadow, apparently – was the more difficult one. It would require a climb of perhaps twelve hundred feet from relatively level country on the far side, followed by a sharp descent to the river. But what's twelve hundred feet to a caribou? Maybe the northern pass had other advantages. Maybe this year, for reasons only a caribou would understand, the shadow was the way to go.

The nine stood on the dividing line between winter and summer. Northward the Kongakut moved unseen beneath a roof of ice; southward it flowed free. Every now and then a section of the ice mantle collapsed, exposing with a thunderous *whuummmp!* another acre of freezing water below.

It was a dangerous spot, and the caribou knew it. Clearly discomposed by their plight, they milled about, measuring ice, then water, then land, then ice again, weighing their choices. From his equipment case Toru removed a lens big enough to see Louisiana. He screwed it to the front of his camera and went to work. Shaun and I grabbed a snack bag, found comfy perches beside the river, and sat back to watch.

And so, there were caribou in the valley after all. Audi had steered us right. Not the thousands I had imagined. Not even a steady stream. But every hour or two or three, a group of five or ten or fifteen. Why they were suddenly appearing – Toru's previous sightings had all been in the hours after midnight – was unclear. Evidently there had been a break in the migration line; now, for some reason, it had been repaired.

The great majority of the animals escaped our attention until after they had crossed the river to the island, and we saw them making their way across the flats west of our campsite. But occasionally we would spot a party where the gang of nine had appeared, which seemed to be the place where all the caribou first came down to the river. From there, a very few chanced a scamper across the ice. That was the quick solution to the river-crossing problem, but one wintry with hazards; if the ice broke while the caribou were on it, they'd be in a pickle. With a good deal of drama these daredevils stepped forward, stepped back, stepped forward again, finally eased their hooves onto the Kongakut's frozen surface. Staying well north of the waterline, the animals herky-jerked across the river, like a car stuck in first gear. They would stroll nonchalantly for a short distance, then suddenly take off lickety-split, then skid to a halt to stroll again. During the stuck portions of these spastic promenades the caribou might pause to sniff the ice; or stand splay-legged, gazing forlornly at their fellows; or cautiously gander about at the pretty scenery; or cock their heads to listen to the water swooshing by a foot or so beneath their hooves; or study the route ahead to gauge how much farther they had to go before they were on solid footing. When the answer to the last question was somewhere in the vicinity of fifty yards, the animals always threw caution to the north winds and took off like racehorses for the finish line. Despite the dangers, the caribou I saw opting for this method of crossing the river all completed the traverse without incident.

Most parties chose water crossings – no piece of cake, but at least free of the threat of burial beneath tons of ice. One afternoon I watched a trio of caribou as they dithered incessantly at river's edge, just a short distance north of the line where the ice had melted and the river ran free. At last one of the three stepped onto the hard surface. The second came up close behind. Together the two moved forward perhaps ten yards along the slippery surface.

For a moment they stood, shakily and irresolutely. With what appeared to be impatience, or perhaps disapproval, they turned and eyed their companion, who continued grazing nonchalantly at the river's edge.

Suddenly the companion jumped straight into the air. It was as though someone had smacked it in the hindquarters with a paddle. Whap! Hitting the ground, the animal spun 180 degrees, then took off straight up the side of the mountain.

The others got the message at once. Scrambling quickly off the ice, they took off after their companion. A moment later the three were galloping upriver, perhaps a hundred yards above the water. They continued along the mountainside for half a mile, then stopped.

What had possessed Number Three? Had it consulted its compass and decided that the direction was wrong? Or had it simply lost its nerve and decided that an inglorious retreat and a powwow with the others were in order?

Again the caribou grazed. Twenty minutes passed. They began to meander down the mountain along a route I had seen no others follow. The path leveled out a few yards from the river's edge.

They were now well south of the ice. One animal leerily put its nose to the river but pulled back quickly, as though the water had a bad smell. The Kongakut, fifty yards wide where I stood, was thundering past at dizzying speed, and the idea that it might have a bad smell, of a sort, struck me as entirely reasonable. Earlier the caribou had rejected an ice crossing as too hazardous; now, contemplating a difficult swim, they seemed to change their minds again.

The ambivalent behavior continued. Twice one of the animals actually lowered a hoof into the water, then immediately withdrew. The group moved to a rocky platform a few yards above the water and pondered their predicament. Then, as suddenly as they had earlier decided to race upriver, they abruptly turned and hoofed it straight up the slope. This time no one led the charge; the bright idea occurred to all three simultaneously.

When they came to the horizontal path they had followed earlier, which ran north to the ice, they never considered taking it. Instead, they crossed over and continued straight up the mountainside. A short distance above, the angle of the slope fell back suddenly, opening into a kind of amphitheater. I had seen other caribou hanging out there from time to time. When the three arrived they came to a halt and once again began grazing.

They stayed for an hour. The last I saw them they were moving north, back toward the spot where they had first come into view, perhaps to try the ice again.

Once the animals had reached the island, by ice or by water, they succumbed to its charms no less than Shaun or I had. Many spent an hour or more making their way across the expanse, grazing, musing, sometimes lying down to rest. This was the second or third wave of the migration, and unlike the pregnant females, which had passed through days or even weeks before, these barren females, juveniles, and immature bulls had time to spare. The great gathering of the tribe was not scheduled to begin for many days, and by the time the caribou reached the island they had less than a hundred miles to go.

Their paths typically took them to within one or two hundred yards of our campsite. Sometimes we would watch from there. Sometimes we would go to them. Toru usually did the latter, always toting a full array of camera gear. He had a slow, easy, zigzag way of approaching the animals that often allowed him to get within thirty or forty yards of them. He seemed to be able to sense when he was nearing the point where they would spook and trot off; just shy of the line he would set up and begin shooting.

It took me a while to get the hang of this slightly tipsy, I-come-in-the-name-of-peace routine. The first few times I tried, the caribou weren't fooled for a second; they knew a rookie when they saw one. They got it into their heads that what I needed was not a little quality time with them, but a humiliating hazing ritual. The moment I would spot one of them and take a few steps in its direction, the animal would signal its cohorts. On a count of three, the entire party would straighten up, gaze disdainfully in my direction, shake their heads sadly, and zoom off in a cloud of dust. Several times I was sure I heard the animals laughing as they galloped away.

With an eye toward improving my skills, I began trailing along a few steps behind Toru, mirroring, as closely as I could, his manner of walking and of holding his body. The animals were no doubt amused by this

ABOVE: *Aerial view of the Brooks Range and coast of the Beaufort Sea.*

BELOW LEFT: *Walt Audi.*

BELOW RIGHT: *Shaun T. Griffin.*

ABOVE LEFT: *The author's arrival at the campsite on the Kongakut River, assisted by Toru Sonohara.* (PHOTOGRAPH BY SHAUN T. GRIFFIN)

ABOVE RIGHT: *Shaun T. Griffin and Arctic char.*
(PHOTOGRAPH BY TORU SONOHARA)

BELOW: *Kongakut River camp.*

ABOVE: *Arctic terns.*

BELOW: *"Toru's Garden."*

ABOVE: *Caribou young on "the island."* (PHOTOGRAPH BY TORU SONOHARA)

BELOW: *Kongakut River flats.* (PHOTOGRAPH BY TORU SONOHARA)

ABOVE: *Caribou cow and calf near the bend in the Kongakut River.*
(PHOTOGRAPH BY TORU SONOHARA)

BELOW: *Caribou grazing on "the island."* (PHOTOGRAPH BY TORU SONOHARA)

ABOVE: *Caribou crossing the frozen Kongakut River.*

BELOW: *Caribou grazing at Kongakut.* (PHOTOGRAPH BY TORU SONOHARA)

ABOVE: *Ogilvie Mountains, Yukon.*

BELOW: *Porcupine herd members foraging near "Caribou Bluff."*

ABOVE LEFT: *Peter Nagano and Richard Nagano on "Caribou Bluff."*
(PHOTOGRAPH BY SHAUN T. GRIFFIN)

ABOVE RIGHT: *Bob Salerno on a view point above Loon Lake.*

BELOW: *Loon Lake, Brooks Range, Alaska.*

peculiar shadow dance. Still, they seemed to appreciate my efforts. Slowly they warmed to me. Even without Toru as a shield, I could sometimes work my way as close to a group as he was capable of getting, and tarry there for ten or fifteen minutes before the animals moved on to a new spot.

If you are not a wildlife biologist or a photographer, as I am not, and if your interest in wildlife is neither scientific nor artistic, as mine is not, then you will probably not find much to remark upon if you watch a caribou for ten or fifteen minutes. The animal will not play games with its neighbors, or groom them, or bite them, or steal things from them, or attempt to mount one of them. It will not make a nest or chase rodents. Caribou are a kind, gentle, harmonious, uncomplaining, tolerant species. They're saints. They're also boring, at least when they're not running across Alaska. Watching a caribou that is not running across Alaska is like watching an old man picking blueberries. Caribou are ruminants, a humble type. Their flagship skill, besides that of finding their way home, is food processing. At this they are masters. When a caribou is relaxed and forage is plentiful, the animal will eat six or seven pounds of vegetable matter a day, matter that a human would find indigestible: lichens, grasses, sedges, willow leaves. When 100,000 caribou gather on the coastal plain in midsummer, this works out to a lot of food – half a million pounds a day or more. The coastal plain is a generous provider.

So is the island. Thanks to fresh forage, which appeared every day, there was plenty for a caribou to eat. This despite the passage of perhaps thousands of herd members since the migration began. Like cows, moose, and other ruminants, caribou work hard at eating and digesting their food. The initial chewing is only the first of many steps that the animal takes to beat a bite into submission. After a mouthful is swallowed, it passes into the rumen, one section of a fancy four-chambered stomach whose complexities make our own stomachs seem like mere garbage cans. After administering further damage, the rumen delivers the food back into the caribou's mouth, as cud, which the animal ruminates at its leisure and at length. Now comes a second swallow. This time the food finds its way to the second chamber of the stomach; then the third; then, at last, the fourth, the portion of the organ that most resembles the human stomach.

None of this makes for good television, and if Animal Planet were forced to depend on films of caribou chewing their cuds to pay the bills, the channel would cease to exist. With little on the outside to engage his interest, then, the caribou watcher is inevitably led inward, into irresponsible, perhaps dangerous speculation. My own ruminations, at my leisure and at length, ranged widely but always returned to what was for me the main topic: namely, the caribou's annual marathon run to *ivvavik*. How did the impulse to undertake this outlandish journey register within the caribou brain? Was it like hunger? Was it weirdly pleasant, like horniness? Or was it grim and duty bound, like the knowledge that one had to get up in the morning and go to work?

And this: What was the nature of the mechanism that guided the animals to their destination? Knowing that Lucky ran all over creation and still managed to end up in pretty much the same place every June, I was unconvinced by the conventional theory that says that migrating is like driving to Yellowstone, a matter of referring mile-by-mile to familiar landmarks, onboard star maps, and so on. The road atlas Lucky would need to pull off such a stunt from every corner of northern Alaska and Yukon would be deliriously complex. This is not to say it couldn't be done but, as an alternative, why not attempt to explain the journey as a function not of caribou pushing but of *ivvavik* pulling: that is, of the destination, not the traveler, directing the operation? In this scenario, *ivvavik* becomes a kind of satellite signal, *beep-beeping* continually on the Porcupine frequency, so that every member of the herd can sense it and run to it. The signal might be physical in nature – a sound or a smell, say, or a strange force like the one that nanoscientists have discovered operating at the subatomic level, which enables an atom in one location to affect the behavior of another atom light years away, despite the absence of any discernable connection between the two. Alternately, the signal might be immaterial – a powerful idea; a compelling philosophy; a god.

Mulling over the arduous nature of the migration, I was reminded of the long and difficult journey that mystics undertake when they set out to find spiritual enlightenment. The path is winding and strewn with pitfalls. Progress is erratic. Successful river crossings lead to avalanche-choked mountain passes, which lead to exhilarating scampers across the ice. The journey never ends, for even if the devout one reaches his goal, being human he is destined to slide back or to lose direction, to descend once again into Yukon winter. There he must recommit to his mission and begin anew. Such a journey is a kind of endless migration between heaven and earth.

Perhaps the trail of the caribou is something like that. Perhaps, like the mystic, the caribou feels the pull of its god at every moment of its life and, in the spring, seeks it with the ferocity of a bodhisattva seeking satori. Perhaps caribou young are taught about the deity, and caribou of all ages dream about it when they dream; perhaps visionaries among them imagine an afterlife in a place something like the windswept shores of the Beaufort Sea.

No stars flickered in the always-daytime sky above the island. Yet each time a caribou spooked when I approached too closely, it spooked toward *ivvavik*. If stars did not point the way, what did? If there were truly a beacon, how did it speak to its followers? Several decades ago, the Princeton psychologist Julian Jaynes published an abstruse, fascinating, outrageous book called *The Origin of Consciousness in the Breakdown of the Bicameral Mind*. In it, Jaynes argued that until the second millennium B.C., humans were essentially automatons that acted not in obedience to their own self-directed wills, but rather to the dictates of inner godlike voices, the same sort of voices that schizophrenics hear. The brain was not unified, "unicameral" as we know it now, but rather "bicameral," its two sides operating independent of one another. The left, logical side interpreted the world, determined courses of action like eating, walking, and sleeping, and then delivered them as commands to the right side. The right side "heard" the commands as the voice of a personal god and acted upon them. Jaynes found what he regarded as evidence to support this preposterous theory in such ancient texts as the early books of the Bible and *The Iliad*, works whose characters manifest no interior, subjective lives. Instead, they blindly obey the orders of gods.

What triggered the switch from bicameral to unicameral? According to Jaynes, a series of environmental calamities several thousand years ago – wars, natural disasters, exploding populations – forced the brain into a better way of coping. So it was that Sumerian tablets suddenly appeared bearing inscriptions like "The good angel who walked beside me has departed" and "My god has forsaken me and disappeared." Consciousness as we understand it – self-aware, self-willed, capable of creating a narrative for one's life – had begun.

The day is warm. The clouds are provocative. Eleven caribou graze on a Sumerian landscape. Suddenly, as one, they break into an easy trot, on a bearing of north-by-northwest. *Ivvavik* is calling.

If environmental calamity can produce higher-order consciousness in proto-humans, why not in animals? Mountain lions, a notoriously reclusive species, have suffered devastating losses of habitat in recent decades. Now a few of the animals are coming out of hiding. In doing so, they are behaving in ways that seem curiously rational. The animals case homes in rural neighborhoods. They stalk hikers. Their occasional attacks on the latter are swift, brutal, and efficient – more like premeditated ambushes than random accidents. Are mountain lions becoming self-aware? Are they consciously orchestrating a solution to their problem? Now, in an effort to ameliorate this nation's onerous oil-and-gas woes, massive environmental stress has been proposed for the Porcupine caribou herd. Caribou are a peaceable species. It's unlikely they would attempt to solve this looming problem the way a mountain lion might. Are there other potential weapons caribou could turn to?

"In the very earliest time, when both people and animals lived on earth, a person could become an animal if he wanted to, and an animal could become a human being." So, long ago, sang the Netsilik Eskimo Nalungiaq:

Sometimes they were people
and sometimes animals
and there was no difference.
All spoke the same language
That was the time when words were like magic.

On a cold, foggy, mid-May morning, a female caribou moves across snowy tundra in northern Yukon. She is late for her appointment. She is exhausted. Her fat reserves have fallen to half their autumn levels. She struggles under the weight and energy demands of the fetus within her. Recent river crossings have been hazardous. The breakup has begun, and now along with frigid waters, the rivers she must negotiate tumble in massive blocks of ice. Emerging from one difficult crossing she comes to attention: in recent days wolves have picked off several of her mates in just such a spot. She continues on, at last giving in to her overwhelming desire to snatch a moment of sleep, even as grizzlies circle.

She arrives at the edge of the Arctic National Wildlife Refuge. Within, can she expect to find . . . well, *refuge?*

She can, though, like any refuge, it will be temporary. As the caribou continues north toward the calving grounds, the wolves and grizzlies fall back, preferring to den farther south. Rivers divide and divide again, diminishing in ferocity with each partitioning; some remain frozen, allowing them to be crossed easily and safely, like country lanes. The terrain levels and simplifies, the way is clear. The air temperature warms to freezing and above – nearly one hundred degrees higher than the female endured during the depths of Yukon winter. She comes to the coastal plain at last and there finds rest, safety, nutrient-rich forage, peace. Among thousands of her kind she stakes out a spacious parcel of real estate she will call home for a month or more. She delivers her calf, enjoys the company of her newborn, the camaraderie of her neighbors. She seizes the opportunities afforded by her refuge by the sea, sleeping without fear (something she has not done for many weeks), feeding voraciously, nursing her young.

The calf grows rapidly. Its mother introduces it to the pleasures and hazards of the world. There are lessons to be given in what to eat and what to watch out for and how to behave and how to recognize each other in a crowd and how to turn the architecture of the herd to the calf's own safety. The smells here are blissful; the views are long and calming. Is it any wonder that the geniality of this place will live in the female's memory, to drive her on her perilous journey again next year and then the next and then the next? To bring one's calf into the world in such a place! *Izhik Gwats'an Gwandaii Goodlit*, the Gwich'in call it: "the sacred place where life begins."

But sacred to whom? To the Gwich'in only? Or might the calving grounds be sacred to all who go there? Writing of the birthplace of a renowned lama in India, the Dalai Lama observed that the location itself became holy simply by virtue of what had happened there. Places become holy, he declares, intrinsically, in their very atoms, when they are witness to transformative events. (The word sanctuary derives from the Latin *sanctus*, which means "holy.") The sanctity of such a place becomes a quality of the land itself. Like topography, scent, and color, it is something capable of being perceived by any creature that contemplates it.

"You feel that there is a spirit in the place, so lofty is the wood, so lone the spot, so wondrous the thick unbroken shade." This is the philosopher Seneca writing of a *templum*, a sacred place in ancient Rome. Wounded Knee, Hiroshima, Ground Zero: can anyone go to such a place and not grasp its transcendent nature?

What then of a spot on the globe where for ten thousand years, untold thousands of caribou have gathered after untold thousands of journeys across hell, to bear their young, to delight in their surroundings, to live together in peace for a time? And then to depart, but with the understanding that all will return when the seasons have circled once again. *Ivvavik* is a testament to history, to faith, and to the possibility of coexistence. Like Robert Johnson's "Honeymoon Blues," it embodies the deepest longings of every living creature: for a good life, for another year. Might not such a place be holy, to Gwich'in, to all people – even to caribou?

*   *   *

In July the mosquitoes arrive, shattering the peace. Then come the warble flies and the nose bots – horrible things! The warble lays its eggs on the caribou's fur; larvæ by the hundreds drill beneath her skin, remaining there till spring, when they reemerge and drop to the ground. Nose bots deposit live larvæ in her nostrils. The larvæ migrate through the nasal passages to her throat, where they may attain so great a mass that by the following spring the animal may have difficulty breathing.

Fall brings hunters to the refuge. No one familiar with the tendencies of government agencies to descend into Orwellian artfulness when they advertise themselves will be surprised to learn that hunting is not only allowed in units of the U.S. National Wildlife Refuge System, it is encouraged. It's true. The U.S. Fish and Wildlife Service, which administers the system, no more guarantees protection from bullets to its customers than the U.S. Department of Defense promises not to strike first. The purpose of a wildlife refuge is to secure safety for *groups* of animals that may visit or make their homes there – caribou herds, for example – but not necessarily for an individual caribou. So long as hunting does not threaten the viability of the group, a portion of its members may be killed. Native peoples have been an integral part of the Arctic ecosystem for millennia, and many continue to depend on the fall caribou hunt in the Arctic National Wildlife Refuge for meat, hides, and tools to carry them through the year. Meat is at its fattest in the fall. Hides show the least damage from warble fly holes. Fall is also the time when antlers reach maximum size, providing a magnet for non-subsistence hunters from around the world. These come in pursuit of the rush that taking down a mature bull is said to provide, and of the trophy heads they will ship home for display in their dens and fraternal lodges.

That hunting can serve two such different purposes – survival on the one hand, sport on the other – is a consequence of two very different views that may be seen when one puts one's eyes to the sights of a rifle. In *Arctic Dreams*, his incomparable meditation on the North, Barry

Lopez makes the case that the northern aboriginal hunter sees an extension of himself – a complex living creature – when he gazes at his prey. As a result of this perceived continuum, the hunter finds himself bound to the animal in a relationship that is charged with responsibility – to the animal, to the hunter, to the hunter's family. The hunt embodies the great paradox of existence: some must die so that others may live. And so the hunter cannot fail to regard his act with anything but utter seriousness. He comes to see his relationship with his prey in spiritual terms: it is sacred, as a child's relationship with his or her parents is sacred, and for the same reasons. The successful hunt allows human life to go on, but at a cost. The Netskilik Eskimo Orpingalik portrayed this tradeoff a century ago, in a song called "Lure":

> Reindeer,
> earth-louse,
> long-legged,
> large-eared,
> bristly-neck,
> don't run away
> from me!
> If I kill you,
> I will offer
> handsome presents
> to your soul:
> hides for kamiks,
> moss for wicks.
> Come happily,
> towards me!
> Come!

Barry Lopez contrasts the northern hunter's view of his prey with that of the sport hunter who is a product of modern Western culture. This person has learned to objectify wildlife, allowing him without compunction to use animals to serve his own ends and to treat them impersonally. Through the sights of his rifle he sees not a complex living creature to which he is inextricably bound, but rather an object to hang on a wall, no different from a calendar or a clock. "We have irrevocably separated ourselves from the world that animals occupy," Lopez laments, of the culture that has given rise to this view. To the northern hunter, he adds, such a view is nearly inconceivable – "analogous to cutting oneself off from light or water. . . . "

For thousands of years, a workable balance obtained between hunter and caribou. With the advent of modern hunting methods, including aircraft searches and the use of radios and high-powered rifles, the balance was destroyed. Today, absent strict limits on numbers of kills by subsistence and non-subsistence hunters alike, the caribou hasn't a chance. In *Caribou and the Barren-Lands*, wildlife biologist George Calef tells the almost unbelievable story of the slaughter of Alaska's caribou herds by hunters during the decade 1965–1975. Failing completely to anticipate the consequences of its actions, the Alaska Department of Fish and Game lifted all limits on caribou hunting during that decade, plus all controls on caribou predation by wolves. The results were disastrous. The Western Arctic herd, the state's largest, lost 60 percent of its members in just five years, plunging from a high of around 250,000 in 1970 to about 100,000 in 1975. The following year a third of the animals that remained, 35,000 caribou, were slaughtered.

Meanwhile, the Nelchina and Fortymile herds suffered near extermination. From the mid-1960s to 1973, 50,000 of the Nelchina's 60,000 caribou were killed. During the same period, the Fortymile dropped by 90 percent; in 1973 a bare 5,000 of the herd's original 50,000 caribou remained. Calef's recounting of these massacres recalls the blood orgies that nearly wiped out the bison in the nineteenth century.

"There were many reports of caribou killed and abandoned," he writes, "of groups slaughtered for only the choicest parts, of uncounted animals carelessly wounded and left to wander and die a lingering death." The Nelchina and the Fortymile herds were particularly vulnerable:

Both these herds crossed roads during their annual migrations. Each autumn when word passed along that caribou were nearing the highways, hunters from Fairbanks, Anchorage, and other towns drove out to "get their caribou." Firing lines formed along the roads. The hills echoed with the scream of two-cycle engines as snowmobiles and all-terrain vehicles carried hunters to the animals.

The results of the state's hands-off policy were catastrophic: between 1965 and 1975, Alaska lost half its caribou.

At the eleventh hour, Fish and Game stepped in. The agency imposed severe restrictions on caribou hunting, including a total ban on the hunting of several herds. In a controversial move, the state also reintroduced aerial hunting of wolves, which had been prohibited for a number of years, a ban the department believed had played a major role in the herd crashes. Whether that was true or not, Alaska's caribou responded dramatically to the policy reversals. By 1985, all of the herds were well on their way to full recovery; many had returned to pre-1965 populations.

For caribou hunters, Alaska is no longer the shooting gallery it once was. But as herd numbers have turned around, hunting restrictions have been relaxed. For the Porcupine, fall remains a hazardous season. Most will survive the hunt. But by the time the animals leave the refuge and head south and east toward their winter range, it will be manifest to all observers that the name "Arctic National Wildlife Refuge" is something of a misnomer. Refuge, yes, but better read the small print: For part of the year. For some of you. Sort of. But stay alert.

Before many years pass, petroleum development may further diminish the protection available to caribou in the refuge. No one knows what effects, if any, drilling would have on the Porcupine. Much of the uncertainty revolves around the question of herd density during calving. Like females of most species, *Homo sapiens* included, caribou females seek space and quiet when they are about to give birth. On the coastal plain they disperse themselves widely. Normally quite sociable, the females become skittish and ill-tempered as their time approaches; if disturbed, they may abandon their chosen spots. Karsten and Leanne Heuer, the "Being Caribou" couple who accompanied a wing of the Porcupine herd on its migration in 2003, found that though they had been accepted with indifference by the pregnant females on the run-up to the calving grounds, they became an intolerable presence once the grounds were reached. The females became restive at any approach by the couple, and the Heuers were forced to stay in their tent to avoid discomposing their neighbors. For thousands of years, *ivvavik* has proven itself spacious enough to accommodate the birthing needs of tens of thousands of these jittery animals. Will it continue to be so if airstrips, worker housing, production facilities, and hundreds of miles of roads and pipelines are built within its perimeter?

Photos of magnificent bull caribou grazing contentedly within sight of the Prudhoe Bay oil fields are sometimes offered as proof that caribou and development can coexist peacefully. Might as well learn about Canada in December by visiting Mexico in May! The photogenic caribou are members of the Porcupine's cousins to the west, the Central Arctic herd. The question is not, Will Central Arctic males feed happily in the vicinity of Prudhoe Bay? It is, rather, Will Porcupine females bear their young happily at *ivvavik*? The coastal plain where the Central Arctic calves is one hundred to two hundred miles wide. The coastal plain where the Porcupine calves is forty miles wide at its maximum, averaging closer to twenty-five miles. The Central Arctic herd is one-fifth the size of the Porcupine herd. Put these disparities together and you have a herd density for the Porcupine that is many times what it is for the Central Arctic, and corresponding far greater space and population pressures.

And if those pressures were to prove too great? Perhaps the Porcupine would have to change its behavior. That could come in the form of lower birth rates, leading eventually to a reduction, perhaps a drastic reduction, in the size of the herd. Or the caribou might abandon *ivvavik* altogether, seeking a new migration route that would take them to a different calving grounds.

Or perhaps the herd would simply learn to love its calamity. Perhaps it will adapt to oil wells and roads, and continue its migration patterns uninterrupted. For the Gwich'in, whose very survival depends on the annual return of the herd, this would be the best outcome, though it is one that few tribal members regard as likely.

During the animal wars of the nineteenth century, when millions of animals were slaughtered in the American West to make way for progress, California condors were sometimes shot simply to see how big they were. Before recovery efforts were initiated in the early 1980s, the condor population, which once measured in the tens of thousands, had plummeted to around thirty.

Development within the Arctic National Wildlife Refuge would be a similar experiment in species resilience. The outcome could be happy or it could be just the opposite. If the latter, a great deal of harm will surely have been done, not only to the Porcupine herd but to the many native peoples whose well-being is linked directly to that of the herd; to the entire Arctic ecosystem and to all the systems that interconnect with it; to the kind of people who never cared about California condors before the early 1980s, and who then, when they learned of the birds' plight, suddenly began to care about them very much – that is, to most of us; most of all, to the idea that we humans fully understand nature and can successfully turn our understanding to our own advantage.

To these concerns I should add one that is quite personal and almost comically self-centered: during the months leading up to my departure for Alaska, I began to tie my hopes for my own welfare to those I had for the Porcupine. The herd's dramatic flight to *ivvavik* became a quest for refuge not only for caribou but for me as well. I needed the animals to get there and to *be there*, in their refuge by the Beaufort Sea, so that I too would be safe for another year.

THE GARDEN

One day, Toru reported that an exquisite patch of wild-flowers had opened on the hillside beyond the creek on the west end of the island. I decided to pay a visit. While I was there, I hoped to do something I had wanted to do since I made up my mind to go to Alaska, which was to experience a moment of pure and complete solitude; *arctic* solitude was the way I thought of it, the kind that might allow a person to see himself stunningly alone in a very big country whose only other citizens were snow and rock and earth.

Toru's garden lay just a mile or so from camp, so I knew quite well that the big country where I intended to carry out this bold experiment claimed two other citizens besides myself, Shaun and Toru, and would therefore technically not be empty. But let's not quibble! The hillside stood on the far side of a sliver of water that represented not merely the physical boundary between the island and the wild country beyond, but the psychological boundary as well. When I crossed the creek I would be on what was, for me, uncharted terrain. Somewhere over there, I hoped, technically or not, I would find the solitude I sought.

Of the many hallmarks of Arctic literature, perhaps none resonates more chillingly in the bones of the armchair explorer than the portrait of profound human isolation in a hostile environment. The materials of that environment – constant danger, ungodly temperatures, hideous diseases – are spectacular; they make your palms sweat. They compose what I referred to earlier as the good parts of the literature of the Arctic. But they're utterly foreign to anyone who hasn't been there. Who can imagine scurvy?

Solitude, on the other hand, is something we all know. And in the best stories of the North, solitude is the element that brings those stories down to earth, providing them with a familiar ring, and the hook we need to forge a connection with the writer's vision. A snowballing string of disasters surely is what draws us into Jack London's "To Build a Fire"; but what makes the story memorable is the fact that the tale's protagonist must meet those disasters by himself, on an endless white landscape that he alone inhabits. No one is going to come out of the whiteness to save him, because no one else is there.

Polar explorers have never been reluctant to admit that their obsession with the earth's frozen wastelands stems, at least in part, from their desire to be alone there, far from the vexations of the world. (Never mind that the earth's frozen wastelands often serve up even more pernicious vexations in return!) Indeed, that was the primary reason given by Admiral Richard Byrd for his decision to spend the winter of 1934 by himself at Bolling Advance Weather Base, on Antarctica's Ross Ice Barrier: in *Alone*, his book about the ordeal that nearly cost him his life, Byrd confessed:

This much should be understood from the beginning: that above everything else, and beyond the solid worth of weather and auroral observations in the hitherto unoccupied interior of Antarctica and my interest in these studies, I really wanted to go for the experience's sake. . . . I had no important purposes. . . except one man's desire to know that kind of experience to the full, to be by himself for a while and to taste peace and quiet and solitude long enough to find out how good they really are.

Like Admiral Byrd, I hoped to taste the rewards of peace and quiet and solitude. But I had an idea that I didn't need a winter alone to achieve those ends; a moment might be enough. I realized that during that moment I might see myself not as a contented cog in the great reliable clockwork of the North but as an insignificant flyspeck in the universal nothingness, and that that could be, well, troubling. What I would find depended very much on which of the two views of the North that had perplexed me across the years was the real place. Was the North, in Elisha Kent Kane's masterfully concise description, "Horrible! *Horrible!*"? Or was it, as the Inuit sings, "a great day that dawns, a light that fills the world." In the hope of finding out, I borrowed Toru's waders and set out for the Far West.

The way led across sandy flats thinly planted in tall, wiry stalks of grass. I took my time. I strayed left and right, hoping to find something I hadn't seen before. In several places I came upon rug-size pools of standing water surfaced in clear windows of paper-thin ice. Standing over the windows, examining their contents from above (stones; weeds; a feather; part of an antler), I fancied myself floating across the island in a glass-bottomed boat. Here and there the path was blocked by narrow streams that crouched in depressions until I came upon them suddenly. Each was outfitted in a handy cobblestone bridge, allowing me – *one, two, three* – to hopscotch to the other side.

Half an hour after leaving camp I came to the creek. I had seen no caribou as I crossed the wide central portion of the island, where the animals usually appeared. The day seemed empty without them. I had grown accustomed to these graceful creatures, poised, plucky, just a trifle vain as they lollygagged over the flats, as though they knew they were being watched and were determined to give the viewer his money's worth; breathtaking in the moment they recalled their mission, skipped lightly, broke into a powerful trot; skipped again, accelerated, now flew, dust spitting from beneath their hooves: two or three bodies leaning into the northwest, now the entire party, bending to the current, adjusting, straightening, like sidestreams entering a great river and resigning to its flow.

The creek, which was perhaps twenty feet wide, moved slowly in black, very cold-looking water. Braids of gray ice filigreed the banks. Not a sound, not even the cry of a raven or a jaeger, heralded my arrival. Rudely breaking the silence, I crashed through a clutch of bushes and stepped down into a pile of dirty snow at water's edge.

The creek shuddered. I wondered if I had disturbed it. It looked sleepy; perhaps it had hoped to doze for a few more days. I took a quick look around, hitched up Toru's waders, and plunged into knee-deep water. Five steps out I entered a soft, cool breeze: the cold water and the surrounding snow and ice had crafted a miniature weather system. The breeze nudged me for a moment, then moved on.

On the far side I thrashed through a tangle of weeds and stepped out of the water. Directly ahead rose a steep snow-covered embankment. On an earlier visit Toru had kindly kicked a zigzag stairway up the bank – eighteen steps by my count. I kicked into the first step, found it solid, kicked again, moved up. At the top I emerged onto a broad, low-angled hillside.

I looked around to see what I could see. The sky was cloudless, fathomless, midsummer blue at the top, fading to late winter at the edges. A light breeze was blowing, warmer than the creek wind; it folded around me like a jacket. It was a grand day. I didn't see any wildflowers but I did notice at once that the footing had changed. The solid earth of the island was behind me; ahead lay tundra, the ground cover of much of the North. I had heard how difficult it is to walk on the stuff; now, as I started up the hill, I found out why. The ground was densely bound in tundra tussocks, miniature haystacks of tough, thick, tightly knotted plant material. Some were a foot tall. Walking on them was like walking on very stiff springs. Tussocks are the dead leaves and stems of the cotton grass plant. Because they are deep and relatively warm inside, they harbor among their twining strands not only freshly sprouting cotton grass shoots, but a mishmash of other plants as well. Tussocks are shelters for homeless plants. Rich in vitamins, proteins, and carbohydrates, they're a major food source for caribou.

I climbed the hillside a short way, to an outcropping of crumbly black rocks. Scattered around and poking from the cracks of the rocks was a wonderful jumble of wildflowers – bluebells, primrose, anemone, and a dozen other species, most of which I didn't recognize. Toru's garden! I almost laughed out loud when I saw it. Adding to the beauty of the spot were wide swaths of crusty lichens that clung to the rocks like coral – some cream-colored, some pumpkin, some the color of dried tomatoes; and pads of thick wet moss that chinked the cracks in the rocks and paved the narrow pathways between.

I cupped a tiny bluebell in my fingers. Such resilience! If I thought for a moment that I measured small and insignificant against the immensity of the North, what of that flea of a flower! Consider its banal biography. That little posy would smile its tiny smile for a few weeks, then die unremarked, leaving behind a few paltry, microscopic seeds. Those would lie cold, dry, sightless, and miserable beneath a heap of snow for the better part of a year; then suddenly hear the alarm, waken, stretch, and bloom tiny again for a few weeks. Why should a bluebell do that? Why should it be beautiful? Neither you nor I will ever see it. What's the point? Do foxes enjoy them? Do tussocks? Rock lichens look and feel like rust but they're actually plants, accidental symbioses of fungi and algæ. They need water to grow. When water is scarce or conditions are otherwise distressing, lichens go dormant. Using this strategy, they can live for centuries. In clumps, tangles, and leafy forms that are easier to get the lips around than the rock variety, lichens too are a favorite food of caribou. Caribou know how to appreciate the North: they eat it! Here is a hundred-year-old lichen the color of cooked carrots. What does it do all day? Does it like living on this rock? The immensity of time or the North, I surmised, does not trouble bluebells and lichens.

I stretched out on a mossy sofa cradled between two boulders. The hillside rose easily to a saddle, then curved upward more steeply before topping off at a summit a few miles to the west and two thousand feet above me. I studied the slope, looking for the easiest way to the top. Suddenly, fifty yards above me, six caribou ambled into view. One was a male with a nifty rack. Spindly legged and top-heavy though the animals appeared, they moved smoothly across the hillside, negotiating the tussocks with the aplomb of tightrope walkers.

Caribou have known this hillside for a long time. Fossils of a caribou ancestor dating back some 1.5 million years have been found a few hundred miles southeast of here, on the Yukon River. I was amazed, and humbled, to think that these determined creatures had walked this path among bluebells and primrose for millennia – that the hillside was *like this* before bronze, before wheeled carts, before pictographs and cuneiform. Across the centuries, no human mind had been needed to ponder the wonders of this place, no human eye to admire its beauties, or ambitions to covet its riches. Do we think that the world is about *us? Please!* But what possible purpose could it have, this tussock-tied hillside of caribou and primrose! Was it simply *to be?* Was purpose a property of matter, like mass and velocity? Was existence intrinsically purposeful, or was more required, attentiveness to a voice in the ear, perhaps, followed by a decision stoically to soldier on? All my guesses at the answers to these questions came up pathetically short of the mark, I was sure of that; I knew only that it was not possible to contemplate the prospect before my eyes and not understand precisely that it had a purpose.

I wondered if the hillside would be the same a thousand years from now, or ten thousand? Peering into the future, as I had into the past, I was suddenly struck by the unsettling thought that solitude can be measured in reference to time as well as to space. The physical I was alone, or nearly so, in the great wide Arctic; the temporal I was alone, too, in a wideness of earthly existence whose horizons reached untold millennia into the past, and ahead as far as I could imagine.

Twice I was stranded. I felt a jab of panic. I had a sudden urge to leap to my feet and race back to the blue tent, to a land that I knew and to friends who cared about me.

Then, as quickly as the feeling had arisen, it passed. In my moment of alarm I had instinctively reached out for the slab of rock beside me, and touched its crumbly face. Immediately, a wave of calm swept over me. I sat with the sensation for a few seconds. I looked around. Then something odd happened. I suddenly had an overwhelming sense not of being alone, but of being *surrounded*, as though I were in the midst of a huge crowd of people. Except that this crowd was not people, it was rocks and blossoms and lichens and air and sky and earth and tussocks and caribou. And the tangy aroma of wet moss. And the pleasant scratchiness of a slab of crumbly rock. It dawned on me that though isolation in time and space had demonstrated only too well that I was indeed very, very small, it had failed utterly to demonstrate that I was alone. On the contrary, it had revealed quite forcefully that my hillside was *teeming* with earnest inhabitants, all going about their business – whatever that was – and that, more important, I was one of them. I was a citizen of the country. The hillside was not across the creek; the hillside was where I lived.

There is no there there, Gertrude Stein famously observed about the city of Oakland. I don't know about Oakland, but I was dead sure that there was a here here in a sloping garden of bluebells by a creek in the Arctic National Wildlife Refuge. Fred and Elaine Meader found it, too, by a far lake in the Brooks Range. And, succinctly and pointedly, Hayden Carruth, in his poem "Particularity":

> this invisible
> hereness where I am,
> where I am
> existing, here, the center
> of mystery.

Perhaps the world's grace, so central to Wendell Berry's "Peace of Wild Things," is simply an expression of the world's contiguousness with itself. Perhaps grace explains how one atom can feel the tug of another light years away and how it happened that I decided to remain in the garden when the urge to flee arose. Perhaps it even explains how Lucky finds her way to *ivvavik*.

Is the Arctic a light that fills the world? Or is it "Horrible! *Horrible!*"? That depends. Are you a citizen of the country? Is this a land you can go to and lie down upon and sink your roots into, as it was for Fred Meader? Or are you a tourist? Is it a land from which you remain separate, as it was for Elisha Kent Kane; an alien place to which you travel to view the sights? Or to make your name, or slay your dragons, or drill a hole and then sell whatever emerges to the highest bidder. Then, having done what you went there to do, do you return to your own side of the creek? Is the Arctic your friend or your enemy? Do you go there to live or to die?

One day, time returned. Walt was due at 1 P.M. Shaun found his watch at the bottom of his pack and calculated that we had two hours to get ready. Hours! What a concept! I gathered my belongings around me – unread books, sleeping bag, empty food containers – and attempted to crush them into my pack. The Law of Expanding Volume kicked in: the pack that had held everything on the way in was too small to hold a lot less on the way out.

At thirty-nine minutes past one, Walt spun out of the sky. A day earlier snow had fallen. Civilization had intervened briefly: if the snow keeps up, I fretted, Walt won't get through! If Walt doesn't get through, we'll miss our plane connections!

But the snow stopped, the day was lovely, and thirty-nine minutes past one was lovelier still. Besides, Walt always got through. The river was down. We walked on dry land to the plane. Toru would stay behind, of course. We thanked him profusely – what more could we do? A moment later he was below us, an indomitable wildflower on a land as big as a sky. We lifted through the rocky gate to the north, where the river tips forward into a tumble, then into a fall. The wideness opened, the Arctic Ocean rose like a great moon on the horizon ahead. Below, chaos became the lay of the land. Rock and ice and snow piled one atop the other, pokes of snow-white mist skimmed over the landscape like flocks of geese. The rock was sharp and sheer; waters multiplied and increased, new rivers emptied out of the mist and cascaded and splashed and frothed over rocks and ice; towers of snow piled and collapsed; waters joined waters and cascaded, splashed, and frothed. It was a shattering of creation into elementary particles. It was the euphoria of the North.

Suddenly I heard Walt's voice: "There's one."

She was alone, picking her way exactingly through the maze. Heart, muscle, spirit, soul, leaper of voids, slicer of wind and storm, explorer, adventurer, pilgrim. Stepping from a tumult of broken rock into an open area, she fell into a trot, as though she were eager to be on her way again. As though she knew exactly where she was going.

PART TWO: YUKON

Winter is toward knowing.
William Stafford

FIRST SNOW

O, to lead two lives! Such was the schizophrenic ambition of the Russian adventuress Isabelle Eberhardt as, more than a century ago, she strove to balance her passion for quiet reflection with her compulsion to explore, under difficult and dangerous conditions, the desert of North Africa. Toward the end of her one, very short life (she perished in a flash flood in Algeria at the age of twenty-seven), she summarized in her journal the two she coveted: "one that is full of adventure and belongs to the Desert, and one, calm and restful, devoted to thought and far from all that might interfere with it." With such a gift, she believed, she might fashion what she desperately sought, "a soul, an awareness, an intelligence and a will."

Eberhardt's inability to choose between a life of thrills and one of placid introspection is not unique among the intrepid. Bored with civilized Concord, Thoreau goes adventuring in northern Maine. There he comes up against unbroken wilderness, which disturbs him. It is "savage and dreary," he reports; it threatens to rob him of his Concord cultivation. He can't wait to get home. Yet no sooner has he done so than he begins to dream of returning to Maine. "Why is home a safe refuge to some and a prison to others?" Elie Wiesel asks, a query that Thoreau or Eberhardt might rephrase as, "Why is home a safe refuge for me sometimes, and a prison at other times?"

For the first few months following my return to Nevada from Alaska, home seemed like anything but a prison. Now a certified sixty and embarking on what I believed to be a new phase of my life, I happily resumed the calm-and-restful portion of the two lives I suddenly found myself leading again, for the first time since my retirement from mountaineering more than fifteen years before. I took pleasure in what I had accomplished during my time away. Topping the list was setting my boots upon, and taking a fair number of steps in, the land of the frozen beard and the blackened toes, something I had wanted to do for decades. Along the way I had seen a ton of caribou, had a blast with Shaun, met and made friends with two very fine men, Walt Audi and Toru Sonohara, explored a small portion of the refuge in great depth, enjoyed grand adventure while doing so and, not incidentally, survived to tell the tale.

That this last was no slam-dunk guarantee was reiterated that very summer, when Timothy Treadwell, a noted friend of grizzlies and founder of the advocacy group Grizzly People, along with his girlfriend Amie Huguenard, was killed and eaten by a half-ton male grizzly in Alaska's Katmai National Park. Treadwell's life and death became the subject of Werner Herzog's acclaimed documentary, *Grizzly Man*.

One day I noticed that the annoying voice in my ear, while still hammering away at others of my unaddressed intentions, had at least let me off the hook on the promise I had made to Fred Meader to go north. *When exactly are you going to do that?* had become *Way to go – you did that!*

As for the enduring peace of mind I had hoped to find on my journey, early results were mixed. Returning home I was hit immediately by real life. Confronted by some family or financial or professional crisis, very often I fell quickly into my old patterns of fear and frazzled nerves. At such times I was the same person I had been before my journey.

Occasionally, however, I was able to recognize those patterns before they drew me into their clutches. When I did, I could sometimes stare down the cause of my discontent by simply forcing a halt to whatever I was doing, taking a deep breath, and conjuring a picture of the hillside beside the creek – Toru's garden. That picture became a kind of visual mantra for me. It had an immediate calming effect.

Curiously, my position as I observed that scene in my mind was not one I had actually occupied as I perched on the hillside that day, gazing back toward the island. Instead, I always found myself somewhere above the scene, peering down at the black rock outcropping and several clumps of yellow and blue wildflowers; in the upper left corner of the frame, six caribou grazed. When I could bring myself to recall that picture, I came into possession of an awesome power, one capable of quelling any disturbance in my life. I absorbed some of the hillside's quiet and peace; just as important, I was reminded of the simple fact that such a place existed, a place where this tired old planet of ours still ran on time-honored rules of balance and cooperation. That was a comfort.

Soon the feeling would pass, and I would return to ground level. What remained was knowledge, ever more certain, that I must nurture the tranquil, eagle's-eye view of the hillside, and that I must make that view my abiding view of the world.

Over the next several months, the Porcupine herd made the evening news from time to time, as one legislator after another and various organizations announced their support, always reluctant, for proposals to open the Arctic National Wildlife Refuge to drilling. I hadn't forgotten that while I had fulfilled one promise to Fred Meader, to visit the North, I still owed him on another; and so, late in the summer, I began to write a book about my travels.

October arrived. One night the moon was cold and silent, as far away as the stars. Shafts of snow, the season's first, angled in from the high west. Watching the night from my front porch, I intuited that a new phase in the caribou migration cycle was about to begin. I could feel it. The sojourn by the Beaufort Sea was over. The herd was drifting toward its winter range. The fall rut had begun. I could practically hear the grunting and snorting of the bulls and the clashing of antlers. I realized that I was not finished with the Porcupine. I wanted to see them again.

The next morning I tuned in to *www.taiga.net*. I was curious to see how Lucky had spent her summer. I had begun to speculate on where those happy hooves of hers would take her over the coming winter. Mexico? The south of France?

From the website I learned that Lucky had reached *ivvavik* late in May, having crossed the Kongakut some seven miles north of the island a week or so before Shaun and I arrived. A mystery was solved: my favorite caribou had assuredly not been one of the seven in attendance at the Grand Fiesta of the Humongous Char. While I was gorging on one of the Arctic's great delicacies, Lucky was chomping cotton grass fifty miles north and west of the island, somewhere near the Okpilak River. True to her wandering ways, she reversed course almost at once and headed back toward the Kongakut. (Because she did not take up residence on the calving grounds, it seems safe to assume that she did not deliver a calf that summer.) Five miles south of the island she recrossed the Kongakut, in rugged mountains. She continued south and east, exiting Alaska, then traversing the panhandle of northern Yukon almost to Northwest Territories. There, at a gravel road called the Dempster Highway, she abruptly changed course and began trending south. Passing safely through Fishing Branch Ecological Reserve, home to one of Canada's largest concentrations of grizzly bears, she entered Yukon's Ogilvie Mountains. There, it appeared, she would settle in for the winter.

In the days that followed I thought a lot about caribou, and especially about caribou in the Yukon and, most especially, about caribou in the Yukon *in winter*. I became a little feverish over the idea of observing such a spectacle. What I knew about the Yukon was not much; of that, probably most was not very accurate. I knew there had been a gold rush in something called the Klondike in the 1890s, but details (or at least, my details) were sketchy. I had seen the famous photograph of the long train of heavily laden miners toiling up a steep, snow-covered mountainside on their way to the goldfields, and from that I had concluded that whoever those men were, they must have been very miserable. But where the mountain was and what exactly had happened in the Klondike, I had no idea.

Then there was the television show that I watched occasionally when I was a kid, *Sergeant Preston of the Yukon*. In every episode ("Revenge," "All is Not Gold," and "Emergency on Scarface Flats" were typical titles), the valiant, long-suffering Preston and his faithful dog King chased down and captured a despicable crook, or several such, thereby securing peace and justice for the territory for one more week. From Sergeant Preston I learned that good was good and bad was bad, that Yukoners who weren't despicable crooks were either gold miners or schoolteachers, that the part of the world where all this excitement took place was very cold, and that you could get your dogsled up and running by shouting, "On, King! On, you huskies!"

Some of the same truths emerged from my most influential source on the region, the Robert Service poems that I fell for as a teenager – poems like "The Shooting of Dan McGrew," "The Cremation of Sam McGee," and, especially, "The Spell of the Yukon." Like the land where Sergeant Preston duked it out with murderers and thieves, Service's Yukon was a brutal, unforgiving place, "the cussedest land that I know." His images are often hackneyed, his music hall rhymes and rhythms, which the poet's enormous audience came to expect, irritating.

And yet some of his lines, somehow, are magical. Though he wastes little ink on the aesthetic and spiritual qualities of the North, Service manages to convey to the reader an exhilarating sense of both. Brutal and unforgiving, yes, yet at the same time majestic and romantic; a place that, despite its savagery, reaches into the heart and takes hold there: a place you long to see for yourself. "There's a land – oh, it beckons and beck-ons," Service rhapsodizes in "The Spell of the Yukon":

> It's the great, big, broad land 'way up yonder,
>   It's the forests where silence has lease;
> It's the beauty that thrills me with wonder,
>   It's the stillness that fills me with peace.

(I might as well admit to a final influence, one just as poetical as Service, and in some ways even more informative. That would be the label pasted on every bottle of Yukon Jack, "the Black Sheep of Cana-dian Liquors," along with the beverage found inside. "Yukon Jack is a taste born of hoary nights, when lonely men struggled to keep their fires lit and cabins warm," reads the lyric on the label. "Boldly flavorful, yet surprisingly smooth." The accompanying drawing, which is vaguely rendered, as though the artist may have had cold fingers, depicts a rather miserable looking fellow outfitted in a coat and hat so thick and so furry that the man could easily be mistaken for a shag carpet. For many years a flask of Jack accompanied me on all my trips into the wild – not because I was overly fond of the sauce inside [although at 100-proof, after the first sip or two that didn't matter much], but because I loved the concept. Many a hoary night I sat by a campfire, struggling to keep it lit. At my side, urging me on, my faithful companion Jack, surprisingly smooth. By the time I became feverish over the idea of seeing the Por-cupine again, I had gone over to a brew called Canadian Mist, but the point had long since been made: the Yukon, as I understood it, was a cold, dark, lonely, yet boldly flavorful place. It seemed like a spot where I might enjoy going on a binge.)

The quiet life drew to a close. The life of adventure beckoned. I began to dream of going north again, to the great, big, broad land 'way up yon-der. The words "Yukon in winter" rattled in my brain when I tried to fall asleep at night. A new picture of solitary me, this time surrounded by an infinity of snow, sparkled in my mind. It hadn't escaped my notice that in the benign surroundings of the refuge the previous June, I'd missed seeing the frozen Arctic of Roald Amundsen and Frederick Cook and Charles Francis Hall. Now I wanted to see it once and for all, that endless landscape of mountains and ice, out of time, bitterly cold, and, I imagined, hauntingly beautiful. And I wanted to see the Porcupine during the calm and restful half of *their* two lives, in that far country where they retooled, added up the previous year's toll, and readied themselves for the great journey.

When to go? Midwinter would be dark, a bad idea. March seemed right. The sun would be back. Days would be bright. Temperatures might be tolerable. Lucky would be stirring.

No one has a right to expect friends to buy into his harebrained schemes, or to join him out on a limb, especially when the limb is in northern Yukon and a pretty short one at that. That I have two such friends is an example of a cup running over. I phoned my old pal David Hertz, in New York City, and asked him what he was doing in March. David somehow intuited that what I had in mind was not spring training or the NCAA basketball tournament. It took him a while to decide, but by the end of the year he had signed on to Yukon 2004.

And, of course, I checked in with Shaun in Virginia City. Since our return from Alaska, six months before, the peripatetic one had traveled to New York twice to visit his son, and to Los Angeles once, but nowhere extreme – no new Paraguays or Thailands on his passport. Needless to say, he was badly in need of an exotic port-of-call. He listened patiently as I described my idea and boldly posed my question. Then he shook his head, as though the answer were obvious.

"When do we leave?" he asked.

SALMON SMOOTHIES

The questions I needed to answer if my newly hatched plan were to have any chance of success were the same as those Shaun and I had faced when we touched down in Kaktovik ten months earlier; namely, where are the caribou and how do we get there? In at least one respect we had an advantage this time around: if we could figure out where the animals were, we might be able to drive to them. That's because there's a road that beats its way practically to the Porcupine's winter doorstep. The Dempster Highway is the only road in Canada that crosses the Arctic Circle. It's gravel for its entire length of some 460 miles, a thin scribble of rocks and pebbles on an otherwise blank slate of very big and very wild country. Around a hundred vehicles a day travel any distance on the road in summer; during the dark winter months the number drops to thirty or so – mostly trucks toting supplies to the hardy souls who make their homes in northern Yukon and Northwest Territories. Drivers are advised to carry extra tires and gas, plus sleeping bags and provisions to tide them over in case they become stranded. Gas and coffee are available at a couple of X's on the map; otherwise the Dempster is as lonely as an old prospector nursing his precious bottle of Yukon Jack. But if you're up for it, you can drive from near Dawson City, in Yukon's mid-section, to Inuvik, Northwest Territories, a town that sits practically on the Arctic Ocean. Along the way you'll traverse a broad valley east of the Ogilvie Mountains. And there, if you're lucky, you might find caribou.

Until a month or so before heading north, I had thought I might be able to fly to the Porcupine by bush plane or helicopter. A few phone calls convinced me of the impracticality of the idea. The distances involved were huge; likewise the costs, far greater than they had been for the hop from Kaktovik to the great bend in the Kongakut. Even if I could have afforded the fare, chances were slim that I or some sharp-eyed pilot would spot caribou in one of the myriad valleys of the Ogilvies, much less locate a place to land nearby. Nor was I attracted to the dangers of flitting about in a small aircraft over big, remote mountains in winter.

One afternoon I checked the maps on *taiga.net*. I was cheered to see that several collared caribou had set up camp beside the Dempster Highway, not far from the spot where the road crosses the Ogilvie River. Better yet, one of the caribou was named Lucky.

Lucky! You go, girl! That settled it: I would search for the herd in a Ford Explorer. Now all I needed was for my favorite caribou and her mates to stay put for a couple of weeks, till I could roll up in my four-wheel drive, pull on five layers of mittens, parkas, and socks, take a nice seat on the hood of the vehicle, and enjoy the view.

And if they didn't? If they moved inland five or ten or fifteen miles from the highway . . .

I imagined standing beside the road with Shaun and David, a black wind howling, wolves howling, trackless mountains howling beyond and above us behind deep cloud . . . alone with my thoughts of Sergeant Preston and his faithful dog King. Would we don snowshoes and take off into the interior? That's what Elisha Kent Kane would do. A day later, would my beard be a mass of ice, frozen fast to my sleeping bag? Would David be forced to cut me out with his jackknife?

And what about bears? We would be within growling distance of

Fishing Branch River, an area famous locally for its large concentration of grizzlies. In an e-mail to my playwright friend, Anne Hanley, in Fairbanks, I happened to mention the grizzly issue. Anne was at the time serving a term as Alaska's State Writer Laureate. The psychological landscape of the North forms the backdrop for much of her work. She knows the physical landscape, too, having canoed and backpacked every corner of Alaska during more than a quarter-century of backcountry poking about with her husband Owen, a virtuoso cross-country skier and, as he likes to bill himself, "America's northernmost pulmonologist." I've tried out many of my Arctic worries on Anne in the past, and this seemed like a good time to resume the custom. At least in March, I mused in my e-mail, I won't have to worry about grizzlies. The animals will be hibernating, of course, as everyone knows.

In her return e-mail, dramatist that she is, Anne managed to reproduce the sound of a tongue clucking. Yes, she agreed, the Yukon bears might still be snoozing. On the other hand, they might not be! The trouble was, grizzlies start stirring in late March, about the time when I would be there. Like most creatures, they're hungry when they get up from their naps. And of course, *as everyone knows*, the first thing a hungry bear does when it wakes up is go looking for a yummy snack.

Anne went on to give me a brief lesson in grizzly economics. Every fall, the Fishing Branch River hosts an extravagant run of chum salmon. The local bears gather by the river for a pre-hibernation salmon orgy. So long as the salmon are running, the bears are gorging. When the salmon stop running, the bears, sated and happy, stumble off to their dens and fall asleep. They leave behind heaps of salmon carcasses littering the banks of the river.

Over the winter, the carcasses freeze in. When the bears emerge from hibernation in the spring, they hightail it to river's edge. There the feasting picks up where it left off, now featuring a main course of what Anne called "salmon smoothies." She said nothing about the advisability of finding myself in the neighborhood during this festive affair, but I got the point she was trying to make.

If I needed any additional thoughts on the wisdom of traipsing about in the Yukon wilds in March, I received them, indirectly, from Dorothy Cooley, a regional biologist for the Yukon Department of Environment in Dawson City. Cooley's areas of interest are many and varied. They include the study of large northern mammals and the effects of climate change on arctic ecosystems. It was her reputation as one of the reigning experts on the Porcupine caribou herd, however, that led me to contact her shortly after deciding that I wanted to see the herd on its winter range. Dorothy was one of the chief architects of the satellite tracking program. She has been involved in the capture, collaring, and monitoring of most of the animals in the project since it began. I went to her with a raft of questions, all of which she fielded quickly, expertly, and uncommonly cheerfully. Too tactful to tell me directly that I had no business hiking into the Ogilvies with my friends, she delivered the message between the lines. One of her e-mails ended with this: "P.S. We're supposed to get to minus forty-five here tonight. How's the weather in Nevada?" With Dorothy's hints and Anne's salmon smoothies as reference points, I concluded at last that a winter search for the Porcupine on foot was out of the question.

Not long after Lucky put down stakes beside the Dempster, she picked them up again. By the first week of March, she and her mates were ten miles from the road and moving farther away daily.

Knowing the animal as well as I did, I wasn't exactly surprised at this development. When did Lucky ever stay in one place for more than five minutes? But I was just about out of ideas. There was still a chance, of course, that uncollared caribou, which would not show up on the satellite maps, might be lingering near the road. I contacted Dorothy Cooley to ask about this possibility. Her answer was not encouraging. She had driven the Dempster a few days earlier, she told me, and seen no fresh tracks. Then, knowing that my options were dwindling, she added this: "It might still be possible to get to the caribou by snowmachines."

Snowmachines? Those noisy, smelly, dangerous, destructive, obnoxious contraptions that occasionally flew by me while I was traipsing through the woods in the winter, sometimes piloted by idiots with enthusiastically extended middle fingers? I had never been on a snowmobile and I regarded them as a menace. Drunken snowmobile drivers in the Lake Tahoe mountains now and then made the local papers after being rescued by sheriff's posses. Then there was the Bambi issue. Snowmobiles frighten animals, that's obvious. It seemed to me that deer and squirrels had as much right to peace and quiet in winter as anyone.

On the other hand. . . .

March was moving along. The window was closing. The caribou migration could begin any day. Yes, snowmobiles were obnoxious; yes, they scared squirrels. But maybe I'd seen only one side of the breed, the obnoxious side. Maybe there was a way to operate a snowmobile that would minimize its inherent evil. In any case, I didn't agonize over the decision for long. Evil or not, snowmobiles were my only hope. Within a few minutes of hearing from Dorothy I had begun a new search. Neither Shaun nor David had ever piloted one of these vehicles either, and certainly none of us had ever driven one into the teeth of Arctic winter. We needed help. Was there anyone in Yukon Territory who could lead three rookie snowmobile drivers into the Ogilvie Mountains on a spirited search for caribou?

I contacted government agencies, backpacking and river-running outfitters, Dawson City and Whitehorse snowmobile dealers – anyone I could think of who might lead me in the right direction. Most of the people I spoke with found my proposal fairly outlandish. Of course, everyone in northern Yukon drives a snowmobile. From November to March it's the vehicle of choice for many. But sensible Yukoners stay on the short and beaten path. Striking off into the Ogilvies, especially with a party of neophytes trailing behind, seemed a foolish and dangerous thing to do.

At last my inquiries led me to one of the organizers of the Trek Over the Top, an annual midwinter tour that sends hundreds of snowmobilers scooting over the snow from Tok, Alaska, to Dawson City, a distance of some two hundred miles. (The club that sponsors the trek also hosts a popular Dawson City Thanksgiving event, in which locals compete to see who is best at bowling frozen turkeys across the ice. Northerners sure know how to have fun!) The man explained to me that while the weather could be nasty, the Trek Over the Top was basically a fun-run over well-traveled terrain. More important, even though he was a trip leader, he admitted that he was not up to the rigors of the trip I was describing.

But he knew someone who was. The man's name was Peter Nagano. A member of the Tr'ondëk Hwëch'in First Nation (First Nation is the Canadian term for Native American), Nagano worked for the Yukon Department of Highways and chaired a government advisory board called the Dawson District Renewable Resources Council. A stalwart for the amateur hockey team sponsored by a Dawson City inn-and-pub called Bombay Peggy's, he had been voted Best Defenseman for 2004 in the Dawson hockey league and Best All-Around in the Yukon Native Tournament. He knows the mountains, my informant told me. He knows wildlife. He's tough as nails. And he rides a snowmobile like Ron Turcotte on Secretariat.

That evening I put in a call to Nagano. He seemed like a nice enough fellow. I told him my plan, what little of it there was. I like caribou, I said. My two friends and I want to see them before the migration begins.

Then I passed along the latest news from the satellite. I admitted that it wasn't good. The few members of the herd that I had any information about were moving deeper into the mountains by the day. By the time we get there, I summed up gloomily, the Porcupine will probably be halfway to Alaska.

There was a long pause. I could practically feel Nagano shaking his head at my naiveté.

"Man, that satellite doesn't know anything," he said. "Come on up. I'll find you caribou."

THE JOURNEY BACK

Shaun, David, and I rendezvoused in Vancouver on the nineteenth of March. A day later, we hopped a three-hour Air Canada flight bound for Whitehorse, Yukon. The plane bore steadily north-by-northwest, passing twelve degrees of latitude beneath its wings as it unveiled the most inscrutable landscape I had ever laid eyes on. Peaks and glaciers, glaciers and peaks heaped and churned in all directions, lawlessly, like a rampaging sea. In the first hour the spectacle was thrilling; sometime during the second it began to wear; during the third, I prayed for deliverance. "The increasing prospect tires our wandering eyes,/ Hills peep o'er hills, and Alps on Alps arise!" Did Alexander Pope take this flight? I had known that the Yukon is very cold and very north, but before this eye-opening flight, I hadn't realized that it is defended by a three-hour-wide border of brutally armored geography. As the plane touched down in Whitehorse, I sensed that I was entering a hidden kingdom reachable only by sky. When the door swung open, I should not have been surprised to see a character from James Hilton's Shangri-La stepping into the plane to inspect my papers.

Follow me, he might have said, the faintest hint of a twinkle flickering in his eyes. *The High Lama has been expecting you.*

From Whitehorse, Highway 2 strikes north for some three hundred miles to a crossroads called Flat Creek, where Highway 5, the Dempster Highway, begins. There are no routes 314 or 159 in Yukon Territory. My AAA Yukon road map shows exactly three year-round paved highways more than a few miles in length – Routes 1, 2, and 3 – and one unpaved – the Dempster. Seven others that are open only part of the year and that carry ascending route numbers through eleven fill out the roster. That's it – eleven roads, most of them closed much of the time. I don't doubt that the challenges facing the Yukon Highway Department are many and great. Simply getting its trucks up and running on a 50 below morning must test the prowess of the department's most skilled mechanics. Highway numbering, however, I take to be a fairly straightforward process.

"We're opening a new road next year. What do you think we should call it?"

"How about Route 12?"

Snow clouds blanketed the sky as we sailed out of Whitehorse in our rented Ford Explorer. The vehicle brimmed in army surplus extreme-cold-weather gear that we had purchased off the Internet – parkas with synthetic coyote fur-trim hoods, balaclavas, mittens upon mittens, triple-wall boots. All of us had identical outfits; at a fashion show we had staged a day earlier in our Vancouver motel, we looked ridiculous – the Three Stooges versus the Yukon. Descriptions of our purchases on the Web assured us that they had been tested to 60 below in certifiably cold places like Greenland and Baffin Island. Given that Whitehorse seemed relatively mild that day – the temperature stood at several degrees above zero Fahrenheit – I was sure that we were more likely to find ourselves overdressed than underdressed when we hit the worst of it in the Ogilvies. Call it looking on the bright side, or maybe just a rookie mistake; in any case, my prediction would quickly prove to be laughably wide of the mark.

North of Whitehorse, Yukon's population density dips to around one lonely person every fifteen square miles or so. The road passes little that it wouldn't have passed a thousand years ago. Now and then I saw a house or a storage shed or some other human-made structure; all looked forlorn and rather loosely attached to the earth, ready to throw in the towel and hightail it out of there at the first sign of trouble. Before the car the road unfurled indifferently, a thin scratch of an engineer's pen joining Whitehorse with the far horizon, little disturbed by traffic, crossroads, or signs. The view through the windshield was of height and width and silence; left and right lay low mountains and frozen rivers and lakes, all heaped in snow and thorny with black scraggly spruces. In the creek bottoms, thin stands of shivering aspens and poplars milled about like unemployed laborers waiting for work. The car drove itself, as though we were being sucked into whatever lay ahead, as though we were being absorbed into the North like a fresh layer of snow.

Our plans were vague. We were to meet Peter Nagano a day later at a spot beside the Dempster, some four hundred miles north of Whitehorse. Nagano had told me we might be able to base-camp in a nearby hunting cabin, but that hadn't been settled the last time I spoke to him. As far as I knew, we'd be cooking over a camp stove, traveling by snowmobile, and sleeping on snow.

In the backseat, Shaun settled in as chief correspondent of the expedition. In an age when communication among members of the species has devolved to hastily cobbled e-mails and shouted cell phone conversations, he remains a throwback, that rarest of birds, a writer of letters, by hand, in slow, honest ink. He maintains far-flung correspondences with relatives and friends, with former students in the poetry-writing workshop he has conducted at the Nevada State Prison for fifteen years, with paupers, scoundrels, and kings. As the recipient of many of these missives, I can testify that the scrawl he has perfected over the years is nearly illegible, but that through patience, fortitude, and the occasional application of a carefully aimed divining rod, the diligent reader can eventually decipher the message; and that the effort is always worthwhile. I have saved all the letters I have received from my friend over the years. They bear postmarks from the ends of the earth, and sometimes beyond. From South Africa he wrote of his visit to Mandela's cell on Robben Island; as Shaun often does, he enclosed a poem, this one honoring the local trash collectors, women who "bend and loop like birds to fruit," each with a child "strapped to her wings." On the road to Patagonia he described the region: "vintage Nevada . . . dry, salt bush, creosote bush, but instead of sand there is an ocean on either side." His defiant habit is part of a larger effort, one that occupies him many of his waking hours, both as an entrepreneur of the arts in northern Nevada and as the head of a celebrated community and youth development agency: to join himself to the world, and others to what they need: writers to writers, homeless to homes, troubled kids to visions and dreams. He is a kind of matchmaker who pairs the unfull with appropriate loaves of bread.

Years ago, finding himself in New York City, Shaun impulsively phoned the poetry editor of *Harper's*, the poet Hayden Carruth. Though the two had never met, Carruth had praised some of Shaun's submissions to the magazine and encouraged him in his work.

"I want to see you," Shaun said.

"What for?" asked the plainly skeptical Carruth. During the ensuing conversation, Shaun managed to prevail. He drove to Carruth's home in upstate New York, and there the two became friends. Now, somewhere near a frosty northern lake, in the shadow of a very cold-looking mountain, Shaun grew quiet, arranged a sheet of paper on his knees, and began a letter to his friend. *"Dear Hayden,"* I imagined him saying. *"I am writing to you from the planet Voldor. . . . "*

Around four in the afternoon, pearly dusk began to fall, along with flickers of light snow. David was at the wheel. Because he was the only person who was paying attention, only he saw what happened next. Thirty yards ahead on the right, a wolf stepped from behind a snowbank and trotted across the road. At the last moment, just before disappearing into the shadows, the animal slowed, turned, and glanced back over its shoulder. As the car sped by, the wolf looked David dead in the eyes.

The driver of the car remains staggered by the experience to this day. Staring into a wolf's eyes, David told me recently, seemed like "an endless look into the mystery of nature." The eyes, my friend insists, were blue.

David and I have known each other for more than thirty years. We have shared many adventures and not a few misadventures, and the fact that he saw a wolf his first day in the North does not surprise me. Amazing things happen to good friends, things that would not happen otherwise. Friendship is a form of energy; it tunes the heartstrings and opens the eyes and the spirit to a world that normally goes unseen. Blue-eyed wolves happen to close friends.

One afternoon, David and I stood midspan on the Rio Grande Bridge near Taos, New Mexico. A golden eagle circled out of the great emptiness above and crossed behind us and then in front of us; and then, satisfied that it had gained our attention, flew beneath us, under the bridge, twenty yards below our feet. (I do not recall the color of the eagle's eyes.) Late one cold winter night near the summit of Slide Mountain, in New York's Catskills, we saved two hikers from freezing to death. And then there was the tranquil summer evening beside Hungry Packer Lake high in California's High Sierra. I sat a few yards from David and watched him drop a fly two centimeters from the nose of a trout so long, so fat, so wise, and so nasty that it had acquired a handle known throughout those parts: Packer Jack. Packer Jack took a sniff at David's Humpy Red or Blue Quill or whatever it was and then pounced.

The battle that ensued was desperate on both sides. At one point, Jack flew ten yards horizontally through the air. Moments later the fisherman was in the water up to his chest, holding his rod high over his head and shouting libelous slogans at his prey. In the end, my friend wore down the old snort, hauled him to shore, and then let him go. But the damage had been done. A new legend was born: Packer Jack had met his match.

David and I met when we taught mathematics at Collegiate School, a private school on Manhattan's Upper West Side. During the day we introduced some very bright and motivated students to the wonders of imaginary numbers and the quadratic formula; after work we abandoned math in order to climb boulders in Central Park or play Ping-Pong at a dive on 96th Street or pull out our topographic maps and plan reckless snowshoe ascents in New York's Adirondacks or New Hampshire's White Mountains. David has spent his life in education. He has served as teacher at several schools, director of admissions and of development at several more, and founder and head of two educational consulting firms. He can teach your kids or run your school or raise a ton of money for it, but he is happiest, I think, when he has his feet up on a porch railing and his fist wrapped around a mug of beer, digging into a thorny question of ethics or politics or baseball with absolutely no hope that he will ever get to the bottom of it. Like those raggedy plane trees that you see thriving in two inches of dirt beside New York City sidewalks, my friend is tenacious, hopeful, neighborly, humbly accepting of his station. He watches the passing parade with amusement and compassion; he shivers in the rain without complaint. He has an exuberant laugh and the face and black beard of a rabbi; which, I have always told him, is what he ought to be.

David has made a career out of optimizing the cards he is dealt. Optimization is something of a family tradition. David's parents, Manny and Silvia Hertz, were Holocaust survivors. Because the two never spoke much about their experiences, David knows only the bare outlines of their stories. What he knows he speaks of with reverence and with awe – not as he might tell a fish story, but as a man who understands searing truth, and how to speak it. He knows that Manny was born in 1903, in or near Kiev. One of seven children, he was apparently the only one to survive the Second World War. At some point, probably in his late teens, he emigrated to Poland, entered the ladies' undergarment industry, had some success, and made some money. He married and had a son and a daughter. David knows almost nothing of this phantom family. He recalls a photograph that Manny kept on his bedroom dresser when David was a child. It shows a beautiful mountain lake somewhere in Poland. In the foreground there is a kayak, and in it are seated Manny Hertz and his son, a man whose name David does not know.

By 1943, the family was living in the Warsaw ghetto. In May, at the height of the uprising, Manny's wife, son, and daughter were murdered before Manny's eyes. Manny was spared, if that is the word; shortly thereafter he found himself in a line of Jews being marched to a train bound for Treblinka. Impulsively, he pulled out a cigarette. Pretending to seek protection from the wind so that he could light up, he stepped out of line into the lee of a nearby building. Instead of returning to his spot with the others, he simply kept walking. He disappeared into the shadows. He was taken in by a Christian woman, who sheltered him for two years. He lived as a Gentile, found a job as a trolley car ticket-taker, and began drinking heavily. Late in the war, when the tide began to turn against the Germans, he joined the Polish army.

Manny was traveling with a group of six or eight other soldiers when he met a beautiful young Jewish woman working in a tavern. Her name was Stasha – Silvia in English. She had recently been liberated from a labor camp. Sometime during the course of a three-day binge, Manny initiated an exchange something like the following.

"Come with me."

"Why would I want to go with you?"

"I'll get you to America."

"Marry me first."

"Okay. Fine. Let's go."

They found someone to perform the ceremony. Silvia traveled with her new husband and his company of soldiers, none of whom knew the couple was married. Soon the others wanted in on the action. One day Manny faced them down, pointing a machine gun at each of his comrades in turn.

"No," he said. "She's mine."

At war's end, the two made their way to Allied-occupied territory, then onto a ship carrying refugees to America. They arrived at Ellis Island in December 1946. David was born two months later.

*   *   *

"I understand myself and who I am as a child of Holocaust survivors," David has told me. "One of the great lessons for me is the resilience of the human spirit. That these people could start new lives and raise children and find laughter and purpose and meaning and go on – what a fantastic lesson to have learned. I've always been extremely grateful for that. It's helped me to understand the strength that lies within each of us. These were normal, everyday, average, commonplace people."

A key event in the formation of David's understanding of the man who was his father took place one evening when David was a kid. Silvia, Manny, David, and David's sister, Raye, were sitting around the kitchen table. Manny said he had an announcement to make. He waited until he had everyone's attention, and then he spoke.

"I renounce hatred," he said. His voice was calm. He looked around the table at each of the others in turn. "It's over. I'm not going to hate anymore."

Manny made good on his vow for the rest of his life, as far as my friend could tell. The effect on David was profound.

"Why then would I ever hate?" he asked me when he told me this story. "If he's stopped hating, what am I supposed to hate?" David mentioned that the word "hate" had come up in the parenting of his own child, as it must for most parents.

"It's a word that I wouldn't tolerate in my own household, and I let my child know it. The word 'hate' has no place."

Manny lived to the age of eighty, Silvia to seventy-nine. Silvia led a busy, productive life but never overcame the terrors born of her wartime experiences. David has many memories of growing up with a mother traumatized by her past. But the story he will tell when asked to remember her is charming and upbeat. The family had just attended a showing of one of the Indiana Jones films at a local theater. Silvia was thrilled by the film. (And perhaps, David speculates, smitten by Harrison Ford!) It was raining when the four left the theater. Walking home, Silvia was euphoric. She took off her shoes and walked barefoot through the streets.

"She just wanted to be a child again," David says. "She said it was the best time she ever had."

During a two-year stint in Seattle, the only time David has ever lived outside of New York City, he fell in love with nature and the outdoors. Once a month during the years we taught school together, we took students hiking in the Catskills. In later years he became an avid fly fisherman. He lives in Manhattan but he has a country home beside a trout stream in the Catskills. A few years ago he and his wife Florence took up kayaking.

One day, at the end of a weeklong backpacking trip in the High Sierra, David and I found ourselves stepping onto the summit of California's Mount Whitney, the highest peak in the lower forty-eight. With us were three friends, Bob Salerno, Steve Shelly, and Terry Word. David listened as the rest of us, in time-honored fashion, took turns bragging about our triumph. Gazing out at a world that now lay at his feet, Steve allowed that, at that moment, he might well have been the highest landscape designer in the world. Terry said he was surely the highest attorney.

A moment of silence followed and then David spoke up.

"I don't know about you guys," he said. "But I know that I'm the highest Jew in the world." The top of the tallest peak in the lower forty-eight erupted in convulsions of laughter, and for a moment I wondered if that grand old mountain would be able to stand up under the strain.

David, Shaun, and I took a room for the night in a motel in the town of Carmacks. In the restaurant next door we were served by a cute girl aching to get out of town. In the bar, along with fifteen or twenty patrons there was, incredibly, a band. They had driven two hundred miles from Dawson City for the gig. Once in midwinter, one of the band members told Shaun, the group drove five hundred miles to play at a bar in Inuvik, at the north end of the Dempster Highway. What musicians will not do for fifty bucks and a chance to preach the gospel of Hank Williams to a congregation of sozzled listeners!

The temperature was 19 below as we headed out of town the next morning for our rendezvous with Peter Nagano. The road was empty. For many miles it paralleled the Yukon River, which lay wide, deathly pale, and still as stone in a beautiful valley to the west. At Flat Creek we turned onto snow-covered gravel: the Dempster at last. Fat parachutes of snow floated down from a chill vanilla sky. We filled up at the gas station, the last one we would see. The proprietor issued the standard warnings, adding that he would be happy to rescue us, if necessary, at a charge of "a gallon a mile." We checked tires, oil, spirits. Nothing lay before us but north. Gleaming mountains, low and distant until now, nudged closer to the road.

We skirted the Tombstones, white opera gloves of elegant pinnacles, marvelous on the western skyline. Forty miles out we came upon a car half buried in a snow drift. We had flipped to a Yukon state of mind: we knew at once that the driver was dead. Shaun stepped out into ferocious cold and wind. He peered through the windshield. Strangely, the car was empty. Disappointed, we moved on. Our vehicle was elegant, warm, steadfast. The earth was an endless prairie of white sliced by a thin shadow, which we followed like a trio of grizzled sourdoughs tracing a vein of silver. *Over there near a frozen creek, a sleeping grizzly dreamed of salmon smoothies. Over there on a rocky ledge, a lynx dozed contentedly, its stomach bulging in cutlets of snowshoe hare. Over there on a snowy mountainside, Lucky sensed a change in the season. She raised her head from a tuft of lichen, turned, drew in a lungful of icy news from the north.*

Making my way across this faraway landscape I had much to fear – mostly the fact that I had no idea what lay ahead, and that whatever it turned out to be could be bad. But snow-covered earth is a kind of benevolence. It's bighearted. It takes apprehension, uncertainty, timidity – the rough, dark textures of the everyday – and wads them up and pitches them under a deep comforter of downy white. In the company of two friends, on an adventure of, for me, mythic proportions, I was aware of none of the trepidations of my ordinary life. Never had I felt such calmness and confidence. Whistling into the unknown, I was ready to tackle the Yukon, ready to chew it up. The Navajo have a word that translates loosely as "to travel back to oneself." I have known about that word for years. Despite its suggestion of retrograde motion, I had always imagined that the word referred to forward linear travel: one moved ahead resolutely, eventually stumbling across a new version of oneself that had somehow been placed conveniently in one's path somewhere down the road.

Now I wonder if the trajectory might not be circular: you spiral around and, somewhere behind where you were, you come upon your former self, a self that is somehow changed. You're a child again, yet not exactly: a creature who possesses something you once possessed – innocence, perhaps, or courage, or joy – but who is equipped this time around to hold on to whatever it was you lost. Maybe migration is a model of this process, provided for anyone who cares to look. Go to *ivvavik*, it says. Then go again. Then go again. See what's there. Maybe it will be worth keeping.

Isn't it true that, when I return home from my friend Steven's cabin by the Yuba River, where I spend time every summer, I always bring something home with me, an old dream or a vow or a plan, or a promise I intend to keep at last? Maybe caribou do that. Maybe *ivvavik* is a place not only for birth but for rebirth, not only for new generations but for every generation. Maybe déjà vu is a spot on the circle that we recognize from the last time around. Maybe, seated with his family around the kitchen table, Manny Hertz found a place on the circle he had been striving to reach for years, a place of nearly inconceivable forgiveness that would allow him a measure of peace at last. Maybe Ralph Waldo Emerson was right when he wrote, "There is no end in nature, but every end is a beginning." Maybe that was why, staring into the blue eyes of a wolf, Manny's son David was able to see endlessly into the mystery of nature. Maybe Thailand and Tunisia and Tajikistan are places where Shaun can begin again, and maybe Shangri-La would be one more stop, but not the last one, on my bumpy journey to a destination called serenity.

We track the East Fork of the Blackstone River, press higher and deeper into the Ogilvies. The Arctic Circle lies just ahead, storied gateway to the ice. The mountains are bare and rounded, heaped like peaches in a bin. The sun burns through the clouds, its light so crisp and pure it shimmers in my bones. I wonder who Peter Nagano is, and I wonder what he has in store for me. Crossing the Blackstone, peeling my eyes for the kilometer post where we are supposed to find this mysterious person, I think of a line by the poet Stephen Vincent Benét: "We don't know where we're going, but we're on our way."

CHEECHAKOS

At that moment, more than one hundred thousand members of the Porcupine caribou herd were dispersed over a huge, oval-shaped swath of land that extended northwest from Yukon's Ogilvie Mountains, across the Mahoni Range, down to the flats of the Porcupine River, and on into the foothills of Alaska's Brooks Range. At the lower end of the oval, perhaps twenty miles from the Dempster Highway, the southernmost members of the herd clustered in groups of one or two or three dozen on low-angle mountainsides flanking some of the myriad valleys of the Ogilvies; their sisters and cousins and aunts in the north-ernmost groupings congregated some two hundred miles to the north-west, in an area the herd had occupied most every winter for the past ten thousand, near Arctic Village, Alaska, one of the principal commu-nities of the Gwich'in Indians. On this day in March, the day of the ver-nal equinox, the shape and position of the oval of caribou looked pretty much as they had since December; the exception was the deep-south sector, in the Ogilvies, which had been narrowing and drifting slowly northward for several weeks. To a passenger in a car moving north on the

Dempster, the fact of the equinox, and the vastness of the encompassing blanket of snow, and the ten-thousand-year reliability of the oval, and the purity of the light, gave the moment a flavor of art in the making, a sense of listening to a kindly and earnest poet reading her rather difficult poem. All the elements of the work were there, but it was difficult to take them all in or even to focus on one, and nearly impossible to make sense of any of them; yet somehow, in their baffling entirety, they were immensely pleasurable. They seemed important. It was possible to imagine that they fit together, forming a cogent whole. Referring to the task of taking in the myriad facets of one of his perplexing and somewhat Arctic poems, John Ashbery observed that "you're getting a kind of indirect refraction from the situation that you're in." On all sides I could feel the glare. This is how the earth works was the situation I was in. *These are the lines. This is the rhyme. It's all of a piece, though you may not see how. Enter into it. Run with the herd.*

There was a turnoff. At its end, above a small mountain of snow, there was a chimney puffing smoke. David swung the car off the highway and aimed in the direction of the chimney. Fifty yards in, we came upon a great thickness of coats and hats and pants and mittens. It was stacking firewood on a sleigh attached to the back of a snowmobile.

The thickness waved. Peter, bundled to the teeth! We hopped out to say hello. In mere seconds the cold and the wind seized my bare fingers and began twisting. I shook hands with Nagano, then dove into the back of the car to locate a pair of gloves. There seemed to be little point in lollygagging or engaging my new acquaintance in a meandering conversation. In the Yukon in March, I'd guess, the citizenry do not spend a lot of time in the out-of-doors taking meetings or shooting the breeze.

A hundred yards farther along the turnoff, to my astonishment, we came upon several buildings. One was some kind of a guesthouse; beside it were several tiny cabins. In short order I learned that I had arrived at the base camp of Blackstone Outfitters, a big-game hunting operation run by a Whitehorse couple named Jim and Adrienne Fink. Because the Finks hosted most of their clients during the fall hunt, the grounds were, at the moment, deserted. But there would be no mistaking the business of the place when the days began to shorten and the surrounding hills went gold and red in the autumn outfits of bearberry, willow, and cranberry, and the sound of gunfire lighted up the wide valleys of the Ogilvies: the walls of the guesthouse were festooned with trophy heads and photos of hunters posed with their kills – moose, Dall sheep, caribou, grizzlies, wolves. A friend of the Finks, Peter had secured one of their cabins for Shaun's, David's, and my use during our stay. Entering the main room of the guesthouse, feeling a blast of blessed heat from an oil-drum stove that stood off to one side, I understood for the first time that my two friends and I were not to be sleeping under the Arctic stars and munching on pemmican; on the contrary, we were to be treated handsomely in entirely civilized conditions.

To help me achieve the goal that had brought me here, Peter had taken on the manifold duties of guide, chef, Ogilvie Mountain naturalist, snowmobile mechanic, and all-around authority on the North. Perhaps forty years old, he looked every bit the amateur hockey defenseman that he was in his spare time: medium in height, stocky, broad shouldered. He had a gliding walk, a skater's walk, purposeful and low to the ground. His face was wide and round, his eyes narrow, his expression somber as that of an old prospector about to put his last match to a pile of sticks at 50 below. In all the time I was with Peter I don't think I ever saw him smile. Like my friend from the Kongakut River, Toru Sonohara, a man with whom comparison was inevitable, Peter didn't waste much time in idle chitchat. When he spoke he did so deliberately and decisively. On first meeting him I thought, here is one serious customer. It wasn't long before I realized that his solemn manner was something of a ruse and that a measurable percentage of what he said was pure jive.

It was in Peter's capacity as all-around authority on the North that, sometime during my stay, he cleared up a mystery that had bothered me for years. He also provided a nice illustration of his laconic, mischievous style. Was it true, I asked him, that it's dangerous to pee at forty below? I needed to know the answer before I went looking for caribou. I didn't want any accidents. Somewhere I had read the reminiscences of an old sourdough, who insisted that upon emerging into Yukon-type temperatures, a stream of urine would freeze instantly into a long, thin, gracefully curving icicle – a Far North version of a McDonald's golden arch. The ice would dangle weirdly on the perpetrator – in extreme cases attaching him to the ground – until someone with a little common sense came along and whacked it off.

Peter looked at me gravely.

"Someone with a little common sense?" I could feel pity emanating from his eyes. "Do you know anyone like that? No, I wouldn't worry about peeing." He went back to whatever he was doing. Then he finished his thought.

"But if I were you, I wouldn't blow my nose while we're out there. The snot'll freeze to your nostrils and you'll suffocate."

When he wasn't flimflamming his guests he was delivering strong-minded opinions on a broad range of local environmental issues. Peter was a member and former chair of an independent public interest advisory body called the Dawson District Renewable Resources Council. The council advises the Yukon government on matters relating to fish and wildlife conservation, forest management, and similar topics of concern throughout Tr'ondëk Hwëch'in First Nation traditional territory. (The Tr'ondëk Hwëch'in often refer to themselves as the Han, an ancient people who inhabited western Yukon and eastern Alaska and from whom the Tr'ondëk Hwëch'in are descended.) Himself part Tr'ondëk Hwëch'in (his father was Japanese), Nagano took a particular interest in questions bearing on management of the Porcupine herd. Like anyone else who had studied caribou census figures collected over the previous several decades, he understood the threat posed to the species by modern hunting methods. Without stringent controls on hunting, natural balances toppled and herd numbers crashed. Earlier I described the Alaska caribou slaughters of the sixties and seventies. Some Canadian herds suffered similar fates. Not long after Alaska's Nelchina and Fortymile herds were nearly exterminated, three Northwest Territories herds were devastated by hunting.

Writing in 1995 in *Caribou and the Barren-Lands*, wildlife biologist George Calef predicted that if no action were taken, the three herds – the Bathurst, the Beverly, and the Kaminuriak – would be wiped out in five to ten years.

In response to such threats, the Yukon and Northwest Territories governments, in conjunction with local tribes, set up strictly defined harvesting zones. Each tribe was told where it could hunt and how many caribou its members could take. The idea was to insert modern controls into a practice that had worked well for thousands of years but was no longer viable. The boundaries were fair and the limits reasonable, Peter said; all parties had agreed to them.

But, he added, not everyone was respecting the system. Some First Nation hunters were invading zones belonging to other tribes; excessive, wasteful killing was still taking place. In the nine years since Calef had made his prediction, herd numbers had continued to fall.

I was surprised to learn that Nagano took a dim view of the satellite collar project, which had taught me so much about Lucky and her mates. It wasn't that he objected to the practice of gathering scientific data on caribou. It was simply that he disliked the means to that end. He spoke with some passion about the fact that test subjects must be chased down by helicopter before they can be collared or their batteries can be replaced.

"How long do you think they chase one?" he asked. "Not one minute. It's half an hour. The caribou run around in a panic. Their tongues hang out. They're exhausted. It's not good."

I recalled my concerns about searching for caribou by snowmobile. Suddenly I felt a lot better about what I'd gotten myself into. It appeared that I'd found the right man for the job. Peter spoke like a man who knew the wild so well that he loved it. I felt confident that he would attempt to do what I'd asked him to do with as little interference in the business of the caribou as possible.

Just how qualified Peter was for the job I learned when he described his participation in a grueling and much acclaimed endeavor called the

Centennial Patrol. Over six weeks in February and March of 1995, a team of twelve very hardy souls retraced a historic Royal Canadian Mounted Police (RCMP) route between Dawson City and Fort McPherson, Northwest Territories, and back again, using snowmobiles and dog teams. The expedition traversed some one thousand miles of punishing terrain in arduous winter conditions. It was organized by RCMP Corporal Peter Greenlaw to mark the hundredth anniversary of the mounted police in Yukon Territory. Team members included several First Nations people. Peter was chosen to represent the Han.

The route taken by the twelve had for centuries been used as a trade run by the Han and the Gwich'in. Beginning in 1895, the RCMP adopted the route for "patrols" to carry the Royal Mail and to bring law and order to remote Yukon outposts that had begun springing up in the Territory, especially after the discovery of gold in 1896. Several spots along the way are sites of the demise of the "Lost Patrol," unfortunate players in a famous calamity of Yukon history.

Late in December 1910, four Mounties – Francis Fitzgerald, Richard Taylor, George Kinney, and Samuel Carter – embarked by dog sled from Fort McPherson, destination Dawson City. Things quickly went badly for the four. They took a wrong turn. Before long they were hopelessly lost. Because they had failed to carry sufficient provisions, they soon exhausted their food and were forced to eat the dogs. They abandoned their sleds and set out on snowshoes. Weather conditions were atrocious. The patrol survived perhaps eight weeks in all, but by mid-February, and only fifty or sixty miles from where they started, the four were dead of starvation and exposure. An attempted rescue by a team under the leadership of Corporal Jack Dempster, for whom the Dempster Highway is named, discovered the bodies late in March.

After the Second World War, the Mounties abandoned the patrol route, and for fifty years it saw no use. When he was posted to Dawson City in the late nineteen-eighties, Corporal Greenlaw, one of those amateur history buffs for whom a hobby becomes an obsession, and then a mission, began research to identify the exact path the Mounties had used in the old days. He led several training runs, covering some 80 percent of the route before undertaking the 1995 journey. During the forty days of the Centennial Patrol, Greenlaw and his comrades camped out in 50-below temperatures, burned vast numbers of calories a day, and lost an average of eight to fourteen pounds each. My new friend Peter Nagano piloted a Polaris snowmobile over those difficult miles – excellent preparation, it seemed to me, for showing me the sights in the Ogilvies nine years later.

Peter set himself up before a stove in the kitchen area of the guesthouse and prepared to cook a midday meal. He spoke glowingly of moose meat, his choice over caribou for its flavor and texture. He asked me to show him the food Shaun, David, and I had brought along to sustain ourselves during the days ahead. I located a couple of packages of freeze-dried chili and some instant soup we had picked up at the grocery store in Whitehorse.

He gave me a withering look.

"My friend," he said, "these are modern times." With that, he expelled me from the kitchen. The guesthouse larder was evidently well stocked, for a short while later the chef set out a beautiful meal on the long dining table that stood to one side of the main room. "Eat up, guys. We've got work ahead of us."

Peter joined us for the feast – moose stew with pasta, pork chops, a tossed salad, biscuits, coffee, and black tea. (While still in the kitchen, Nagano came across a few bags of herbal tea that someone had left behind. "Goddamned hippie tea!" he shrieked. He snatched the bags from the counter and fired them into a wastebasket.) I ate with no less amazement than I had felt when I first laid eyes on the guesthouse. Because we and the chef were still breaking the ice with one another, the conversation around the table was at first painfully polite. Then David passed around the just-published *Sports Illustrated* swimsuit issue, which he had brought along as a housewarming gift. A good choice: the magazine turned out to have been written in a universal language. By the time we finished the meal, the house was warm, the ice broken.

A snowmobile is a big, heavy, loud, fast, fiendish machine. A *cheechako* is a newcomer to the Yukon. Not far from the guesthouse, in an open area several acres in extent, Peter introduced three *cheechakos* to the art of snowmobiling. The stakes were high: the following day the party was due to strike out into the Ogilvie Mountains on these very machines, on a mission of epic importance.

Zooming around the narrow track he had laid down on the snow with his craft, Peter set a high standard for showmanship and craft: now seated like a proper pilot; now half-standing, one knee on the seat, head and shoulders angling forward over the windshield into boreal wind, man and machine hurtling down a straight stretch at terminal speed; now plowing up and through a deep drift, exhorting the beast beneath him like a jockey approaching the finish line at Belmont; now coming out of a treacherous corner, leaning far to one side to counterbalance a ton of iner-tia on the other, harmonizing sundry competing forces, steering as easily as he might have on a bicycle; now (I think I remember) leaping a wide gap between two hillocks, his fingers gripping the handlebars lightly, like paintbrushes, his feet flying straight out behind him. It looked so easy!

And on flat, hard-packed straightaways it was. But in deep, soft snow, where it was imperative to keep up one's speed and one's nerve, it was maddeningly difficult. Slowing down, growing timid in my approach to a corner, sensing the power of the machine beneath me, I inevitably ended up stuck in the snow at a humiliating angle, engine howling obnoxiously beneath me. Peter would show up and signal for me to hop off. How patient he was! Saintly! With two engines now bellowing at our sides, he would mime the escape routine: Stand on the high-side running board.

Goose the throttle. Jump and yank and throw your weight around like an enraged sumo wrestler. If that doesn't work, kick the sonofabitch in the ass. Then steer sweetly back onto the straight and narrow.

Then he would zip off, carving magnificent figure-8s and -9s and -453s in the snow, leaving me shaking my head. Like any new skill, this one was easy to understand in theory but devilishly hard to execute. While I waited for my frost-impaired synapses to wire up the new circuitry, I despaired of ever learning to ride. Compounding the problem was the fact that I had quickly become aware of a danger associated with the sport that I had never thought of before. My machine weighed close to five hundred pounds. Several times as I spun out on a banked curve, the mass of screaming metal heaved up and nearly rolled over on me. The first snowmobiling skill I really nailed down was that of leaping out of the way as I was about to be crushed to death.

Not long after starting I was sweating heavily – this in below-zero temperatures. The only pleasure I took in the proceedings was watching David, who was having as bad a time of it as I was. Only Shaun took to the enterprise with ease. Bare minutes after firing up his engine, he was riding like a pro.

After perhaps an hour of this torture, we returned to the guesthouse. In the final minutes, I had begun to make some headway. Nevertheless, I was frustrated and angry. Worse, I was exhausted. Peter had said we might be looking at forty or fifty miles of travel the next day, some of it on steep slopes, all of it in deep, unbroken snow. I was beat after an hour of driving around in a circle. Would I be physically and mentally up to the challenge? In the preceding months, I had considered and solved a welter of problems, any one of which might have prevented me from realizing my dream of reuniting with the Porcupine in the Ogilvies. That I might be thwarted in my effort because I couldn't pilot a snowmobile was a possibility so absurd and so seemingly improbable that it had never entered my mind. Now I wondered if that was the snag that would trip me up.

Having seen Shaun's performance, I was confident he could keep up with Peter on any terrain. It occurred to me that it might make sense for me to turn over my aspirations to my friend. I wondered: could I be satisfied warming myself by the guesthouse stove all day while Shaun raced over hill and dale with Pete? Could I be happy for him, and for myself as a member of the team, if he were to return with the news that he had found the herd?

Neither David nor I had much to say that evening. We laid out the clothing we thought we might need the next day, loaded up our day-packs, and retired early.

I awoke before the others, to snow flurries and an overcast sky. Determined to see a bit of the countryside, I bundled up and went for a walk. The temperature stood at 25 below. I was relieved to discover that I had the right outfit for the party. All those army surplus greens and browns really worked! Tromping along under three layers of polypropylene, two pairs of mittens, an Eskimo parka with a synthetic-fur-lined hood and a polypropylene balaclava beneath, and multilayer Arctic boots, I was toasty warm.

I traversed the snowmobile park to the Dempster Highway, which looked less like a highway than a hodgepodge of animal trails, and crossed to the other side. As I moved along, I tuned in to the rhythm of cold fresh snow squeaking beneath my boots. My first thought was of worn wind-shield wipers dragging on a dry window; then, warming to my surroundings, the sound of poor little baby mice being crushed underfoot. Finally I heard the voice of the snow itself: *Ouch! Ouch! Ouch! Ouch!*

Before me a few scraggly spruces and scattered pokes of willow grass interrupted what was otherwise an enormity of lush, exhilarating white. The Ogilvies are low, bare, gently arching mountains – in winter, vanilla ice cream scoops with their bottoms sheared off. The tallest reach no more than a few thousand feet above the valleys, which flow like glaciers, wide and smooth, between the peaks. I stood for a time on a level stretch that funneled, in the distance, into the valley where Peter would lead the caribou seekers in a few hours. Some of yesterday's vexation had worn off. I felt uneasy about what lay ahead, but stirred by the landscape. Because of the overcast, no shadows delineated the contours of the valley; it was hard to make out the ups and downs and rights and lefts. But the route looked manageable – wide and easy-rolling in the foreground, sloping genially upward to a saddle between two elegant sugarloaves. What lay on the other side was a mystery. But I suddenly knew that I would never forgive myself if I were to turn my dream over to Shaun. I wanted to see for myself what was up on that saddle and beyond.

What a wonder that animals lived – thrived! – in that otherworldly world before me, which looked so impoverished. A few minutes before, I had seen a pair of ptarmigan, fat, white, and shiny as teapots, shooting the breeze near the guesthouse.

"What will we have for breakfast this morning, my darling?"

"I have no idea! Anyway, it's your turn to peck!"

Now as I scanned the face of a low hill rising a short distance to my right, my eye caught movement near the ridgeline. I'd left my field glasses behind but it didn't matter: in the icy air I could see what was going on with stunning precision. A red fox was crossing the slope. Dolphinlike, in a series of graceful, satiny leaps, she vaulted from one spot to the next, across fifty yards of snow. As she neared the edge I lost sight of her. Then I spotted her again, bounding back across the hill and a bit farther down.

Whatever are you up to, little fox? Breakfast business, no doubt. And what is on the menu? Moles? Shrews? Oh, no – ptarmigan!

Well, she seemed ready for the day. So was I. I returned to the guesthouse to discover that preparations for launch were well under way. David seemed chipper. Shaun was raring to go. Peter's brother Richard had arrived to join the party on the great hunt. A bit taller, leaner, and grayer than Peter, Richard, who sometimes worked as a hunting guide for the Finks, was, like his brother, a virtuoso player of the Yukon backcountry. He greeted me warmly, then commenced a funny denunciation of, of all people, New York Yankee owner George Steinbrenner, for laying out a ton of cold cash to steal Alex Rodriguez from the Texas Rangers. (In the Yukon, hockey rules, of course. But baseball has its adherents – fanatics is probably a better word. Among them are Richard and Peter Nagano, who sometimes play the game on snowshoes.)

Richard was more animated than Peter, and equally droll. Unlike the three cheechakos, the brothers looked as though they had done their clothes shopping for the day at Eddie Bauer. Both wore thick, quilted suspender bibs, black with sky-blue knee cuffs. Richard had on a red fleece vest, and over that a sensational yellow-and-black parka. Pete's jacket was heavy fleece the color of caribou calf. Both wore the famous vapor-barrier "Mickey Mouse" boots developed by the military during the Korean War. Mickey boots, like Mickey's feet, are bulbous and clumsy looking. They're white rather than the mouse's preferred yellow or orange, to camouflage them against the snow.

The men fired up the snowmobiles for an extended warm-up period. As I watched the two prepare for the journey, meticulously, joking all the while, any remaining doubts I may have had about what I was about to do evanesced into frosty air. I realized that this was to be just another day in the wilds for the Nagano brothers, but one they were eager for. I felt the same way.

While waiting for our conveyances to heat up, we retired to the guesthouse for a bite to eat. Peter moved immediately to the kitchen. I told him that David, Shaun, and I were fine – we'd rustle up some instant oatmeal and dried fruit for ourselves. The commander of the expedition glared at me.

"Don't mess with me!" he barked. "I'm making breakfast!" In short order he laid out pancakes, sausages, and scrambled eggs for all.

By 10 A.M. the temperature had risen to -16; a heat wave, except for the fact that on straightaways we'd be hitting speeds in excess of forty miles per hour, generating a windchill that I didn't want to think about. Peter loaded up an assortment of emergency items, including a satellite phone and a rifle, the latter a precaution against early-rising bears. The sky was cold, gray, and choppy. It looked like a stormy ocean and there seemed to be waves crashing at the edges. There was no wind. Puffy snowflakes filled the air, dropping straight out of the sky. Around ten-thirty Peter jumped on the lead vehicle, pulled down his goggles, and took off.

THE PORCUPINE
IN WINTER

Caribou have been around in North America for a long time. They successfully negotiated the last several ice ages, an item of family history recalled in their classification as chionophiles – "snow-loving animals." "Everywhere they travel and in everything they do," George Calef has written, "the caribou must contend with this omni-present blanket of the northern land. They may be conceived in the snow, born in the snow, and die in the snow."

Nature has done a superb job of equipping the species to contend with these cold facts. For much of the year, the food caribou need to sustain themselves – mostly lichens, with the occasional lingonberry or horsetail thrown in – is buried beneath a layer of snow. (Not necessarily a deep layer: the Arctic has a dry climate; annual snow accumulations may be far less than in the snowy states of the lower forty-eight.) To figure out where the food is, the species has evolved a powerful sense of smell. With it, caribou can detect fodder buried beneath a foot of snow. To reach the food, the animals dig slant-sided holes, or "craters," with their superbly adapted hooves. The bottom surfaces of the hooves are concave. The surrounding toe pads, which are soft in summer, grow tough and sharp-edged when temperatures plunge. In winter a caribou's hoof becomes a tool – a shovel. With it, the animal can hack through all but the hardest-packed snow. (When a caribou walks, its hooves, which are outsized and nearly as wide as they are long, act like snowshoes. This distributes the animal's weight evenly over the wide areas of its hooves, lessening the chance that the legs will broomstick into the snow.) In the depths of January, a caribou may spend twelve hours a day excavating craters; it may dig a hundred of these before accumulating the ten to fifteen pounds of forage it needs to survive.

Even that amount would not be enough – especially for pregnant females eating for two – were caribou not among the most efficient protein processors on the planet. Lichens are low in protein. No other ungulate can survive on them. Protein synthesis requires nitrogen, which is found in the waste product urea. Instead of passing all of their urea out of their bodies, caribou recycle as much as 60 percent of it during the cold months, allowing the nitrogen it contains to be used again. Even at that, and even under the best conditions, the typical caribou loses 10 to 20 percent of its body weight through the winter. (For an entirely different reason – wolf predation – half of caribou calves do not survive their first winter.)

To meet the austere temperatures of the Arctic, caribou have evolved a coat that has long been prized by northern peoples for its superb insulating qualities. Fur covers practically the entire body of the animal, including the ears, the tail, and, nostrils excepted, the muzzle. The coat consists of two layers. On top is a layer of long guard hairs containing large, honeycomblike cells. Below is a layer of fine wooly hair. George Calef points out that, in tandem, the two layers do such a good job of trapping warm air that even when temperatures hit rock bottom, caribou do not shiver; nor do they require more than a minimal increase in metabolism to maintain their body temperature of 105 degrees Fahrenheit.

To further conserve warmth, caribou operate a so-called "counter-current" circulatory system in their legs. Arteries carrying warm blood to the legs run alongside vessels returning to the heart. Some of the outgoing heat is transferred to the incoming vessels and transported back to the animal's trunk. If the legs needed heat as much as the rest of the body does, the system wouldn't make sense. But they don't. Caribou legs spend the bulk of their time in snow. As a result, the legs have adapted to far lower temperatures than has the rest of the animal. Indeed, normal caribou leg temperature is 50 degrees, compared with a normal body temperature of 105. Because the temperature differential between the outside air and the legs is far less than it is between the air and any other part of the animal, some heat that might be lost from the head or torso will, in the legs, be conserved.

Even in the worst conditions, when the wind is howling, bitter cold is somehow seeping under the celebrated double-layer coat, and the normally efficient countercurrent circulation system seems in need of a tune-up, caribou can turn to a last-ditch plan they have hammered out over the eons: they excavate shallow beds in the snow, curl up beside their comrades, and pray for deliverance.

Decades of musing over what I imagined to be the true nature of the North had persuaded me that it must be one of two places: either the radiant expanse that lit a fire under Fred Meader or the nasty one that several times nearly iced Elisha Kent Kane; light or dark, your choice in Arctic brews. It hadn't occurred to me that there might a third possibility, the one I discovered mere minutes after jetting away from Jim and Adrienne Fink's guesthouse by the Dempster Highway, hot on the heels of an amateur hockey player by the name of Peter Nagano, who was piloting a snowmobile as though he were Wayne Gretzky attacking the enemy net on a breakaway: a thrilling, exhilarating North, a place of spicy, silvery, frosty air, electrifying scenery, wildly beating hearts, and a palpable sense that the earth is acutely, shimmeringly alive. Some say the world will end in fire, some say in ice. On the evidence of that day in March, I'm pretty sure it began, at least, in ice. Flying over the snow, I was utterly oblivious to danger or to the disastrous consequences of an accident, totally consumed by the business at hand – the need to hold the beast beneath me in check, to follow the trail religiously, to protect my hands and feet and eyes – gazing out at a white starry world through orange-tinted goggles, smelling and feeling my surroundings over the roar and jitterbug of the engine, I was drunk on the idea that the planet I inhabit is one helluva fine place to spend a life.

In the early going there were mishaps. Not five minutes from the starting line I steered off Peter's track and went screwball in deep snow; David coming up behind me did the same. Presciently having been placed fifth in line, Richard dug us out and got us rolling again. Within minutes the same thing reoccurred. Part of my problem was poor visibility. With no shadows to guide me and my eyeglasses fogging beneath my goggles, I was constantly missing turns or veering off the pathway. Self-rescue should have been a simple matter of steering back onto the track. But I had returned to my timid ways of the day before. Instead of boldly reclaiming the road, I lost heart; a moment later I'd be stuck in a quagmire of snow. I managed to work out the fogging problem by clearing a small air opening under my goggles. But the third or fourth time David and I spun out, I began to wonder if the two of us had any hope.

By then, Peter and Shaun were far ahead of the pack. Sensing that something was awry, they circled back. Peter was clearly peeved at David and me. Dutifully he went over the basics again. He decided to bring Richard to the front of the pack. There, with Shaun's assistance, the brothers would track and re-track difficult sections of the route until the foundation was passably solid. And they promised to stay in view of the two rookies in back. With my vision clearer, with the frontrunners in sight, perhaps I could follow more easily, and David too.

Starting out again, I bore down fiercely; I don't know if I've ever concentrated more intently on executing flawlessly a suite of technical maneuvers. The consequences of failure were, of course, only too clear to me.

Somehow my single-mindedness paid off. Over the next ten or fifteen minutes, the mystery went out of the machine. Its movements began to make sense beneath my hands and feet. I started to feel comfortable. My confidence grew. Now began a dreamy, effortless span of time and miles that didn't end until, many hours later, I pulled up in front of the guest-house at the end of the day and doused my engine. Crossing a rolling upland, traversing beneath an icy palisade, scooting up a gnarly slope, I seemed to be sailing over the snow like a low-flying bird. Two thousand miles north of Carol and Jake and the emerald waters and cherished pine forests of Lake Tahoe, I felt at home, as though the vast crazy snow dome inside of which I found myself were exactly the right place for me to be. Even on treacherous stretches, even on downhill straightaways with the throttle full-out, I felt fearless and invulnerable.

David was not so lucky. After dumping several more times, he agreed to climb aboard with Peter and be a passenger for the remainder of the day. He accepted his fate without whining and without shame. He knew why he was here, and it was not to be an Indy-500 driver. Was it such a bad thing to hitch a ride with Peter Nagano, veteran of the Yukon Centennial Patrol?

In a valley between two misty mountains, on a long, lonely moonscape of treeless white, we bid goodbye to David's beloved snowmobile. How, I wondered, would we ever find it again? That dismal spot looked exactly like a thousand others we had passed. Peter and Richard seemed utterly untroubled as we sped off into bewildering nebulousness. I never saw either man pull out a compass or a map; I'm sure they had neither. They appeared to know every inch of this almost featureless maze. At day's end, after more than forty miles of travel, and returning home by a completely different route, we rounded a corner, sailed down a slope, jetted along beside an ice-covered creek, all in poor visibility. Suddenly, perched ahead of us on a square of snow, like an antique ottoman on a polar-bear rug, was David's faithful snowmobile. Maybe if I had traveled those confusing alleyways as often as the Naganos had, I would have known my way around, too. Or maybe the brothers had a sixth sense about the North. In any case, I would have trusted them to lead me anywhere, even to *ivvavik* and back.

With David settled in behind Peter, we continued west from the highway. Several times Peter and Richard left the three cheechakos parked somewhere while they scouted ahead. Those long minutes, in bleak surroundings, were bitterly cold. We'd snack, stomp our feet, wish we were wearing caribou fur! Light snow fell throughout the day. Luckily there was little wind. Could I have bucked a bad wind? I was glad I didn't have to try. Soon we'd hear the distant buzz of two engines, then spot two dots far off on a gray, sunless slope. By their movements I could sometimes make out the lay of the land. Where all appeared smooth and flat, the lead vehicle would suddenly swing one way or another, betraying the contours of the slope. Arriving beside us, Peter would deliver some news. He thought we should go this way, or that. Why? I had no idea. He and his brother seemed to be enjoying themselves. Before taking off again we five would stand around shuffling in the snow, and Richard would have a smoke and complain good-naturedly about the Los Angeles Lakers or describe some of his own adventures, like the trips he had taken to Ottawa to see relatives. As for Peter's travels, he allowed that he had been to Anchorage but that was about it. He offered no apologies. "Why should I go anywhere else?" he said. "I've got everything here." Then we would take off and a few minutes later we'd be little dots on a mountainside, just as Peter and Richard had been.

I was by now handling my machine with something resembling artistry. Sometimes we would head straight up or straight down a steep slope. Those episodes were great fun, and easy, because the vehicles were stable front to back, the direction of travel. The figure I cut was thrilling – spellbinding. Watching me would have been like watching Leonard Bernstein conduct "The Flight of the Bumblebee."

But traversing left or right along a slope was scary. To keep the contraption from tipping over I'd stand and lean far to the uphill side, hopping up and down, if necessary, to offset gravity. Only once did I come close to biting the dust. Approaching the crest of a hill, I took the final yards at too steep an angle. I felt the snowmobile start to slip. Instead of panicking or slamming on the brakes, I jumped off and ran alongside my baby a short ways, steering with one hand while I allowed the vehicle's forward motion to counterbalance its urge to tumble. Reaching a more level stretch, I grabbed the handlebars, jumped on sidesaddle, and continued as though nothing had happened. I've never in my life been so proud of myself.

For several hours we pressed on over darkly beautiful terrain. Around two o'clock we stopped for the third or fourth time while the Naganos scoped out the road ahead. This time only Richard returned. He signaled for David to climb aboard with him and for Shaun and me to follow.

We set off along a level stretch, then moved left up a slope, across the top of a ridge, and down slightly to a shelf on the side of the ridge. A short distance away, a slab of pearly mountainside hung from a choppy sky. Approaching, I saw Peter kneeling in the snow beside his snowmobile. His elbows were braced on the seat and he was peering through field glasses at the mountain.

He signaled for the rest of us to turn off our engines and join him. I walked to his side. My heart was pounding. Without lowering the glasses he pointed at a spot midway up the slope. I saw spots – rocks, I assumed, or trees, though I hadn't seen a decent tree all day.

I remembered being here before. Not here, exactly, but in a place more like this than any place I had ever been. *Standing beside the Kongakut River, gazing across the water at a far-away gathering of nearly invisible specks. Toru had passed the field glasses to me...* and now Peter did the same.

"Caribou," he said softly, as though he were afraid that the distant creatures would hear him. He paused while I adjusted the glasses and homed in on the amazing scene before my eyes. Then he spoke again: "I told you we'd find them."

*   *   *

We stayed for half an hour. The animals were so far off it was almost impossible to tell much about them except that they were, in fact, caribou. There were two groups, one of about a dozen, the other, slightly higher on the slope, of perhaps ten. Peter told me that caribou gather on ridges and mountainsides during the winter, rather than in the valley bottoms, for the simple reason that, higher up, strong winds whisk away some of the snow cover, making it easier for them to find fodder. Below, as I knew from personal experience, the snow buildup could be prodigious; that delicious patch of lichen you had your heart set on might be a long way down.

I wanted to be nearer the action, of course. But in at least one respect, my distant prospect provided an advantage I might not have had at closer range. From my lofty perch I could see, along with caribou, a many-mile sweep of wild, desolate country. Above, a frozen sky appeared utterly disengaged from the goings-on below. In all directions the view was alarming. The terrible isolation of the spot was manifest. The cumulative effect of this delirium of cold facts was to produce a heartwarming realization: plunked down teeny-tiny in the middle of that stark and lonely world, on the forlorn flank of a remote, snowy mountain, surrounded, protected, and gladdened by exactly nothing, without a tree or a warm bed or a shock of decent forage in sight, there was a phalanx of caribou, *alive and well!* This was miraculous! I shook my head at the absurdity of the idea. But there was no mistaking that the animals were there; moreover, I knew well enough that they had been there since long before it ever occurred to some bumptious pharaoh to build a pyramid or some genius hunter-gatherer to plant the first patch of rye. Is the world an awesome place? Picture this: *the Porcupine in winter!*

Standing beside me, Peter suddenly turned his attention to a stretch of terrain a few hundred yards below our position and a good distance to the west. Through field glasses it was possible to see that something was moving across the snow. How my friend had spotted it with his naked eye was a mystery; even with glasses I could barely make it out.

"Wolverine," he said. He explained that although he couldn't see the animal's features clearly enough to identify it, the loping motion was a dead giveaway. With his hands Peter imitated a wolverine moving on snow, a smoothly connected series of bounding leaps, like the hand-springs a gymnast might use to cross a mat during a floor routine.

I was happy. With the help of a lot of people, I'd somehow connected the dots and come full circle. I felt an enormous sense of relief, of a dream fulfilled. I thanked Peter for taking me to that place, wherever it was. I wanted him to know that, as far as I was concerned, he had discharged his end of the bargain and could now relax.

"I'm done," I said. "I'm happy. I can go home now."

He looked at me as though I were crazy.

"Done?" he said. "You may be done with me, my friend. But I'm not done with you."

Moments later he hopped onto his snowmobile and took off alone. Twenty minutes later he was back. He signaled for the rest of us to saddle up and follow him.

We motored along the top of the ridge, then steeply and thrillingly down into a gigantic bowl perhaps a mile wide. The floor of the bowl was dead level and fathomless with snow. Moving across without foundering required enormous care. On the far side a shallow depression snaked into a curtain of fog – a creek bed lined with rotten snow. Peter gunned his engine and shot across the depression. Beyond, we ascended to the lip of the bowl, then sped a short ways over a level stretch. Ahead I could see our apparent destination, an isolated knoll rising a few hundred feet above the surrounding terrain. As we started up the flank, we passed through a sparse garden of what appeared to be unopened umbrellas poking upward through the snow – evergreen tips, as it happened. A cheery touch by the landscape architect, one I had noticed throughout the day whenever we encountered an abrupt change in elevation.

The knoll, on the other hand, was unlike anything I had seen. Constant winds had swept it clear of snow. The ground surface was rough and rocky. Scattered about were some good-sized boulders. Working our way upward over the rutted surface, we were forced to slow to almost walking speed.

Just short of the summit, Peter stopped. He motioned for the rest of us to park and follow him. We fell in behind him as he hunched down and quietly moved to the top of the knoll. At the top he stood and peered over the edge. A moment later I did the same.

A wonderful sight met my eyes: perhaps seventy yards below, at the bottom of a gentle slope, several dozen caribou grazed. Another group of about twenty fed a short distance to the north; eleven more were gathered in the opposite direction. Many of the animals sported modest sets of antlers. I could see their white manes and their white rumps and the splayed-leg way they had of standing when they weren't eating, and I was pleased with myself, because I recognized those peculiarities from history, my history, and that seemed to give me cachet in matters caribou.

No words passed among the five observers at the top of the knoll. Each found a spot and settled in to watch. I snapped a few photos, then sat down on an accommodating rock that had thoughtfully been placed there for my convenience.

For a few minutes the animals seemed unaware of our presence. Then one in the central group caught a scent or a movement and quickly passed the news to the others. Each tensed in turn; you could see the realization passing down the line, like a breath of wind moving across a field of tall grass. A few of the caribou galloped off a short distance, then halted.

When it was clear that there was no immediate danger, no charging grizzly or leaping wolf to ruin the afternoon, the feeders returned to their business. From time to time one would lift her head to take a gander at the men on the hill – more out of curiosity, it seemed, than fear. Shaun soon took it upon himself to move down the slope toward the central group. He was able to halve the distance between the top and bottom of the knoll before the caribou spooked. There he stopped, at the edge of the zone of intolerance. In a short time the animals grew used to his presence and resumed feeding.

It was evident that, thanks to bare ground and an abundance of fodder, we'd come upon a prime grazing area. This made it likely that all the animals we were observing were pregnant females or juveniles, the standard winter arrangement in such a spot. After the fall rut, adult bulls, barren females, and some of the younger bulls lose their antlers. Pregnant females do not. This gives them a huge advantage over the others when it comes to appropriating choice feeding areas. On the winter range, the pregnant females take the best spots for themselves, their fetuses, and their yearlings. The others, even bulls far bigger and stronger than themselves, they chase off to marginal feeding grounds. The groups remain separated throughout the winter; expectant mothers do not see their comrades again till after they deliver their calves at *ivvavik* in June.

Blissfully lounging on my agreeable rock in that sublime spot, I snacked on moose jerky and enjoyed the show: my old pal Shaun, off on another madcap journey, this time down a hillside into the Yukon nowhere; snowflakes twinkling out of a morose sky, as though they were happy to be on their own at last; yearlings jousting, bleating, and annoying their moms, like kids everywhere; a bullying female usurping a blue-ribbon feeding area from her thoroughly cowed neighbor; and, beneath it all, earth's creaky gears cranking along as dependably as ever. It was a dreamy afternoon – like a day at the beach, only colder. It occurred to me that Lucky might be goofing off somewhere down there at the bottom of the slope, so I contacted my telepathic messaging service and sent a communiqué. Alas, there was no response.

The knoll marked farthest west for the exploration party that day. As the hour grew late, the surrounding light became brittle and chill. It seemed odd to leave the animals in that forlorn spot, but we did. (Peter had worried that I might want to remain on the knoll by myself for the night. A confession: the thought never occurred to me.) On the way home, Shaun's snowmobile stopped cold and would not be restarted. We left it in a spot no more distinctive, to me, than the one where we had left David's vehicle earlier in the day. Shaun climbed aboard behind Richard, and for a brief period the party was down to three vehicles. Then, on cue, in a valley between two misty mountains, on a long, lonely moonscape of treeless white, we came upon David's snowmobile. Shaun hopped on. With the rest of us he steered into our morning tracks. Then, in something of a daze, we headed downslope on the long, final, euphoric miles that separated us from home.

That night the temperature fell to 40 below. The next morning was blustery. A storm seemed immanent. But amazing things happened that day, a day in which we clocked another fifty miles in the wondrous Ogilvies. Beside the guesthouse there was a sixth snowmobile – just what we needed to make up for the one Shaun had been forced to abandon in the wild. Crucially, David had been visited during the night by the ghost of Dale Earnhardt. My friend slipped into the driver's seat of snow-mobile number six and, like *that*, drove like a champion. (I retain a vivid picture of David's being thrown from his vehicle on a downhill run somewhere that second day, somewhere very far from his Central Park West apartment, and the snowmobile going on without him, and him running alongside with a fierce expression on his face, and then *leaping* like a Hollywood stunt man and landing *kerplunk!* right on the seat, and taking up sweetly exactly where he had left off.)

We headed out at midmorning. Richard towed a sleigh that we would use to collect Shaun's disabled snowmobile when we found it. Somewhere, Peter zigged where he had zagged the day before, and we entered a new kingdom of snows.

The miles that followed were as thrilling and as beautiful as it would be possible to imagine. In the early afternoon the sun peeped through the clouds, just as we drove onto an immense tableland, a placid ocean of blinding white that stretched as far as the eye could see. It was possible to move across this ocean at tarpon speed and we did, heedless of the traffic laws. At last we came to the base of a tall bluff. I understood that we were going to go to the top of the thing, but I couldn't imagine how. The route looked foolhardy, like something a teenager might try.

Peter called a halt to inspire the troops. He explained the plan. He and Richard would go first. They would lay a bombproof path up the slope, the wildest we had attempted. Richard had two suggestions for the cheechakos: (1) be bold; (2) drive like hell.

All I remember of the next few minutes is a staccato of four-letter words pouring from my mouth and a sure sense that the five hundred pounds of steel on which I was riding would, at any moment, be riding on me. But the path was sure and the leadership sound. In short order the entire team stood safely atop the bluff, gazing out at magnificent views to the horizon in all directions. In the near distance the great table-land flowed outward in waves, a high sea to anywhere you please. Beyond rose mountains upon mountains, blazing in pure light.

A few yards from where we stood lay signs of a different sort of drama: strewn about in a vaguely defined circle were the scant remains of a caribou – a few bone fragments, part of a hoof, some clumps of fur. At several spots along the circumference, a clue to the perpetrator's identity: wolf scat.

The south side of the bluff consisted of a series of steep-sided snow bowls. It took me a few moments to realize where Peter had brought us. Call it Caribou Bluff, if you will, for in each bowl there were multitudes of caribou. Multitudes more ranged below, on the sloping run-out to the tableland. The entire formation on which we stood was something like a very large vanilla ice cream cake festooned with sprinkles, except instead of sprinkles it had caribou.

Peter said that he ascended the bluff perhaps once a year and that he rarely brought others with him. It was evident from his manner that the place had a hold on his heart. I stood with him in silence and in awe, unable to account for the incredible good fortune that had brought me together with such a man, and with Richard, so amiable and so steadfast. We each had a bite to eat and then we fired up our engines. For the next hour, our quintet wound slowly down and across the face of the bluff, from one bowl to the next, in and out, around and among the animals. We darted in close enough to arouse their interest, but almost never so close as to unnerve them. At each turn we came upon a crowd of onlook-ers. Once, scooting along a straight stretch beneath an escarpment,

I looked up and saw a dozen heads peering over the edge at me. We came around a bend, and there were a hundred caribou; we zipped up a slope, and there were a hundred more. It was exciting to approach a blind spot, not knowing what we would find on the far side. Sometimes a dozen caribou would be waiting for us, and they would scarcely look up. Other times a few would spook, then quickly give in to a famous family tendency toward curiosity. They would stop and turn around and then trot back in our direction, their heads cocked. Several times we stopped to take photos, or simply to gaze at the panorama of wildlife, and to wonder if the animals knew they would be leaving this place in a few days, to begin the long trek to *ivvavik*. And if they did not know, how would they find out, and how would they know the way?

Those were the last caribou I would see on my travels. I think about them often, especially when I read about yet another proposal to open the Arctic National Wildlife Range to oil and gas development, on the very spot where many of the animals that I saw that day would bear their young, two months and many miles later. The common denominator of all such schemes, it seems to me, is their vulgarity. Oil development on Alaska's coastal plain is roughly analogous to public defecation at Ground Zero. It is crude, it is profane, and it is profoundly ignorant of history. That should be bad enough. But no. Undeterred, many advocates of development cheerfully take on the added habit of duplicity, dismissing as worthless and expendable lands in which they themselves have no personal interest, at the same time extolling as heaven on earth lands in which they do. Ronald Reagan was the first president to recommend oil and gas leasing for the Arctic National Wildlife Refuge. Now hear Mister Reagan, a few months before taking office, on why he intended to maintain the land on his 688-acre California ranch in its untamed, natural state: "Everybody has his own Shangri-La, his own way of getting away, and this is ours." No one would have blamed Mister Reagan for opposing oil exploration on his beloved ranch, were oil to have been discovered there. And no one would blame Vice-President Dick Cheney – a prime mover behind efforts to open the refuge to drilling – for opposing oil exploration and development on the Snake River, one of his beloved Wyoming fishing holes. Cheney grew up in Wyoming and has fished its streams avidly since he was a kid. "I love the setting where you get to do it," he told *Outdoorsbest* online magazine. Fishing, he said, takes you

> to some of the most beautiful places in the world in terms of setting. But I have just as much fun with a day on the Snake an hour from the house, and I take just as much satisfaction from it. I've always firmly believed in the old saying that a day spent fishing is a day that doesn't count against your total time in life.

Nor would President George W. Bush's first secretary of the interior, Gale Norton, another prime mover, be faulted for opposing oil and gas development in some cherished corner of her home state of Colorado, where, whenever possible, she repairs to hike and ski. As she told *Outside* magazine, explaining the source of her affection for such places: "Growing up in Denver, I'm sure it started with loving the Colorado mountains."

Ten thousand trips to ivvavik, *my friend – and you say enough? And who exactly are you? Someone who understands the world? I see! Tell me this: Why, then, are you blind to its majesty?*

Years ago, my father, who was an Episcopal priest, told a story in one of his sermons that I'm reminded of when I picture roads, drilling pads, and airstrips on the calving grounds of the Porcupine caribou herd. I was probably eight or ten at the time and not in the habit of listening closely to my father's sermons. Yet so powerful was the message of his story that I heard it clearly on that long-ago Sunday morning, and I've never forgotten it. It seems that an old monk was showing a group of American tourists around a great European cathedral. At the end of the tour the group came to a side chapel, where a candle was burning. The monk explained that it had long been one of the duties of his order to tend the flame.

"How long has it been burning?" someone asked.

The monk smiled. "A thousand years," he said.

There was a gasp from the assembled, and then silence. Then, while the others watched, one of the tourists walked over to the candle and cupped the flame in his hand.

"A thousand years," he said. "That's long enough." With that he blew out the flame.

Will that be the headline when the calving grounds are opened to drilling? *Officials say, That's long enough!*

But perhaps the story of the thousand-year flame was apocryphal. Never mind. Other flames far longer lived than that one are routinely extinguished: of that there can be no doubt. Mayan ruins are looted, cave paintings defaced, antiquities destroyed. During the early days of the Iraq War, Baghdad's National Museum was pillaged, resulting in the destruction or disappearance of priceless artifacts four thousand years of age and older. Such atrocities are not confined to foreign lands. In 1964 a geology student studying ice-age glaciation on Nevada's Wheeler Peak set about collecting tree-ring data from some of the bristlecone pine trees on the mountain. Bristlecones are known to be very old, and the student theorized that knowledge of their ages might assist him in dating contemporaneous glacial phenomena. He chose a tree known as WPN-114, which grew at an altitude of 10,750 feet in a glacial cirque on the northeast face of the mountain. The student made several holes in the tree with a twenty-eight-inch increment borer, an instrument that would have allowed him to take a sample of the core without harming the tree.

Unfortunately, he was unable to get a clear reading with the borer. His only other option was to examine a cross-section of the trunk under a microscope. With that in mind, he asked for permission from the U.S. Forest Service to cut down the tree.

Permission was granted. With the help of Forest Service personnel, the student chain-sawed the bristlecone. Subsequent counting of its rings established that the tree was about 4900 years old. That made it, to the best of anyone's knowledge, the oldest living thing on earth.

It is true: WPN-114 was very old, and its downing was a tragedy.

But it was not the oldest living thing on earth. Not by a long shot. Terns have been migrating between the Arctic and the Antarctic since long before WPN-114 took root on the bleak northeast slope of Wheeler Peak. Fin whales have cycled between Antarctica and the coast of South Africa, monarch butterflies have plied the airways between California and northwest Mexico, for just as long. The Porcupine caribou herd has staged an endless journey over mountain and river, from Yukon's Ogilvie Mountains to Alaska's north coast and back, for at least ten thousand years; there is evidence that the true time span may be many times that number. The Porcupine's grand journey began in the unfathomable mists of prehistory, in a nursery of ice. It grew and prospered during fat times and waned during lean, engendering a unique narrative as surely as does a people or a nation. The chronicle of the Porcupine lives and breathes today where it has always lived and breathed, in a vital, enchanting corner of the world. Who now claims the authority to snuff it out?

Two weeks after I returned home from the Yukon, about the time that the Porcupine's 2004 run to Alaska shifted into full gear, Lucky's battery went dead. After broadcasting her day-to-day locations for almost seven years, her transmitter fell silent. Her last known position was 64.947°N, 139.030°W, which put her about twenty-six miles east-northeast of Jim and Adrienne Fink's place, and just a few miles from the spot I called Caribou Bluff. That left only Donner and Blixen, of the original ten caribou captured in 1997, still transmitting their latitude and longitude coordinates. In the meantime a new generation of test subjects had joined the satellite collar project – Aurora, Helen, Tundra, Lynetta, Iola, Arnaq, Cocoa, Catherine, Rocky, Isabella, and Pingo. A year later seven more were added, and the list continues to grow.

By my calculations, at the time of her disappearance Lucky had put some 25,000 miles beneath her hooves – a circumnavigation of the globe, more or less. She probably put on a few more after the satellite lost track of her, though perhaps not many. She was, after all, getting up there in caribou years. As I write these words, twenty months later, she may well have seen *ivvavik* for the last time.

If so, she had a pretty good run, and she saw a lot of the world. I like to think that I spotted her that last day, up there in one of those glorious bowls of snow, not far from the top of the world. I like to imagine that even now she's okay, just being Lucky, racing for the next bright horizon, and the one beyond.

PART THREE:
CLOSING THE CIRCLE

Meanwhile the wild geese, high in the clean blue air,
are heading home again.
  Mary Oliver

GREAT LAND WITHIN

Late one afternoon in March 1963, a scatter of caribou moved onto the frozen surface of Loon Lake, a seven-mile-long body of water located some eighty miles north of the Arctic Circle, in Alaska's Brooks Range. Watching from the window of a one-room cabin at lake's edge were a former Ph.D. candidate in philosophy at Boston University named Fred Meader and his five-year-old son Dion. The elder Meader stood to one side; Dion knelt center-window atop a stool. On the table beside the boy was a large pot of boiling water, which Dion's mother, Elaine, had placed there for cleaning the dinner dishes.

The Meaders were the sole human inhabitants not only of the lake but of a chunk of mountainous terrain bigger than the state of Connecticut. Their nearest neighbor lived fifty miles away. In those days before the Alaska pipeline, there wasn't a road within two hundred miles of Loon Lake. A day earlier, the Meaders had been visited by a bush pilot named Andy Anderson, who checked in on the family once every month or so from his home base in Bettles, a dot on the map some eighty miles to the south. Except for Anderson, Fred, Elaine, and Dion never saw a soul at this time of year. When their visitor's plane disappeared over the southern horizon, the solitude that the Meaders had come to this desolate place to find would be complete until Anderson returned sometime in April.

Dion's role as an interested observer of the activity on the ice was no offhand matter; it was of a piece with the way he spent most of his time. He had an affinity for the animals of the northern forest. Except for his mother and father, wild animals had been his only playmates since his parents brought him to Loon Lake nearly three years before. Dion's senses had become attuned to the habits and moods of the creatures of the Brooks – caribou, lynx, wolf, moose. He knew when they were around. He could track them with a prowess that astounded his parents. He kept a pet raven, a fox, and a weasel, which he regarded as his equals. Dion Meader was something like Kipling's Mowgli, except that Dion was a real kid.

Before long, the caribou left the ice and moved into the forest. Fred stepped away from the window. From his kneeling position atop the stool Dion began to move. As he did so, he lost his balance. Instinctively, he reached for something to break his fall. His fingers found the only object within reach, the pot of boiling water that his mother had placed on the table. As Elaine looked on in horror, the child grabbed the edge of the pot and pulled the water over on himself.

Dion was dressed for March in the Arctic, but his heavy clothing did little to protect him: he sustained first-, second-, and third-degree burns. With her child screaming in her arms, Elaine struggled to remove his clothes. Plasma was draining from the boy's body. Trained as a nurse, Elaine did what she could to calm her son and to tend his wounds, but it wasn't much. She knew that he was likely to go into shock.

Fred and Elaine Meader were mature, reasoning adults who had made a decision to excuse themselves from what they regarded as the abjectness of the modern world only after years of intense thought and preparation. Any consequences of their decision, however unfortunate they might be, could at least be said to have resulted from their own actions and no one else's.

The same could not be said of their child, who was innocent in the matter. His parents' rejection of modernity and all of its imperfections also meant their rejection of its benefits, including its possible lifesaving benefits. Now it appeared that the loser in this trade-off might be Dion Meader. Help was a long way off. A hike to Bettles was out of the question. Fred had injured his knee in a recent accident and was in no condition to attempt the long and probably vain walk through Arctic winter, with no road to guide him. If the Meaders were going to save their child, they would have to turn to the ancient ways of the wild to do it.

Elaine wrapped her son in a blanket and took him into her arms. Night descended on the lake. Dion asked his mother to sing to him. He was a boy, she later recalled, whose experience of wild nature was personal and profound. The natural world of the Arctic was his friend, his teacher, his context, his address. He connected "with the magic of the stars," she said, and when he saw the northern lights on his birthday, he took them to be a gift created especially for him. Life was the earthly expression of a benevolent universe, an expression that was synonymous with joy. Now with his own life in jeopardy, Dion settled into his mother's arms. She began to sing. She lifted her voice, not a big one, and sent it out into the great darkness, from her little cabin at the end of the earth. She sang and sang, through the night, till the first rays of sunlight lifted over the mountain to the east. As she sang, she imagined an airplane landing on the lake and taxiing to the front of the cabin.

One of the many aspects of the human drama of the North that captured my fancy when, as a young man, I fell in love with Arctic literature, was the frequent willingness of its players to exchange the dictates of causal logic for magic and mystery. Experienced at the outer edges of the physical conditions that humans are capable of surviving, Arctic life quite naturally lends itself to the strange and the inexplicable, as though a dollop of each might warm up the temperature a few degrees. Even in modern times, tales of the North often have a supernatural quality about them. Inuit and Gwich'in hunters converse with animal spirits; explorers and adventurers in jams see phantom ships hurrying to their rescues; university-educated men and women pay attention to their dreams and send out tiny songs into the night, with no small confidence that their melodies will come to rest in useful places. Awe-inspiring optical phenomena like the aurora borealis, halos, and coronas are common in the North; for anyone who might be beaten down by cold or hunger, they can be taken as a sign that all is not lost. Similar conditions explain the supernormal audibility that is sometimes reported at these latitudes, which can allow normal conversations to be heard miles away. The word "arctic" itself derives from the Greek *arktos* – bear – a reference not to polar bears or grizzlies but to a fantasy in the night sky, the constellation of the Great Bear.

In 1818, in pursuit of a £20,000 prize offered by the British Parliament for the discovery of a Northwest Passage to the Orient, the explorer John Ross entered Lancaster Sound, a body of water separating Baffin and Devon islands in the Canadian Arctic. Had Ross continued in that direction he might have won the prize, for he was precisely on route with the Northwest Passage eventually worked out by the Norwegian Roald Amundsen, during the years 1903–1905. Ross, however, turned away, because he saw a range of mountains blocking the sound. He named the range the Croker Mountains, after the First Secretary of the Admiralty.

There were no Croker Mountains. What Ross saw was a mirage, likely the result of a phenomenon called looming, a bending of light rays that causes objects beyond the curve of the earth to appear to float above the horizon. The existence of the Croker Mountains was disproved a year later, but not before Ross had blown the prize. Such mistakes, Barry Lopez cautions the dreamer who hopes to fully explicate the North, "serve as a caution against precise description and expectation, a reminder that the universe is oddly hinged."

Elaine Meader understood the odd hinging of the North. In 2003, as part of a mammoth undertaking called Project Jukebox, a nine-thousand–interview oral history project conducted by the University of

Alaska, Fairbanks, Elaine talked about her years at Loon Lake with Karen Brewster, a research associate at the university. Elaine allowed that when she and Fred went to the lake, she believed that "there was a mystery somewhere in [human existence] that we couldn't analyze rationally." Her desire to grow closer to that mystery was central to her decision to reject the confinements of the modern world and to enter into the greater natural world. She was, she said, "staking my life and meaning on that." Repeatedly she stated that her experience of the Arctic wild was fundamentally "spiritual" – enough times, in fact, that one comes away from the interview wondering if unbelief might be a phenomenon confined primarily to the world's temperate zones.

Shortly after Elaine, Fred, and Dion took up residence at Loon Lake, they were visited by a distant Brooks Range resident, a wolf trapper, and his wife, the latter an Inuit who apparently was tuned in to the same spiritual wavelengths as Elaine. The couple flew to the lake in their own plane to welcome the Meaders to the neighborhood. After paying their respects, the trapper and his wife departed and never returned. When Dion pulled a pot of boiling water over on himself, more than two years had passed since the Meaders had seen the couple.

But on the night of the accident, in her cabin far from Loon Lake, the Inuit woman became disturbed. She told her husband that she was receiving "a very strong message" that something terrible had happened at Loon Lake. "We've got to go to the Meaders," she insisted. "They need our help." Her husband was experienced enough in such matters to know that it would be a mistake to dismiss his wife's intuition. Early the next morning, the two took off for Loon Lake.

At first light, Fred laid out an SOS sign of evergreen boughs on the lakeshore. A short time later, he and Elaine heard the sound of an airplane engine. The craft landed on the lake exactly as Elaine had imagined and taxied to the cabin. The trapper and his wife loaded Dion onto the plane and flew him to Fairbanks. The boy spent several weeks in a Fairbanks hospital but recovered completely.

*   *   *

During the late sixties and seventies, a small but influential back-to-the-land movement flowered on the West Coast. The premise behind the movement was that people can and should learn to live in harmony with wild nature – in particular, the wild nature of northern Alaska. The protagonists who showed that not only could this be done, it could provide the foundation for rich, fulfilling lives were Fred and Elaine Meader. At intervals during their seventeen years in the Brooks, they traveled to the lower forty-eight, where Fred lectured and showed slides and films of life at Loon Lake to enthusiastic audiences of disaffected Americans. He became something of a cult figure. As a result of his and Elaine's influence, Alaska today is home to an appreciable number of men and women who were so moved by Meader's performances that they pulled up stakes in places like Bakersfield, Ukiah, and Ashland and went north. I met half a dozen of them during my time in Alaska. All of them had heard that I had come down with my own case of Fred Meader, and they wanted to tell me their stories. Few of Fred's followers entered into the North as completely as he and Elaine had. But full immersion was not what the couple had in mind for everyone. Respect for, closeness to, and responsible husbandry over the Arctic wild were more like it. By engendering those values in hundreds of people, and hundreds more of their progeny – people who today live not in tiny cabins in the Brooks Range but in houses and apartments in Fairbanks and Anchorage, and whose love for the Alaskan wild is fierce and uncompromising – the Meaders can be said to have succeeded in their mission handsomely.

Fred and Elaine were the hearts and minds of the Loon Lake movement; Dion was the soul. As he grew into a young man fully conversant with the wild, a young man *of* the wild, his parents began to entertain hopes that he would carry on the tradition they had started when they were no longer able, and take it to some as yet undefined higher level. They feared for his socialization, however, so as he grew older they began to bring other children to the lake for extended periods to provide companionship for their son. One, Sean McGuire, spent several years residing with the Meaders, arriving when he was ten. McGuire recalls those years as the most blissful of his life. He and Dion fished, hunted, roamed the mountains, talked to the animals – Dion always the teacher and prime translator. Dion was, McGuire recalls, "as pure a naturalist as you could be."

Whatever Fred and Elaine's hopes for their son may have been, they were not to be fulfilled. In the fall of 1974, three years before Fred's death on the Koyukuk River in Bettles, Dion drowned in Loon Lake. He was seventeen. The loss that his death represented for his parents is unimaginable. That it might have been prevented but for a series of unlucky happenstances can only have compounded their grief. Fred and Elaine were in California at the time. Several other teenagers were staying at the cabin with Dion. Earlier, the party had taken the only three canoes at the lake to Trout Lake, a location a good distance away. There they shot a moose. By chance a helicopter carrying some geologists landed nearby. They offered to fly the teenagers back to the cabin. All but Dion accepted. He paddled home alone, leaving two canoes behind. He reached the cabin without incident. Critically, there was now only one canoe at the cabin.

On September 18, well into Arctic fall, Dion heard a plane at the other end of the lake. He had a letter that he wanted to get to his parents, so Loon Lake postal service being what it was, he jumped into the lone canoe and set out for the far end of the lake. He carried no life jacket. But he knew canoeing, Elaine said later – for practically his entire life, a canoe had been "part of his body."

About a mile from shore, he was thrown into the freezing water. No one knows what happened. The best guess is that the thwart on which he was sitting snapped and the canoe overturned. Dion took hold of the canoe and began kicking toward shore. His friends heard his cries for help. Lacking a craft from which to mount a rescue effort, they attempted to fashion a raft by lashing together some driftwood pieces. But the wood was green, and the raft sank as soon as it was launched.

Dion made good and, under the circumstances, superhuman progress. But the frigid waters of the lake at last began to take their toll. Some thirty minutes after going into the water and perhaps one hundred yards from shore, he dropped below the surface. From an agonizingly close distance away, his friends watched helplessly. Five weeks were to pass before they could get word out to Fred and Elaine about what had happened.

Elaine has stated that both Fred and Dion had strong premonitions of early deaths. Shortly before his own demise, watching from a canoe near the shore of Loon Lake, Fred had seen a caribou near the cabin. He studied the animal intently and lovingly, overwhelmed by a sense that it was the last caribou he would ever see. As for Dion, describing his own conviction that he would not make it to age nineteen, he told his mother that he was horrified by the idea of a "cement box." "I want to be a flower or something," he told her. His body was never recovered from Loon Lake. He became, in his mother's words, "part of the lake."

Following Fred's death in 1977, I exchanged several letters with Elaine. In one, she wrote of her early years at Loon Lake, and of gradually coming to feel at home in the North. She described that burgeoning feeling as one of "intimacy with the ways of the wild, a love and understanding of those ways." In the years before she and Fred made their decision to leave civilization behind, she wrote,

> The horizon of that love and understanding was always receding from us. Fred and I felt a lifetime in the wilderness could only increase the mystery and love. . . . I realized that the world of consciousness within us – of love and emotion – was not separated from the greater world of the wild outside of us. The world of rock, stream, and creature is made of that same love and emotion.

The belief that the materials of the world, animate and inanimate alike, are somehow mysteriously linked is common in indigenous cultures. By the time Fred Meader died, the environmental movement in the United States had progressed far enough that American conservationists were eager to quote Wordsworth and Emerson on the subject and, most famously, John Muir: "When we try to pick out anything by itself, we find it hitched to everything else in the Universe."

But Elaine's idea that connectedness extends to worlds *within* and *without* struck me as new and powerful. Certainly she wasn't the first person to detect the basic outlines of this order. Carl Jung, Pierre Teilhard de Chardin, hip theologians like Matthew Fox and Thomas Berry, normal everyday Buddhists and Native Americans preceded her.

But Elaine seemed to be going a step further. She wanted to bring emotions into the continuum and to make them central: love, joy, fear, anger – emotions are one with rock, stream, and creatures. For her, the natural world is *made* of them. In her letter she used a phrase that came to her in a dream to express this unity: "great land within." She suggests that, just as the yawning universe numbers among its elements each of us, tiny but somehow significant, so too we carry within us lands of boundless dimensions, along with all the inhabitants thereof. Science might scoff at such a notion, but not anyone who has ever experienced a sudden epiphanic surge of understanding, or seen in a wildflower or a sunset the contours of hope or love.

Elaine went on to describe her belief, forged from seventeen years' living off earth's bounty, that death is not the end for the animals that the subsistence hunter kills for food – that, indeed, the worlds of the living and the dead are connected too.

> Death is not tragedy. The spirits of these animals survive and are around us as we work. Our feelings of respect and gratefulness and even our joy are important to the caribou whose bodies have become our food.
>
> I do not believe Fred's death is a tragedy. I only know that both he and I have to let go, at this sharp turn in the road, of all our plans for the future, and approach our new lives with faith. These feelings are the greatest gift I can give him now, because then our strengths merge and support each other, as they have in this lifetime.

Two daughters were born to Fred and Elaine late in their stay at Loon Lake. Heather was three at the time of Fred's accident; Dawn was four months.

> I will teach my little girls that they have a "spirit daddy," and that he loves them and can help them from his side of life, and that through our spirits we can all keep in touch, and learn from and grow with each other.
>
> When I "lost" my son three years ago, I learned that the most important thing in the world was not lost, and that was the spirit of love and joy within us and between us. [Since Dion] passed over, it has been both Fred's and my experience that our relationship with Dion did not end, but that the relationship has grown and changed only in different ways than if he were here.

Following her husband's death, Elaine announced her intention to stay on in the Brooks and to raise her daughters there. But she soon recognized the impracticality of the idea. More important, she understood that a new phase of her life had begun. Within a few months she made the difficult decision to leave Loon Lake behind. With Heather and Dawn in tow, she emigrated to northern California. Two decades earlier she had left the nursing program at Boston University. Now she harbored a wish to return to the healing professions. She went back to school, and in 1987 received her Ph.D. in psychology. In the years following, Elaine Meader-McCausland (a conjunction of Fred's name and her own maiden name) worked as a practicing psychologist in redwood country north of San Francisco. Her primary interest in her practice was in archetypes and the unconscious, work that connected her, she said, with the spiritual roots she developed in the wilderness. As she explained, "My communication with spirits at that lake and in those mountains was not that different from what I do in my life now."

Elaine returned to Loon Lake in 1979 and 1984. Sixteen years passed before her next visit. She now spends time there every summer. Peering into the future, she envisions the lake as a place where people will come for extended periods of contemplation and exploration, to get in touch with the same forces she encountered there. In her 2003 interview with Karen Brewster, Elaine outlined her plans for the time she has remaining:

> My work for the rest of my life will be spiritual work. . . . I have to say that Dion is my biggest guide. After a number of years it became apparent to me that he was with me in my work and is part of my whole search, which is still a spiritual search.

She said she hoped to reach a "spiritual understanding" of the work we must do as humans in order to solve the onerous problems we face and to rein in our destructive nature, so that we can "save our world and our future."

> I believe that is happening. . . . We have to keep working at our answers and keep practicing our spiritual tools in order to go through the transformation as a species that I think we're destined to go through.

Nearly half a century ago, Elaine and Fred Meader's belief that the world was headed in the wrong direction sent them on what some who knew them regarded as a bizarre mission north of the Arctic Circle. They went to save themselves, but what they found, at least one of them believes, may one day save us all.

A VOW FULFILLED

On a chilly, early-summer afternoon, a de Havilland Beaver crested a circle of spruce-mantled mountains in northern Alaska and descended into the interior, toward the blue-black waters of Loon Lake. At the north end of the lake, where the plane touched down, the surface of the water rocked in a thin layer of ice. Steering northwest, the pilot navigated a path around the obstruction. In shallow waters he cut the engine and allowed the Beaver to drift to shore.

From a jumble of paraphernalia scrunched into the rear of the plane, I extricated my backpack and stepped out onto one of the plane's pontoons. One step ahead of me, my friend Bob Salerno tossed his pack into a thicket of vegetation at lake's edge and hopped to the ground. A moment later I did the same. With that, I made good on my promise to Fred Meader to visit him at Loon Lake. As it happened, Fred was no longer resident physically at the lake, having for a quarter century lain under a pile of rocks a few hundred yards from where I now stood. But under the circumstances it was the best I could do, and I was happy.

A month or so earlier, I had located Elaine in California. I had lost track of her in 1978, before she made her decision to relocate to red-wood country. With our reconnection began a new series of letters and, this time around, e-mails. Only now did I learn of the new and bountiful stage of her life that had begun after I last heard from her, one whose measure in years had come to exceed the seventeen she spent at Loon Lake.

One evening we spoke by phone. I told her of my plan to visit the lake with my friend. She at once offered us the use of the cabin that she and Fred had called home during their early years in the Brooks Range. Now as I stepped ashore and sensed the immensity of the mountains, the waters, the stillness; most of all, the *mosquito* that had just landed on my neck – I posted a silent and heartfelt thank-you note to Elaine for her generosity.

For the next week, Bob and I canoed the placid waters of the lake, climbed and explored the nearby mountains, solved the world's problems during happy hours that sometimes lasted somewhat more than an hour, slept sound as dormice in the tidy log cabin at water's edge that Fred and Elaine cobbled together from the remains of an old prospector's cabin that long-ago autumn of 1960. Bob was the ideal partner to join me in tackling these difficult challenges. Like the giant porcupine that spent his days wandering the forest, his nights curled up cozily in the canoe beside the cabin, Bob has one foot planted firmly in the wild world, the other in the world of the civilized and the urbane. He reveres Henry David Thoreau and Gustav Mahler equally. Given the choice among a hike in the Adirondacks, a lecture on particle physics, and a concert by the Kronos Quartet at Carnegie Hall, Bob would fall to quivering pieces, unable to decide. A former marathoner, he's logged thousands of miles in wild country across the land, always with five pounds of literature crammed into his backpack.

When he's not wearing out a pair of hiking boots, he's selling them; or at least he might be if Gucci made hiking boots. Bob is a lifer in retail at the very highest levels. When I met him he was senior vice president of Bergdorf Goodman, the super-high-end designer emporium at 57th and Fifth in New York City, where the ladies lunch, heads bow at the mention of the names Armani and Donna Karan, and thousand-dollar handbags fly off the shelves faster than Fritos at 7-11. Bob was responsible for all operational, financial, and administrative functions at the store. He claims that his colleagues at BG were mystified by his occasional withdrawal to places like the High Sierra and the Brooks Range, rather than sensible spots like, say, Sedona or Costa del Sol. The photos that he brought back documenting what he had seen and done during his bizarre sallies into forests primeval confounded many. What, no golf? Not even an herbal bath? Bob, who does not play golf, has a white, neatly trimmed beard, thinning auburn hair, and a wit dry and salty as cocktail cashews. He complains way too much on the trail but, because for some reason he attracts every mosquito and gnat in the neighborhood, I regard him as the ideal hiking companion.

Despite the long passage of time since the Meaders made their home in that magnificent spot, it became clear to me during those blissful days walking in their footsteps that, like the forests that bound the mountainside behind the cabin and the wild creeks that thundered into the lake, Fred and Elaine were still part of that haunting landscape. Their images were sewn into the very fabric of the place. Earlier I mentioned the Dalai Lama's notion that locations can become holy, intrinsically, in their very atoms, when they are witness to transformative events. It seems to me that Loon Lake is such a place. Here, two bullheaded, stoical, visionary individuals reminded the rest of us of something that humans once knew but that has been pretty much forgotten the world over: people and Planet Earth can live together in peace.

One morning, Bob and I threw day packs over our shoulders and set out up the flanks of the mountain that rose steeply to the west of the cabin. For the first half hour, we beat our way through a massive landslide of rocks, dirt, mud, and upended trees that overhung the cabin like a giant nose on the mountainside. Within, the thing was a mess, a primal coming undone of creation; neither of us was sure that we weren't about to sense a subtle shift beneath our boots, then begin a slow, unhappy ride to the lake, perhaps picking up the cabin on the way by.

Above, the mountain grew amicable. We moved upward on soft,

damp earth, leaping friendly brooks, traipsing through gardens of blue anemones and sphagnum moss.

The forest thinned. After two hours, we emerged above the tree line. The sky was steely blue, the way obvious. We entered a zone of slabby rocks interwoven with brilliantly blooming wildflowers. I thought inevitably of Toru's garden, three hundred miles to the northeast. As I stepped onto the peak's south shoulder I was greeted by a stunning view down into the watershed of a river that, as far as I knew, had not labored sufficiently in the cause of progress to have acquired a name. Even from several miles away, the roar was audible – a thunderstorm on the horizon. South and west through canyons unknown the waters flew, white streamers pluming behind like tail feathers.

The former marathoner plowed on ahead. Trailing by fifty yards and needing someone to converse with, I recalled Elaine's idea of a conscious universe. *A moment later I came upon a bed of purple forget-me-nots. They appeared to be enjoying themselves. Why deny them a voice? We talked. They explained their purpose in life (I would reveal it here but I was sworn to secrecy). When I began to describe my own reasons for being there, they wagged their heads. Don't bother, they said. Enjoy the view. Anyway, we already know.*

From the mountain's rocky summit, Bob and I enjoyed a grand panorama of the central Brooks Range. Barely visible on the northern horizon was 7,500-foot Mount Doonerak, an unnerving (for a former climber) spike of ice that's named for an Inuit spirit. Doonerak has a name, but in all directions rose mountains that did not. Few have felt the bootsteps of climbers. In time-honored fashion, Bob and I used the view as a kind of travel brochure to spur plans for future adventures and misadventures. Let's go there and then there, and then let's float a raft from there to there! Bob is one of those people who sees places like the Brooks Range and the Colorado Rockies and his beloved Adirondacks no matter where he stands. Sometimes he'll phone me from his office in New York, and we'll make small talk for a minute or two. Then suddenly he'll mention Alaska or Nevada's Black Rock Desert, and I'll know he's had a sighting.

Just a few miles to the north of where we stood was the boundary of Gates of the Arctic National Park. Fred and Elaine worked hard for the creation of the park, driven by their belief that, without protection in the National Wilderness Preservation System, Loon Lake and vast portions of the Brooks Range were doomed to development. Thanks in part to their efforts, the park was created in 1980, an eight-million-acre master-piece of visionary legislation. Fred died not knowing the crowning irony, that at the last minute his beloved lake would be cut from Gates of the Arctic and thereby denied the protection wilderness designation would have provided. The owners of pending mining and real estate claims convinced the boundary-drawers that the area was unfit for wilderness status. Today the fruits of that decision – a road, mining operations, vacation homes – spread south from the lake, vivid testimonials to Fred and Elaine's percipience.

One afternoon the Beaver returned. Inside were two passengers, Elaine and Fred's older daughter Heather and her partner Ryan Eme-naker. Heather was the vanguard of the family summer-visitation party; her mother and her younger sister Dawn would be arriving in a few weeks, both for extended stays.

Heather was five months old when Dion drowned. She was three when her father died. Because Elaine departed Loon Lake soon after Fred's death, Heather has scant memories of her early years there. She returned for short visits when she was five and nine, but it wasn't until 2000, when she was twenty-six, that she began to go back regularly and get to know the place as the home it had once been. Like her father, she is tall, wiry, erudite, strikingly earnest. She exudes purpose – understandably so, because, as it turns out, she has one. Words tumble from her, serious words. She is ready to engage anyone with a moment to spare in a lively, intense conversation about the sad state of the world and – this is what distinguishes her from your run-of-the-mill malcontent – what to do about it. She has short jet-black hair, a beautiful smile, and a cheery, utterly open manner. I felt we were friends the moment we met.

She remembers her father as "two gigantic legs."

"I was standing between them," she told Bob and me one afternoon as we sat at lake's edge tossing pebbles into the icy waters. She laughed at the memory. "I had a little hatchet and a little piece of wood, and I was chopping the wood." Another recollection was more telling. Fred had caught a fish. In its stomach, in famous fish fashion, there were little fish. In a kind of warm-up for the work she would take up two decades later, Heather sided with the little fish.

"I took them out of the fish's stomach, ran down to the lake, and tried to revive them."

Heather's life in the world beyond Loon Lake centers on issues of social justice. I got an inkling of this when I glimpsed the book she was carrying when I first saw her – Volume 2 of the autobiography of feminist-anarchist Emma Goldman. No mere petition signer or sign waver, Heather has stood on the front lines of some of most hotly contested political battles of our time. She has taken a lead role in the fight against World Trade Organization policies, joined permanent encampments in northern California to forestall the logging of old-growth redwoods, and traveled to Black Mesa, Arizona, to aid the so-called Navajo grandmothers in their struggle to avoid expulsion from their land. To support herself and pay for her schooling, Heather takes employment in fields consistent with her political beliefs. She had, for example, worked in a care home for the elderly; before that, she counseled parentless teenagers who could not be placed in foster care because of legal or behavioral problems. Heather was about to enter college near her home on California's North Coast. She planned to major in women's studies and eventually work with young women on the street.

Listening to the words of this remarkable young woman, I found it impossible not to think of her parents and of their megalomaniacal goal of saving the world. Heather didn't dispute the comparison. She did, however, point out a fundamental difference between Fred and Elaine's approach to the problem and her own.

"What my parents did is probably no longer possible," she said. "I don't think I could leave the world the way they did. My soul is here at the lake, but my heart is intimately connected to the struggles of the world out there. They needed to separate themselves in order to do what they thought was right. I need to stay intimately connected, to work from within to try to keep pieces of the world intact."

Along with Fred and Elaine's utterly serious approach to life and its complications, Heather inherited their passion for the wild. Despite having been back in the Arctic for only a short time, she was thoroughly at ease there and luxuriated in her home away from home. She chopped wood like a lumberjack, usually with a blue bandana wrapped around her head. She tolerated mosquitoes without grousing, canoed boldly, spoke of blizzards and grizzlies with a fondness that amazed me.

"All the clutter of the world falls away when you're here," she said. "The lake centers you emotionally and spiritually. The world and society disappear." Heather regards Loon Lake as a refuge to which she can repair to gather strength and nerve. "It's as if this place with all its intense life and death cycles touches on the pure essence of existence. Whenever I leave I take a part of that with me. We need places like this to rejuvenate us for the trying times ahead."

One evening, Bob and I decided to invite Heather and Ryan for dinner. For the main course we turned to our huge store of freeze-dried backpacking foods. Of all the skills the serious backcountry traveler must master in order to survive in the wild, none are more critical than that suite of steps known collectively as "reconstituting the meal": choosing the aluminum foil package of desiccated comestibles that is perfect for the occasion; adding the correct amount of water; stirring and shaking with the recommended degree of robustness; finally, keeping nearby the proper medications for treating the stomach ache that is almost certain to ensue. I was fortunate to have as my partner in the preparation of the evening meal a man whose understanding of these requisites was second to none. So committed is Bob to the art of the freeze-dried meal that, years ago, he began keeping a log of his backpacking dinners, together with a pithy review of each. So, for example, on the evening of August 13, 2002, the featured dish, lasagna, was "tasty and filling but needs oregano badly." The next night, Sierra chicken was "pretty bad. How many chickens do you see in the Sierra?" A night after that, turkey tetrazzini was "best with cognac." Bob has recently instituted a rating system that involves the awarding of ice axes to each product tested, with five axes being tops. He will sometimes solicit opinions and ratings from his companions, but he reserves the right to make final judgments himself. The man, it must be said, is a brutal critic. Most meals he has sampled have garnered lowly ones and twos, with the occasional three. Bob has yet to stumble on a five-axe meal, but he remains hopeful.

On the night of the grand banquet in the Brooks Range, my partner and I decided to throw caution to the winds and head south of the border – Mountain House Mexican-Style Chicken with Rice (two axes) and Richmoor Natural High Chicken Fajitas (three axes). *Olé!* It was hard to imagine that Heather and Ryan were not vegetarians, but since we had no vegetables we decided not to ask. Why chance spoiling the evening? Whatever their persuasion, our guests ate heartily and without complaint, and did not ask to read the ingredient lists on the sides of the packages.

Early the next morning, Heather, Ryan, Bob, and I walked up a hillside a short distance from the "new" cabin, which Fred and Elaine had put up as their family began to grow. We paused in a beautiful setting overlooking the lake, the spot where Fred was interred in 1977. Heather told some stories about her dad. Then she placed a white rock on a circle of rocks that marked the site, as she does each time she visits. The rest of us followed her example. A light breeze floated by, leaving in its wake a blush of summer warmth. In that instant I believed everything Fred had told me about the Arctic – the kindness of the place, the peace it offered to anyone who cared to come and look.

I knew there would be times when I would question that presumption. After all, the benevolent garden which, during his lifetime, Fred had extolled so convincingly was, simultaneously, the plot of cold earth that took him long before his time. The North, I was beginning to understand, was neither wholly light nor completely dark; it was, rather, a little of both – bipolar, if you will. If in some sense it could be taken as a model for the condition of my mental and spiritual health, as I had gone to it believing that it could, then peace was never likely to find a permanent place in my life; but neither were anguish and despair. Like caribou circling between the trials of winter and the raptures of summer, each would come and go, ebb and flow.

On that amicable prospect overlooking Loon Lake, in that serene moment, it was light that flowed. In that moment I could join the Inuit hunter in his timeless celebration of the dawning of the great day – not ultimately a song of day and of light, but rather one of wonder and hope – of the gift that allows anyone anywhere to say, let's go there and then there, and then let's float a raft from there to there. And maybe when we arrive, we will find rest at last.

It's not easy to bury someone in the Arctic. Just a few inches below the earth's surface lies a layer of permafrost that's nearly impenetrable. As a result, the depth of the grave usually falls somewhat short of the recommended six feet. To make up the difference, the burial party heaps rocks and dirt on from above, forming an easily recognizable mound that may rise a foot or more above the earth's surface.

Besides its shape, Fred's grave differed in one other noticeable way from what one might see in a normal, manicured cemetery. Around the periphery of the site lay the sparse ground cover and stunted growth that are typical of Arctic latitudes. But the mound itself supported a spectacular riot of foliage. Wildflowers, willow seedlings, luxuriant mosses and lichens, alder shoots, plants of a dozen varieties sprouted upward and outward in twenty different directions. I saw no orchids, but orchids would not have looked out of place on that exuberant pile of dirt and rock. Irrepressible in life, Fred remained so in death. *Welcome to the Arctic, old friend, he said to me. You have come at last! Now look: Do you see how glorious it is? I told you so!*

In the great dome above, a fine day was rolling into place, a silver-blue day, a silky breeze of a day, a day that's hard to remember for anything in particular, and impossible to forget. Heather and Ryan scooted off down the hill, to save the spiders, I suppose, or, God help us, the mosquitoes.

Less ambitiously, Bob and I headed for the old gray canoe and an intrepid exploration of the hard-charging creek we had seen spilling from a canyon half a mile to the east. Within minutes we were willow buds on the lake, moving in easy unison with its rhythms and its melody.

The Arctic!

With each sweep of my paddle, all I could think was, Oh, how glorious it is!

ACKNOWLEDGMENTS

None of the journeys that I describe in these pages would have been possible without Carol and Jake, my sine qua nons, and without the arrival on the scene, quite miraculously, and at a moment when it appeared that my plans might never take wing, of an anonymous and exceedingly generous benefactor. To that person or persons I owe a debt of gratitude I can never repay and will never forget. I'm grateful, too, for timely aid from the Nevada Arts Council and the Sierra Arts Foundation, both essential players in northern Nevada's thriving arts community.

Nor could I have logged a single mile without the steadfastness and good cheer (mostly) of my several traveling companions, who apparently understood what they were getting into when I broached my idea to them, and who joined up anyway; and with whom I enjoyed adventure and misadventure such as I never could have imagined possible. Let me here name them for all to see and admire: Shaun Griffin, David Hertz, Bob Salerno, Peter Nagano, and Richard Nagano. Then there is the re-markable photographer and adventurer Toru Sonohara, who accidentally wandered into my story in an obscure corner of the Arctic National Wildlife Refuge, and who proceeded to enrich my experience of the North a hundred-fold. I'm proud that some of Toru's marvelous photographs grace the pages of this book. Each is a testament to his art and to his indomitable spirit. (Toru can be contacted at *dance-with-bear@ mercury.dti.ne.jp.*)

Many people pitched in to help when they learned that I liked caribou but didn't know much about them. For their expert assistance, I would particularly like to thank Stephen M. Arthur, research biologist with the Alaska Department of Fish and Game; Don Russell, research manager with the Canadian Wildlife Service; Remy Rodden, conservation education coordinator with the Yukon Department of Environment; Martin Kienzler, satellite data technician with the Yukon Department of Environment; and Jim and Adrienne Fink, proprietors of Blackstone Outfitters in Whitehorse, Yukon. Dorothy Cooley, regional biologist with the Yukon Department of Environment, deserves special mention. An authority on the animals of the North, Dorothy fielded countless questions from me, from the arguably reasonable to the absurd: What were the satellite coordinates of the caribou known as Lucky on October 7, 2001? When do females drop their antlers? What do you think of the idea of my friends and me backpacking into Yukon's Ogilvie Mountains in winter? (Answers: 67.268°N, 141.079°W; after they give birth; not much.) My questions usually went out to Dorothy in the early morning; her thorough, definitive, and cheerful responses were back by 9 A.M. She was a superb resource, and I count myself fortunate to have found her.

I owe one large mountain and several mid-size rivers to my friend Steven Nightingale, novelist, sonneteer, champion of morning stars, caster of lifelines. Steven's words and wit, his constancy, his ideas and stratagems (the bulk of them quite impractical) inspired and sustained me, especially during the darker times. I'm grateful, too, to David R. Godine and the remarkable people at David R. Godine, Publisher, especially Carl W. Scarbrough, Susan Barba, and Sue Berger Ramin, for their virtuosic talents and their unwavering belief in this project. To Anne and Owen Hanley, two northern lights, I extend my deepest thanks. These wise and indefatigable Alaskans hosted my various companions and me, often under conditions of great grime and cursedness, at their beautiful Fairbanks home on occasions too numerous to recall. They fed and clothed us; they loaned us bear barrels; they explained mosquitoes. Perhaps best of all, they brought us together with a force of nature named Sean McGuire. In the late sixties, at the age of ten, Sean took up residence with Fred, Elaine, and Dion Meader at their remote cabin in the Brooks Range. There he remained for several years, living as close to the earth as it is possible to live. As a result, he became an evangelist, the good kind. In 1978, to draw attention to the Alaska Lands Bill then before Congress, he walked seven thousand miles from the Yukon River to Key West, Florida, a journey that took him ten months. Thirty years later, he remains one of America's fiercest advocates for wild-land preservation. I'm grateful to him for his peerless example and for his generosity toward me. If you desire an otherworldly experience, book a room at Sean's Cloudberry Lookout Bed and Breakfast in Fairbanks. On a chill winter evening, climb the steps notched into the great spruce log that spirals upward through the roof of Sean's utterly fabulous log-and-glass house. You will reach what the proprietor calls his "aurorium" – his aurora viewing tower. There, you may converse with the night.

I learned most of what I know about caribou from three books. I commend them to anyone who wishes to know the animal: *Caribou and the Barren-Lands* by George Calef, the gold standard of the genre; *The Mammals of Canada* by A. W. F. Banfield, authoritative and massively detailed; and *Arctic National Wildlife Refuge: Seasons of Life and Land* by Subhankar Banerjee and six other essayists, as beautiful and ardent a work as you are likely to find. Taken together, the three provide a fine example of the ideal William James sought to achieve in his writing, and to which I aspire in my own: "The union of the mathematician with the poet, fervor with measure, passion with correctness, this surely is the ideal." I should add that, if anywhere in this book passion has won out over correctness, and errors of omission or fact resulted, they are entirely my responsibility.

My boundless debt to and admiration for the visionaries Fred and Elaine Meader will be evident to anyone who reads this book. Although my story gained in complexity as it went forward, it began with a simple idea, which was to repay Fred for changing my life. With her daughters Heather and Dawn, Elaine Meader continues the work that she and Fred began half a century ago of preserving the Arctic wilderness. Interested readers can learn more about these endeavors at *http://northernlight legacy.org*. Heather's stunning photographs of the North are on view at that website and at her own: *http://www.hmmphotographs.com*.

At the Meaders' request, I have changed the names of certain geographical features that are central to their story, and to mine.

More on my journeys north, and on other journeys of mine, real and imagined, can be found at my website: *http://www.robertleonardreid.com*.

SUGGESTIONS FOR
FURTHER READING

The literature of the North can be as chilly and forbidding as its subject matter. Herewith, sixteen volumes from that sometimes wintry bookshelf that have welcomed me warmly (the Jack London is an exception) and made me want to know more. Because most of these works were published decades ago and may be hard to find in their earliest editions, I have not listed the original publishers or publication dates. Most of the books are widely available in more recent editions, and the interested reader should be able to track them down without difficulty.   – R L R

Subhankar Banerjee, *Arctic National Wildlife Refuge: Seasons of Life and Land*. Six meandering, exigent essays, plus Banerjee's photographs, which document with irrefutable clarity the sublime, endless, heart-aching beauty of the North.

A. W. F. Banfield, *The Mammals of Canada*. From fringed bat to collared lemming to least weasel to caribou, Canada's mammals are herein weighed, measured, counted, and exhaustively described. Without Banfield, I would not have known that a caribou's top speed is forty-nine miles per hour or that the animal has thirty-four teeth, including six incisors that are small and flexible. Somehow, I'm glad to know that. Richly illustrated with color plates, drawings, and maps.

Henry Beissel, *Cantos North*. The whole history of the Canadian North – Vast blank canvas of a land / hung tattered at the top from fixed pole / and stretched below along a single latitude / taut into the framework of two oceans. . . – told in one astonishing, deeply satisfying poem.

George Calef, *Caribou and the Barren-Lands*. The work without which my own could not have been written. Sumptuously detailed, handsomely and usefully illustrated by the author's remarkable photographs, this authoritative account of the life cycle of *Rangifer tarandus*, the North American caribou, is a sympathetic and readable portrait of the species by a wildlife biologist who knows the animal better than anyone.

Frederick Cook, *My Attainment of the Pole*
Charles Francis Hall, *Narrative of the Second Arctic Expedition Made by Charles F. Hall*
Elisha Kent Kane, *Arctic Explorations*
Fridtjof Nansen, *Farthest North*
Robert E. Peary, *The North Pole*
Toward the finish, newspapers across the land characterized it as "the race for the North Pole." In fact, it was more like an interminable death march played out over many decades, across the whole wide canvas of the Arctic. Each fresh expedition struck confidently north; years later it returned dejectedly south, not so fresh, and minus any number of its original cast of characters. Net gain: a few degrees of latitude, a modicum of knowledge concerning what needed to be done better next time, and fortunately, a thick, chest-thumping expedition account. I've listed here several of my favorites. Contained therein are enough vanity, violence, heroism, cowardice, betrayal, madness, tragedy, triumph, and duplicity to inspire half a dozen Coen brothers's films.

Loren Eiseley, *The Immense Journey*; *The Star Thrower*. Not strictly North-oriented, but essential to any appreciation of north, south, east, or west. Strange, brooding, wondrous essays by our most compelling scientist-wonderer. Eiseley makes even pigeons seem numinous. Few writers have so acutely sensed the transcendence of the ordinary, or understood so precisely the dead seriousness of being alive.

Donald R. Griffin, *Animal Thinking*. As a puppy, my golden retriever learned to stand at the back door and bark when she wanted to come in. Recently, she began barking to alert me that, while she intended to remain outside lounging in the sun, the family cat was at the door and would like to come in. Goldie began doing this spontaneously, without lessons and without liver snacks. I do not consider it a trick. A generation ago, behaviorists insisting that animals were little more than instinct-driven machines would have characterized my story as sentimental claptrap and branded me a liar. Today, thanks to a revolution in the way we understand animals that began with *Animal Thinking*, the mouse-in-a-maze crowd no longer rules the roost. Donald Griffin, a distinguished zoologist, risked ridicule and ostracism when he wrote this brave and compassionate tome; doing so, he opened the door to throngs of researchers who had long suspected that instinct was insufficient to explain much of the behavior they observed in animals. My own speculations on the inner lives of caribou and Arctic terns owe their origins to Griffin and to my first encounter with this book a quarter-century ago.

Jack London, *To Build a Fire*. Vivid, boreal prose, and the North at its most unforgiving. Carry extra matches.

Barry Lopez, *Arctic Dreams*. Perhaps it is no more possible to understand the North than it is to understand Thelonious Monk or the Bartók string quartets. For those who would make the effort, this is as close to a Rosetta stone as they are likely to find. Composed in a fever of hope, the book has now, two decades later, a haunting, end-of-days quality;

one hears dying gulls and the cry of the ice. Exhaustively, sometimes numbingly detailed, Lopez's masterwork comes to us as an urgent communiqué from a wise man on a distant planet, imploring us to draw close and pay heed.

Robert Marshall, *Alaska Wilderness: Exploring the Central Brooks Range*. Three-quarters of a century ago, Robert Marshall, a man with prodigious physical powers and the eye of a visionary, walked into Alaska's Brooks Range and found something worth saving. His account of his deliverance is an exhilarating portrait of an ancient time, one when every footstep was an unveiling of the unknown. Marshall inspired a legion of followers. By championing his preposterous notion that wild is free, they changed the geography of the American mind.

John McPhee, *Coming Into the Country*. The book that introduced Alaska to the rest of the nation. Classic McPhee – meticulously researched, adroitly composed, maddeningly balanced; and alas, thanks to the writer's consummate success at documenting a moment in time, decidedly dated. Still, the issues he was tackling in 1976 – tradition versus progress, self-determination versus government meddling, energy development versus wilderness preservation – remain with us today, thirty years the worse for wear. And his depiction of a perennial American failing is astute and timeless: we discover paradise, we fall in love, we lose sight of what we have, and with messianic zeal we set out to destroy it.

John Muir, *Stickeen*. John Muir, a vast Alaskan glacier, a stormy day, a "small and worthless dog": presto, the best dog story ever written. In this true account, as in much of what he took on, Muir proved himself decades ahead of his time. His Stickeen is a thoroughly realized creature, possessed of a complete set of emotions, hitched, like everything else in the universe, to Muir, to me, and to you.

ARCTIC OCEAN

BEAUFORT SEA

Prudhoe
Bay

Deadhorse

Kaktovik

COASTAL PLAIN

Alaska Pipeline

IVVAVIK
NATIONAL
PARK

Inuvik

NORTHWEST
TERRITORIES

BROOKS RANGE
1999

VUNTUT
NATIONAL
PARK

2002

ARCTIC NATIONAL
WILDLIFE RESERVE

1997

Arctic Village

Old
Crow

Fort
McPherson

Kongakut River

OGILVIE MOUNTAINS

2003

Porcupine River

2001

Eagle River

Fort Yukon

ARCTIC CIRCLE

CANADA
UNITED STATES

Yukon River

Dempster Highway

ALASKA

Ogilvie
River

YUKON

2000   1998

Fairbanks

Alaska Pipeline

Dawson
City

Lucky's October Locations
1997–2003